11893

D1276231

The Story of Rock

The Story of

ROCK

SECOND EDITION

❂ CARL BELZ ❂

New York   OXFORD UNIVERSITY PRESS   *1972*

Third printing, 1977

Copyright © 1969, 1972 by Oxford University Press, Inc.
Library of Congress Catalogue Card Number: 77-183870
Printed in the United States of America

Preface to the Second Edition

Many changes have taken place in the world of rock music since the first edition of this book in 1968. Established artists have continued to work, but new groups and individuals have appeared, and events such as Woodstock and Altamont have made international headlines. I have tried to account for these developments in a new last chapter. In addition, the past three years have witnessed the publication of numerous books dealing with the history of rock, its personalities and its special meaning. A bibliographical essay treats a selected number of these publications and is intended as a guide to further reading.

Naturally, some of my own thoughts and feelings about rock have changed during the past three years. These are reflected in the additions to *The Story of Rock* mentioned above, and in some changes in the original text. Two of these changes are worth mentioning here. First, I have deleted certain negative comments about the Rolling Stones, in particular those referring to the relation between the Stones and the Beatles. Second, I have deleted a chapter called "Rock and Fine Art." I have done so because it is now clear to me that the Beatles' "White Album" does not have the significance for the broader history of the music that I initially claimed for it in that chapter. However, I continue to be convinced of the album's significance for the Beatles' development as a group, and I have therefore incorporated parts of the "Rock and Fine Art" chapter into my original discussion of the Beatles and their music.

As in the case of the first edition of *The Story of Rock*, many individuals have helped in the realization of this one. While I cannot mention all of them, I would like to express special thanks to Norma Rothenberg, Don Weller, Cary Rudman, Bill Cohon, and Walter Soule.

Preface to the First Edition

Rock is here: a large and extraordinary musical area whose character and history are only beginning to be charted. This book is one exploratory study. Its purpose is to outline the whole area of rock's development, but it presents a definite point of view, almost an argument, and this is announced in the first sentences of the text.

The book makes certain assumptions about its own limitations, and I wish to clarify these at the outset. In mapping the character of rock music, I make no attempt to define it precisely. The most persistent feature of rock has been its beat. Generally this beat has been heavy, but at times, particularly in ballads, it has been soft. Rock has been influenced by country music, by the blues, by classical music, by calypso, by traditional folk styles, and by a variety of other musical conventions. But in each of these phases, the beat has been present and has given the music its own character. As in the case of jazz, any listener who wants rock defined specifically is probably unable to recognize it.

A second feature of this book concerns its scope. While attempting to outline the entire rock history, I do not presume to deal with every rock artist or record. Each listener knows his favorite rock examples, his "Top 10" for any particular year. My own tastes are expressed throughout the text, and the discography which follows it constitutes my selection of rock "classics." Generally, however, the book concentrates on the broader themes and meanings of the rock development. I hope that the reader will test these concepts against his own listening experiences and against his judgment of artists and records I do not consider specifically.

Another fundamental assumption of this study is that rock has existed primarily on records. In this, the music is rather different from jazz and from the traditional folk music to which it is related. Although jazz and other types of folk music exist on records, they did not originate in that medium. For the most part, they originated and developed through live performances. Rock, it seems to me, has generally done the opposite. Records were the music's initial medium. Admittedly, there were always live performances, but they have become really important to the music only in recent years.

This study cannot claim to be internationally comprehensive. Before the 1960's, rock was primarily an American music. Since the early sixties, however, independent rock traditions have developed outside the United States, most notably in England. This book devotes considerable attention to English music, especially to the Beatles, but it does not concentrate in depth on the background of the English scene or on the musical and social developments which took place there before 1964. Rather, I begin my treatment of English rock in 1964, and I consider the impact of that music on American rather than British audiences. Like the history of the music in England, rock's relation to jazz in the United States, as well as to Negro blues, are formidable subjects in themselves, and they lie outside the scope of this book. And I must stress that the present historical study concentrates on the art of rock as opposed to its sociological, political, or economic aspects.

There is plenty of writing available on the subject of rock. Periodicals such as *Crawdaddy* treat it exclusively, and others, including *Time* and *Life*, offer regular features on one or another of its practitioners. Nevertheless, rock remains a sprawling and unclear phenomenon upon which little critical structure has been imposed. Confusion about the identity of the music is partly responsible for this situation. Many essays on the subject discuss the music in enthusiastic terms, but fail to describe clearly the inherent character of the music itself. This tendency reflects the folk nature of rock: the music is considered exciting, important, and meaningful, but it does not encourage discussion of why these terms are aesthetically valid.

The folk character of rock probably accounts further for the sociological bias which most writing on the subject assumes. Throughout its history, the music has had such an immediate, direct impact on its audience that the character of the audience itself quickly becomes the subject for discussion. Most popular literature dealing with rock during the 1950's stressed juvenile delinquency, just as it stresses hippydom, drugs, and mysticism during the 1960's.

These remarks are not intended to undermine sociological studies, nor to deny that rock provides a rich store of evidence for the investigations conducted by that discipline. I simply wish to emphasize that my own approach represents an alternative: that is, it considers the music *as* art and *in terms* of art. My concern is with the ways in which the music emerged and has developed, with the stylistic directions it has taken, and with the evidence it provides for an understanding of folk art, fine art, and popular art in general. Admittedly, the social, economic, and the political import of the music cannot be dismissed entirely. But those aspects will be subordinate to my concern for the *art* of rock, for it is in terms of art that the present study finds the music most meaningful.

The primary source for studying any work of art, is, of course, the work itself. For the history of rock the primary sources are records. But of the thousands of records which have been issued, which ones account for the mainstream of the music's history? A critical history, including a history of rock, is constructed on the basis of which objects the critic experiences as being the best he has encountered. In the process whereby a number of critic-historians devote their attention to a common group of objects, a consensus of which are highest in quality may emerge. Over a period of time, and as new objects are created, this consensus may dissolve or shift its focus. With rock, no real consensus exists which can be said to take the entire history of the music into consideration. While I hope this study will constitute a beginning for such considerations, I cannot presume that the history I present is founded on anything but the records I personally feel are possessed of the highest quality.

A secondary source for organizing the history of rock is provided by the charts of best-selling records. A plethora of such charts exists. They are published by radio stations and teen newspapers throughout the country, and they are contained in the periodicals of the music and entertainment industries, notably *Billboard*, *Cash Box*, and *Variety*. Of these three, *Billboard* emerged as the most consistent and reliable source for the present study. *Billboard's* major attribute is its comprehensiveness: The magazine lists records which were popular on a regional as well as on a national level, new releases, albums as well as singles, and more records in each stylistic category than any other publication of its kind.

The charts of best-selling records have several important functions. Before citing those, however, I wish to emphasize that the charts list only the *best-selling* records—not the records which, at any particular moment, are necessarily artistically the best. While the charts have been an invaluable secondary source in the writing of this history, in other words, they do *not* provide its basis. If that were the case, my book would constitute the history of popular art instead of folk art. A clear understanding of this distinction must therefore be maintained whenever references to the charts are made.

A primary function of the charts is to document records with regard to their dates of issue, their artists, labels, and publishers. In addition, the charts enable us to estimate the *kind* of acceptance given to an individual record: They reveal the geographical area where the record first became popular, the time-span during which its popularity continued, whether it achieved an instantaneous or gradual success, and if it provoked intermittent or constant interest. Along with their basic information, then, the charts reflect broader patterns of the music's development. Through the period of the 1950's and 1960's, for instance, they show the extraordinary increase in the number of newly released records per week, the equally extraordinary increase in the total number of artists and groups within the music business, and the fact that the more recent records enjoy a lifespan of popularity which is only a fraction of that enjoyed by records during the early 1950's.

Apart from information, the charts of best-selling records also provide material of another sort. I am referring to their bizarre, often poetic, conflation of song titles, group names, and label identifications. The montage of these elements possesses a distinct appeal because of its spontaneity. If the charts thereby approach poetry, however, the poetry is folk-like in character. It unconsciously reflects the spontaneity of the music, and it unknowingly reveals how the music has developed a sophistication of its own. During the 1950's, a group could call itself Danny and the Juniors, Little Joe and the Thrillers, or Vito and the Salutations. But in the 1960's, the names have become more sophisticated—and less direct—in their references: Moby Grape, the Jefferson Airplane, Canned Heat, Good Soup. In this way the charts point to the development of rock in its larger stylistic implications.

In using *Billboard* musical charts, I also adopted this magazine's general categories of musical style: Pop, Country and Western, and Rhythm and Blues, each of which it listed separately. But this presented an immediate problem. Neither *Billboard* nor any of the trade periodicals listed rock as a distinct idiom. The charts were unable to classify a style which, in its sprawling catholicity of sources and influences, appeared everywhere in the lists and blurred their former distinctions. My contention is that the music included elements from each of the three traditional fields, but emerged as a style which was separate from any one of them. In tracing rock history, the charts therefore have a dual function. On the one hand, they provide a rich source of documentation, while on the other, they reveal certain internal limitations. As they do, moreover—as records begin to appear simultaneously on two or on all three of the charts—they reveal the beginning of a revolution in the history of music.

In describing the sources, influences, and stylistic character of rock, I have also employed three main chronological divisions: from 1954 through 1956; from 1957 through 1963; and from 1964 to the present day. The first period describes the emergence of rock from sources in the Pop, Country and Western, and Rhythm and Blues traditions. This period concludes with a treatment of Elvis Presley, whose style shows a unity of the three sources. The second period treats the gradual expansion of rock and its ability to subsume a variety of sub-styles and innovations.

Among these is a popularized version of historical folk music which reaches a peak of development in the work of Peter, Paul and Mary. Since 1964, particularly in the music of the Beatles, rock has taken a new direction: A combination of self-evident worldliness with an artistic sophistication has led the music away from the folk ways of its past.

My primary acknowledgment is to Kurt von Meier, with whom I spent many hours discussing the ideas contained in this study. Without those discussions, the book could not have been realized.

I am also indebted to several people for advice during the initial writing of the manuscript, particularly to the following: Chris Hampton, Richard Comfort, Charles Kessler, Charles Lutz, and Sue Ginsburg, who also assisted in the research. Many students at both Mills College and Brandeis University should be cited for their patience and co-operation in providing a sounding board during the evolution of my ideas. I can list only a few of them: Jaymi Goodenough, Beverly Ross, Barbara Monning, Surpik Zarakian, Sally Argo, Jim Balanoff, Steve Bloom, Gregory Prestopino, Ed Spiro, Sylvia Weiser, Stanley Kramer, Bart Goldman, Steve Gillmor, Fred Finkel, Eda Warren, Caryl Weinstock and Danielle Frankenthal. Several friends provided an initial inspiration for the book, largely because of the intensity of their personal interest in its subject: Deb Wye, Roberta Bernstein, Sarah Kelly, Mary Bell, and Liz Needleman.

Finally, I am indebted to two other persons: my editor, James Raimes, whose advice was invaluable in many ways, particularly in the distilling and clarifying of my thoughts about rock; and my friend and colleague, Gerry Bernstein, who provided constant encouragement during the difficult months of putting the manuscript in its final state.

Contents

"This Is Dedicated To The One I Love"

The Story of Rock

Introduction: Rock as Folk Art

The underlying contention of this study is that rock* is a part of the long tradition of folk art in the United States and throughout the world. However simple or obvious this thesis may seem at first, it nevertheless involves a number of complicated issues concerning the history of art, the relationship between folk art and fine art, and our notions about the creative act in either domain of expression. The fact that rock first emerged, and has since developed, within the area of popular art only complicates its relationship to the folk and fine art traditions. It is to this general question—of the distinction between folk art, fine art, and popular art—that I wish to address these introductory remarks in order to clarify the position of rock in the larger history of art.

Distinguishing between folk, fine, and popular art has become extremely difficult in the 1960's. We live in a culture which is determined to question the validity of such

* "Rock and Roll" is sometimes used generically to describe the whole movement studied in this book and sometimes to describe a particular type of music within the movement. I have avoided the term and use the accepted generic term "rock" throughout.

distinctions and in which such questioning has provoked some of the best artistic statements since World War II. The complexity of this situation is partly due to the phenomenon of Pop Art, a fine art style which has been directly stimulated by popular or mass culture. Pop paintings and sculptures draw their inspiration from billboards, comic strips, advertising, and supermarkets, and sometimes look deceptively like the original objects in our predominantly man-made environment. Similarly, certain developments of theater—particularly the "living theater," "happenings," and "environments"—encourage the notion that the entire panorama of life can be viewed as a work of art. In the face of all this, drawing lines between art objects and non-art objects, or even distinguishing between different *classes* of art objects, might seem a less important task than describing a seemingly delightful situation in which anything can be art and maybe everything is. For the critic-historian, however, these distinctions are fundamental. Rock has been considered as popular art, folk art, fine art, and even non-art. Which, in fact, is it?

The vast and current interest in rock might be viewed as a feedback from such phenomena as Pop Art. Taking a hint from the fine arts, the adult public has begun to appreciate material which was previously alien and embarrassing to the critics of modern American civilization. Such appreciation, however, is a development of the 1960's. The development of rock particularly during the first decade of its history, took place in the absence of such appreciation. The music emerged in response to a series of changing values and vital needs—not as the result of a sophistication gleaned from art galleries, museums, or periodicals. Its history, moreover, must be seen as a youth movement and as the reflection of a way of life radically different from the one which prevailed before the 1950's. When rock emerged, it spoke to these new values, to this youth, and to this changed way of life. But it did so in its capacity as a voice *of* the people rather than an art which talked *about* them from a detached and self-determined vantage point. On an immediate level as well as in its ultimate significance, the music has been a confrontation with reality rather than a confrontation with art. This distinctiveness of function marks rock as folk art rather than fine art.

The difference between the functions of folk art and fine art cannot be regarded as absolute or necessarily clear-cut. All art, it can be argued, arises in response to vital needs and reflects a changing way of life from generation to generation. Further, all art is admittedly concerned with reality. At this level of generalization, folk art and fine art become alike. But folk art and fine art are not so similar when we consider which elements are more or less important in the creation and appeal of each.

In the modern period the most advanced media of the fine arts have become increasingly conscious of their respective and unique identities. Painting, for instance, has consistently involved itself with questions of the intrinsic nature of its expression: its flatness, its shape, its opticality, and so forth. Furthermore, these questions have evolved into an explicit *content*. In other words, the most successful expressions in the medium have tended to force the viewer to recognize that he is looking at a painting, a work of art. Moreover, by recognizing its particular medium in this way, the individual work compels its viewer to recognize that the object of his experience—in this case, the painting—is also distinct from other kinds of realities and from life in general. To put it another way, fine art declares itself as being different in kind from life. This is not to say that fine art ignores life or is irrelevant to the concerns of reality. Rather, any fine art expression confronts life, and has meaning in terms of it, only by engaging in an immediate confrontation with itself. In this sense, fine art is conscious of its own being, and, more generally, conscious of art.

In folk art, "art-consciousness" does not occupy the primary role that it does in fine art. A folk idiom's immediate concern is with issues of life and reality and with an overt expression of those issues. It is not aware of the identities of the separate media that it may employ. In the sense I am trying to define, a folk idiom employs different media unknowingly; it regards the identities of these media as being passive, like entities that need not be confronted in themselves. More simply, the difference between folk art and fine art can be stated in the following way: The work of folk art says of itself, as it were, "this is reality," while the work of fine art says "this is a picture of reality." In no way, of course, does this distinction imply that one type of expression is of a higher quality than the other.

The distinction I have just made must be cautiously applied. It might very well be rejected by the artists themselves. But, however fascinating and enlightening an artits's remarks may be, they constitute a different area of concern, that of autobiography. A given artist—someone, say, whom I consider the producer of fine art objects—may contend that he never thinks about "art" when he is making a picture. Similarly, the Beatles have frequently commented that they do not *intend* all the meanings the critics find in their songs. Such statements are perplexing unless we understand that they belong to the domain of autobiography. The emphasis in the present study is upon neither autobiography nor biography, but upon the works of art themselves and upon their inherent character as experienced objects. Such an emphasis is not simply capricious, nor is it meant to undermine the significance of other types of studies. It merely represents a method for relating works of art in an historical context, and, more important, for understanding the meanings those works compel in our experience of them.

The ways in which rock relates to the fine art-folk art distinction are apparent in various aspects of the music itself, in the fabric of media which has surrounded it, and in the responses it elicits. In the early days of the *American Bandstand* television show, for instance, a panel of three or four teenagers periodically reviewed newly released records. The record was played, the audience danced, and a discussion of the song's merits followed. This discussion invariably contained remarks such as, "It's got a great beat. . . . I'll give it an 80," or, "You can really dance to it. . . . I'll give it an 85." The panelists never talked about the artistic properties of the record: the way the song was structured, the relation between its structure and meaning, its manipulations of the medium, the implications of its content, or any of the kinds of issues that are central to a meaningful statement about a work of fine art.

No one who appreciated or understood the music ever expected such questions to be discussed, for they are not part of the folk response. That response is spontaneous, and it is directed to the thing-as-reality. In other words, the connection between listener and song is an immediate one; no aesthetic distance separates the two, no gap that would provoke art-consciousness. With rock, as with any folk idiom, a consciousness of art is unnecessary for grasping the full impact of a particular work. This fact probably explains why the *Bandstand* panelists, however "uncritical" they may have appeared, were usually accurate in naming the best—that is, the most folk-like—of the new records.

The adult audiences and the popular press who condemned rock in the 1950's did so because they did not understand the identity of the music they heard. They failed to grasp the essential difference between folk art and fine art, a difference teenagers unconsciously took for granted. Adverse critics of the music complained that it was crude and primitive, that it used poor grammar and improper enunciation, and that its lyrics were literary nonsense. Even in the 1960's, on his *Open End* show, David Susskind continued the effort to embarrass the music by reading the lyrics of some typical rock songs as if they were examples of fine art poetry. This sort of criticism was as futile and irrelevant as an art historian's criticism that a painting by Henri Rousseau had awkward perspective or that its human figures were out of scale with the landscape.

Folk art is neither aware of, nor concerned about, the kinds of manipulations that constitute "proper" effects in the fine arts. The rock artist's "crude" enunciation sprang naturally from his spontaneous effort to express something real. Yet, the grammar of "Doncha jus know it" or "I got a girl named Rama Lama Ding Dong" does not alone transform a song into folk material. Artists in the fine arts have used unconventional or slang expressions for centuries, from Shakespeare to the present day. What distinguishes the folk artist is that he uses such expressions unconsciously rather than for a desired artistic effect. Unaware of the option at his disposal—between art and reality—the folk artist plunges naturally, though unknowingly, into the latter.

Just as rock does not "become" folk music simply because it includes certain kinds of grammar or sentence structures, its folk character is not assured by the use of particular musical instruments or by a devotion to specific subject matters. A common misunderstanding concerning these questions arose during the latter 1950's and continued into the 1960's. Groups like the Kingston Trio and individual singers like Joan Baez inspired a popular movement which seemed to equate folk music with songs telling a story or conveying a moralistic point and accompanied

Dick Clark's *American Bandstand* in the early 1950's

by the acoustic or solo guitar. To its enthusiastic audience,
this type of music was pure, eschewing the so-called falsi-
fications of recording-room manipulations. As such, it appeared to offer an alternative to the crude and primitive
style of rock. The artists and audiences of this new trend
failed to realize, however, that folk styles change. The
acoustic guitar may have been all that was available to the
folk artist of the 1930's, but his counterpart in the 1950's
and the 1960's could work with electronics, with echo
chambers, and with complicated recording techniques.
Folk music could change its cloak—just as folk art
changed its materials between the stone carvings of Cy-
cladic culture, the bark paintings of Australia, and the oils
of Rousseau.

A dramatic reflection of rock's essentially folk character
is apparent in the large number of one-shot successes in
the history of the music. A group or individual produces a
high quality record on its first effort but fails to repeat
that success. Although the group or individual artist generally issues a second or a third record, these follow-ups
rarely achieve the special blend of ingredients that gave
the initial song its impact. The explanation for this phenomenon—for the fact that the follow-ups are so often artistic failures—is directly connected with folk art's lack of
art-consciousness. When the rock group produces its first
record, it is not concerned with style or structure, but,
rather, with a sense of immediate impact, with what the
Bandstand panelists call "the great beat." With the second
or third record, however, the group seems to become aware
of *art*—that is, with the artistic character of the first record. The group tries to duplicate the elements of the first
record with only minor or barely perceptible variations.
Yet, as they try for artistic consistency, their folk orientation
generally betrays them: Not really understanding art, or
the complex blend of aesthetic decisions which produced

the original sound, they produce an object bearing only superficial resemblance to the first record. In this instance, the folk artist's lack of art-consciousness plays an ironic role in his creative life: At a time when he consciously believes he is making art, he is merely producing reproductions of his own original and unconsciously creative gesture.

Rock history substantiates the notion that the realities in a particular song carry greater significance than the art of that song. This further suggests that the realities exist and are felt on a day-to-day basis. That is, rock's past is generally experienced as being part of the present rather than a part of history. Its history, in other words, is not usually pursued as an end in itself. While many songs may be remembered from the early or middle 1950's, their artists are usually forgotten. In such cases, the very term "artist" has a radically different meaning from the way it is used in the fine arts. In the latter, the artist is regarded as an individual whose significance and responsibility are linked with the production of a number of objects which are vital to our understanding of art. But with folk art, the relevance of the object-as-reality assumes greater importance than the artist who was responsible for its production—as if that artist only *happened* to have created the record. Hence, we cherish and recognize numerous songs in the folk music tradition, but we do not feel compelled to connect them with particular artists. In the fine arts, such a connection is demanded by the works, and scholars labor for years to discover the names of the masters whose art has survived without evidence of authorship.

That the relevance of rock songs is experienced in terms of day-to-day realities is shown by the numerous polls of "all-time favorites" conducted by local radio stations across the country. These polls usually list 300 songs; of that number, however, more than half are examples from the same year as the poll or from the year preceding it. Contrary to what many disk jockeys say, these figures do not prove that rock has improved over the years. Rather, the polls demonstrate that the current songs are simply more *real* than the older ones. The lists of "all-time favorites" reflect only today's memories of realities which existed when the various songs were originally experienced. The albums of "Oldies But Goodies" are similarly folk-like in their stress upon experienced realities: They thrive because they enable listeners to relive the past in the present, not because they inform their audiences about the art of the past.

I have suggested that folk artists, in contrast to their fine art counterparts, tend to be anonymous in relation to the works they produce. Yet, rock has a distinctive style of anonymity. While the artists of still remembered songs are frequently forgotten, the writers of those songs are even more generally nameless. Rock has only recently granted significance to these figures. Through most of its history their names have merely appeared parenthetically beneath the song titles. Moreover, even the groups who are currently most popular remain tinged with folk anonymity. Most listeners know the Rascals, the Hermits, the Doors, and other groups, but I wonder how many listeners know the names of the individuals who compose those groups. Teenage newspapers and magazines seek to combat our ignorance with their feature stories on one or another group and its members. But, as time passes, even these efforts seem futile in the face of the relentless thrust of folk anonymity; and they *are* futile because the experience of a folk music reality is ultimately more pressing and immediate than the name of the artist who produced it.

This anonymity is one of the differences between rock

and jazz. Jazz is a music of great individualists. Further, its roots reach far back into the beginnings of the twentieth century, and its stylistic manifestations have been more varied than those of rock: New Orleans jazz, Chicago jazz, swing, be-bop, and modern jazz *each* represent a whole movement, one that is more expansive than the development so far of any of rock's sub-styles. Finally, improvisation has always been far more important in jazz than in rock. Nevertheless, they share a common ancestry in the blues tradition of America, and they share a folk delight in spontaneity of expression.

Perhaps the greatest difficulty in distinguishing rock as a folk idiom lies in the fact that the music is so closely linked to the enormous and complicated commercial music business, whereas generally works of art in the larger folk tradition are not at all closely related to popular art. This has caused the adverse critics of rock to say that the music has been forced upon a gullible public by some mercenary wholesalers of bad taste. In addition, these critics feel that the artists themselves are exclusively interested in financial rewards and are unconcerned about the quality of their music.

Suspicions like these are based on the fallacious assumption that the quality of art and the salability of art are mutually exclusive. Such a point, however, does not immediately dispel the suspicions themselves. Admittedly, many rock artists have earned fortunes through the sales of their records. My question, at the same time, is whether such evidence provides any meaningful explanation of why rock came into being in the first place, or why it has continued to exist. Rock artists have won and lost commercially, but the experience of the music itself has continued to possess vitality. I cannot imagine any artist who would not *enjoy* the benefits of commercial success, but both folk art and fine art can be originated and can survive without it. On the other hand, popular art does depend on commercial success in order to exist. That is, popular art *must* be popular, whereas folk art and fine art need not be, although they *may* be at any given moment. This demand for popularity is linked to the fact that popular art invariably has a product to sell: The product may be a bottle of shampoo or a new automobile, but it may also be non-material, such as diversion or escape, the "look" of reality or even of art. Popular art has many guises, but unlike either folk art or fine art, it is not self-sustaining.

Popular music, the Tin Pan Alley tradition, or *kitsch* music, has the appearance of fine art but fails to engage in the creative or artistic problems of fine art. *Kitsch* feeds parasitically upon fine art, but only after the latter has passed through its experimental and innovative stages. *Kitsch* represents an institutionalizing of the fine arts, and its product is therefore only the "look" of art. These products may be pleasant, enjoyable, and entertaining—the records of Frank Sinatra, Perry Como, and Andy Williams, and other leading exponents of *kitsch* frequently are—but they are not fundamentally concerned with artistic creation. Rather, they adopt the style of a work of art after it has come into being elsewhere, and they refine it and make it palatable for audiences who could not understand it in its original form.

Popular art avoids an encounter with reality just as it avoids an encounter with art. It succeeds by selling the "look" of reality. So although rock emerged in the same domain as popular music, it cannot be classified simply as popular music. Admittedly, the task of separating the two types of music is occasionally problematic, particularly at those points in rock history where an artist's work, Elvis Presley's for instance, undergoes a transformation from folk art to popular art. But generally the distinction is clear.

I have tried to outline some of the qualities of rock which show that it is folk music. In doing so, I am aware of the risks in generalizing about so large a body of material: Many exceptions can no doubt be offered to my central thesis. More important than the exceptions, however, is the undeniable fact that the music has changed considerably since its beginnings in the mid-1950's. Its history reveals dramatic changes in its attitude both to subject matter and to technique. And developments in the late 1960's further suggest that the music may be changing in its relation to the folk art-fine art distinction. It has been folk music through the greater part of its history; but to say that it is folk music today is more difficult. A separate chapter must be devoted to this issue and to its implications; but that discussion must take place at the conclusion of this study, after a fuller examination of the development of the music itself.

The Beginnings of Rock:
1954 through 1956

1954: A Critical Turning Point

Until 1954, the larger area of popular music consisted of three general fields: Pop, Rhythm and Blues, and Country and Western. Although the three areas were not separated in the strictest sense, a variety of factors nevertheless isolated them from one another. Each field had its own group of artists and record companies, a series of radio stations on which its music could be heard, and an audience to which it made its strongest appeal. Each field had a distinct musical style and an artistic tradition which was generally taken for granted by both its artists and its listeners.

With the emergence of rock, distinctions among these three fields became increasingly fluid, and an integration of their previously separate artistic elements took place. From 1954, this integration became a constant and unrelenting force in American popular music. Before 1954, the phenomenon had been only sporadic and isolated. During the early 1950's, for instance, certain records from the Rhythm and Blues or the Country and Western fields had crossed the traditional barriers of the taste market. Songs by the Weavers, Hank Williams, Les Paul, Louis Jordan, and Sonny Till are examples of this pattern. Yet they were only prototypes for a trend which proceeded without interruption during and after 1954. In order to clarify the significance of this trend, however, I must describe the character of the three fields in relation to this critical year.

The Pop Field

Among the three broad fields of the music industry in 1954, the Pop field was the largest in terms of its audience, the number of artists it included, and the size of the record companies which issued its music. It was the only field which could claim to represent listeners in all parts of the country, and it therefore provided the greatest potential rewards for an artist who wished to succeed on the basis of national recognition and large-scale commercial success.

The Pop field in 1954 was defined and dominated by a handful of record companies known at the time as "majors." Among the majors were Capitol, Mercury, Columbia, Decca, and RCA. For each of these companies, significantly, Pop music represented only one facet of an enormous industrial enterprise. Their artistic repertories included jazz and classical music along with Pop, and each firm produced albums, tapes, and occasionally their own record-playing equipment in addition to single records. Through established connections with radio and television, the majors also possessed promotional facilities which could bring national attention to a new song within a period of several days. Thus, an artist's association with one of these companies meant that he was afforded the widest possible market existing in the music business.

With their complicated and established industrial structures, the major companies represented the conservative branch of the music business as it existed in the early 1950's. This conservatism was reflected in the charts of the period's best-selling records. A typical chart, for instance, would show the 25 most popular records in the country. Of that number, however, two or three versions of the same song were frequently found among the top ten records. In addition, the songs at the top of the charts generally remained there for periods of twenty or twenty-five weeks. Finally, the charts were almost exclusively dominated by the labels of the major companies, and by artists whose names were familiar to listeners in nearly every part of the country.

Such a pattern of stability was changed dramatically by rock. Where a handful of well-known artists had dominated the charts, rock introduced an enormous number of new groups and individuals. Although many of these achieved only a single success on the national level and afterward seemed to disappear completely, they nevertheless represented an undeniable expansion of the range of talent within the Pop field. With each new group or individual, furthermore, a new record label also appeared. Thus, the market came to be shared among small and large companies alike instead of being controlled by the majors alone. There was a new competition within the music industry. Correspondingly, the charts of best-selling records changed more rapidly at that time than at any time in their previous history. Songs went from the bottom to the top of the charts in the space of several weeks and vanished just as quickly. Rock revolutionized the commercial structure of the Pop field, transforming it into what many people in the business felt was chaos and unpredictability.

But rock altered the larger stylistic character of the Pop field just as it altered the field's commercial structure. In 1954, the Pop style was represented by Perry Como, Eddie Fisher, Kay Starr, Joni James and others who extended the ballad tradition of the 1940's into the new decade, just as

Andy Williams and Jack Jones, among others, extended it into the 1960's. The style of these artists was *kitsch*. With its folk character, rock provided an alternative to *kitsch*. And as rock became successful and developed, it forced radio stations, listeners, and trade periodicals like *Billboard* to single out *kitsch* as "good music" or "easy listening music." Although the two styles continued to be listed together, rock's presence in the Pop field implied that the "goodness" of Pop music could no longer be taken for granted.

Thus, the Pop field has contained two major musical styles since the advent of rock: a popular art style and a folk art style. The former has been labeled "good music," while the latter has not been labeled at all. The implication, particularly in the trade literature which commented on the emergence of rock in the 1950's, was perhaps that the new trend constituted "bad music." More relevant, however, was the implication that the writers did not understand what they were listening to. Was it just a fad? Was it a new direction for the entire Pop field? Would it last? Could it honestly be called "bad music"? Such questions persisted in the 1950's, particularly in reference to the overall picture of the Pop field. But they were questions which unconsciously assumed that rock was popular art instead of folk art. The new music was as confusing to the critics of the Pop field as it was disruptive to its commercial structure.

Another characteristic of the Pop field in 1954 was its predominant whiteness. It was not exclusively so: Nat Cole, the Mills Brothers, the Ink Spots, and others commanded large audiences in the Pop market. But during the early 1950's, rather than bringing the Negro folk tradition to Pop music, their music generally appealed to the same *kitsch* sensibility as did the music of white artists. Rock changed that. Since 1954, the Negro contribution to the general field of American music has made itself increasingly felt; in fact, the history of rock is largely synonymous with the development of Negro music within American culture since that time.

I have presented the outlines of the Pop field as it existed in 1954, the year in which nearly all of the above developments occurred. However, one final development must be cited. Before 1954—that is, before the emergence of rock—the Pop field reflected and appealed to adult tastes and values. The *kitsch* tradition belonged to adults, just as the industrial structure of Pop music was formed by adults for the benefit of adults. Today young people direct their own record companies and publish their own songs. In the early 1950's, however, youth had to adjust to adult tastes if it wished to partake of adult culture. In comparison to the crazes linked with the rise of Elvis Presley or the Beatles, even the youth craze which accompanied Frank Sinatra's initial popularity in the late 1940's was an extension of adult values. The Frank Sinatra craze was quickly absorbed by the adult market because Sinatra's style was adult. But rock has always belonged to youth.

The Rhythm and Blues Field

Although the Pop field possessed the largest audience and the most expansive industrial structure at the time of rock's emergence, the Rhythm and Blues field possessed the richest assortment of the artists who were to mold the new music's stylistic character. Throughout the 1950's and into the 1960's, the work of these artists provided the strongest and most consistent reason for the quality and appeal of the music itself. However, the Rhythm and Blues field experienced radical and sometimes problematic changes for which the enormous popularity of rock was largely responsible. Rock exposed the Rhythm and Blues tradition to a larger audience than had ever been aware of it, and stimulated an unprecedented industrial growth within the field.

In the early 1950's, the Rhythm and Blues field was largely composed of independent record companies, or "indies" as they were called in the music business. For the most part, the indies enjoyed only a fraction of the business which was enjoyed by the majors of the Pop field. Although the indies outnumbered the majors, each one contained fewer artists, and the activities of each were often restricted to only single records or to one musical style. The independent company's promotion and distribution facilities were similarly limited, usually to a handful of cities or to one region of the country. Thus, an artist associated with one of these companies was simply not offered as broad a market as an artist associated with one of the majors.

During the decade of the 1950's, the situation of the independent record companies changed remarkably. In a period of phenomenal growth, several of the indies—Atlantic and Imperial, for instance—attained the size and stature of the older, major firms. In addition, the total number of indies increased each year. This growth pattern parallels exactly the expansion of the rock style. The new music, that is, existed almost invariably on the labels of the independent companies, not on the labels of the established majors.

The connection between rock and the indie companies has real significance in the music's history. During the 1950's, for instance, there was repeated criticism that the new music was being forced on the public—especially youth—by record companies and disk jockeys. The development of the indies dramatically refutes these criticisms. Without expansive promotional facilities, the indies were

in no position to force their music on a broad audience.
While several of them attained major status, the great majority of indies enjoyed the same one-shot commercial successes which were characteristic of the artists they represented. The indies survived and developed only because
the public *wanted* rock music.

As the individual indies grew and as their number rose
during the 1950's, the structure of the whole Rhythm and
Blues field changed accordingly. Although the field had
been dominated by indies before 1954, its development
had never been so rapid, and it had never reached such a
large national audience.

The restricted nature of the Rhythm and Blues field before rock is also apparent in the fact that it appealed traditionally to a Negro market. Until 1949, Rhythm and Blues
was called "race music" in the industry, which suggests
the extent to which the distinction was taken for granted.
But even though the Rhythm and Blues term was adopted
in that year, the race distinction did not begin to blur until
the middle of the 1950's. With the emergence of rock,
however, there was not only a steady penetration of Negro
artists into the Pop charts, but of white artists into the
charts of best-selling Rhythm and Blues records as well.
Although this integration persisted into the early 1960's, it
is an interesting fact that Negro artists came to dominate
the Rhythm and Blues charts again by the middle of the
1960's. In this sense, the charts reflect social developments
outside the music itself.

In 1954, the music of the Rhythm and Blues field was as
different from Pop music as were the two fields' commercial structures. Basically, the difference was between the
folk character of the blues and Pop's *kitsch* character.
Needless to say, a long and deep tradition of Negro blues
existed before rock emerged to make it available to a large
national and international audience. The blues was after

all a fundamental element of jazz. But to the Pop audiences of the early fifties, Rhythm and Blues itself sounded different from anything they had heard, and they responded to the music's folk authenticity and hard beat. To the Negro audience, Rhythm and Blues was their own music. But rock changed that situation: It made the sound of the blues more familiar to the general Pop market, and this commercial exploitation made the Negro people who had grown up with the blues feel that their fundamental musical heritage had been wrenched from them. This helps to account for the development I mentioned earlier, of Negro artists and audiences reclaiming the blues in the 1960's.

The Country and Western Field

Country and Western music is unique among the three fields which contributed to the amalgam of rock's style. Throughout the history of rock development, it has remained the most self-defined in its artistic character, and its commercial handling has changed the least.

Like the Rhythm and Blues field, the Country and Western field traditionally occupied a position somewhat on the periphery of American popular music. It too represented a folk tradition which had occasionally made an impression on the Pop field. By the middle of the 1950's, however, it was neither as strange nor as new to the ears of the popular listening audience as was Negro Rhythm and Blues. Through the long-standing popularity of Western movies and, by the fifties, the revival of this genre on televison, the music of the Old West was quite familiar. Even before the 1950's, it had certainly been popularized by Gene Autry and Roy Rogers, for instance, and Country and Western songs were usually lumped together in the popular imagination under the heading of "hillbilly" or "cowboy" music. However, these traditions were accepted and respected in a way that the Rhythm and Blues tradition was not. And when their artists made themselves felt as contributors to the new rock tradition, they did not provoke as much controversy as the Negro artists did.

In terms of its industrial structure, the Country and Western field did not expand considerably during the years of the rock development. By the 1950's, the field seems to have been fairly content with the scope of its audience and with the commercial handling of its music. It possessed a long-standing chain of radio stations and programs, as well as an established circuit of in-person performance sites. For record promotion and distribution, many of its artists enjoyed the benefits of being affiliated with the same major companies which dominated the Pop field. All of these features existed before the advent of rock in 1954, and they gave the Country and Western field a degree of established conservatism which persisted throughout the decade and continues to persist in the 1960's.

The conservative character of the Country and Western field became clearly apparent as rock developed during the 1950's. At a time when the Pop and Rhythm and Blues fields were undergoing some radical changes and were experiencing some extensive interpenetrations—Rhythm and Blues charts reflecting Pop tastes, Rhythm and Blues artists gaining acceptance in the Pop field, and mutual stylistic influences occurring between the two fields—the Country and Western field remained relatively static. Very few of the patterns which apply to the Pop or Rhythm and Blues fields in the 1950's can be applied to Country and Western. And when the Country and Western charts reflected the rock style—in the records of Elvis Presley, Carl Perkins, the Everly Brothers, Jerry Lee Lewis and others—it was invariably through artists who had their origin in the

Country field itself. Artists who started in the Rhythm and Blues or Pop fields were never found in the Country charts. Given the apparent fluidity of the other areas of the popular music world at this time, this was remarkable. Although a comparable self-defining exclusiveness later appeared within the Rhythm and Blues field, it did so only in 1963 and 1964, after almost ten years of rock development in an opposite direction.

What the Country and the Rhythm and Blues fields already shared in the early 1950's were their respective traditions as folk music. The Country and Western tradition included many different types of expression, a number of which varied according to geographical region or traditional occupation: There were cowboy and railroad songs, sea chanties, and country blues, to name only a few. As rock emerged, the Country and Western artists who helped to shape the new music continued some of these traditions and eschewed others. The younger generation used fewer of the older conventions of Country and Western material —religious subjects, for instance, or songs telling about nature—but it continued the tradition of the country blues and ballad, and it used the beat of the older country generation which was much lighter and quicker than the Rhythm and Blues beat. In addition, the younger generation kept alive the tradition of the guitar as a folk instrument—a tradition which is evident in all of the country-inspired rock of the 1950's and which has assumed even greater significance in the music's more recent development.

Early Rock: Crossovers and Covers

The first rock record is the original version of "Sh-Boom" by the Chords. Issued on the Cat label, a subsidiary of Atlantic, "Sh-Boom" occupies a unique position in the history of popular music: It not only heralded the style of the new music, but the history of its success established the pattern followed by nearly all of the successful rock records between 1954 and 1956.

"Sh-Boom" made its appearance in the Rhythm and Blues field early in the summer of 1954. By July of that year, the record had generated enough sales across the country to break into the national chart of best-selling Pop songs. It was not the first Rhythm and Blues record of 1954 to achieve such a distinction. The Crows' "Gee" had done so several months earlier. But "Gee" never reached the top ten—which "Sh-Boom" did after three weeks on the charts —and, further, "Gee" did not stimulate nearly as much general enthusiasm in the field of popular music as did "Sh-Boom."

An index of this enthusiasm lies in the number and variety of "cover" versions that were made of "Sh-Boom" as soon as its impact on the national audience was realized. The largest-selling cover was issued by the Crew Cuts. It was released during the week in which the Chords' version reached the Pop charts, and it reached the top ten itself just one week later. Clearly, the song had stimulated an immediate and phenomenal excitement—with a variety of both artists and listeners. It was also covered by Billy Williams on Coral Records and by Sy Oliver on Bell, both of whom were Pop oriented; in addition, it was covered by country artist Bobby Williamson, so that it even penetrated the Country and Western market, although not in its original version. By the fall of 1954, "Sh-Boom" reached England's top twenty chart, and, still in the same year, Stan Freeberg used it as the inspiration for one of his many successful parodies of popular culture.

The Stan Freeberg version of "Sh-Boom" is of more than passing interest. The parody appeared after the two best-selling versions of the song, and it drew elements from both. Through its lyrics it made references to the Rhythm and Blues origin of the Chords' record and to the Crew Cuts' popularized cover of the original. In ridiculing both versions, however, the Freeberg parody failed to distinguish between them as different types of artistic expression. In other words, it failed to define the new music as folk art or popular art, Negro or white music. Instead it presented "Sh-Boom" as senseless and incoherent, and it expressed consternation as to how this song could provoke such extraordinary interest. This experience of consternation regarding rock was shared generally by adults during the early 1950's. However unconsciously, Freeberg's parody therefore revealed an important aspect of rock; in appealing to the puzzlement of adults, it marked the new sound as a youth expression.

What happened to "Sh-Boom" happened again and again to other songs throughout 1954 and 1955. An unknown song, by an unknown group, on an unknown label —unknown, at least, by the larger Pop audience, although not necessarily unknown by the Rhythm and Blues audience—emerged in the Rhythm and Blues field, broke into the Pop charts, and was covered by Pop versions. The Spaniels' "Goodnight, Sweetheart, Goodnight" was covered by the McGuire Sisters; the Penguins' "Earth Angel" by the Crew Cuts; Fats Domino's "Ain't That A Shame," the El Dorados' "At My Front Door" and Little Richard's "Tutti Frutti" were all covered by Pat Boone, and there were many other examples.

Significantly, there was a tendency for the Pop covers of these early rock songs to outsell the originals—at least this is the evidence offered by the Pop charts in which two or more versions were competing at the same time. Such a pattern may seem strange, even incredible now, since the original versions are remembered while the records by Pat

Boone, the McGuire Sisters, and the Crew Cuts have been forgotten. During the early 1950's, the promotion and distribution facilities of the major record companies, which were much greater than those of the indies, probably helped to bring about this situation, since the major companies were generally responsible for cover material. But the foreign-sounding character of the new music—that is, as it was then experienced by a majority of listeners— must also have enabled the Pop-styled imitations to capitalize on the rock innovation. After all, the unsophisticated Pop audience was still conditioned to the older Tin Pan Alley musical tradition and could hardly have been expected to adjust their sensibilities overnight. That they adjusted rather quickly is demonstrated by the fact that, by 1956, the cover versions no longer dominated the Pop charts. By that time, the records by Chuck Berry, Fats Domino, and Little Richard stood alone in both the Pop and the Rhythm and Blues listings. In 1954 and 1955, however, the Pop audience was eager for the new material, but unable to accept completely the authentic versions.

The cover situation indicated some of the competitive turmoil generated within the industry by the new rock music. Both the established record companies and their artists quickly felt the pressure which was being exerted by so-called "unknown" groups and individuals. The very effort of the major companies to meet this competition— by producing their own style of rock or by imitating the originals—suggested that the new music was not a freak occurrence of taste, but that it had struck a profound response in the national audience. As the majors attempted to elicit this response, they generally produced records which today are only curiosities in the history of American music: Perry Como's "Ko Ko Mo," Eddie Fisher's "Dungaree Doll," or Kay Starr's "Rock and Roll Waltz."

While their established artists were failing to adapt to the new music, further, the majors were failing to discover new exponents of rock. The reason for both phenomena was that the major companies were oriented toward the past—toward the diluted and sweetened values of *kitsch*, instead of toward folk values. The artists and organizations which had formerly dominated the music business did not understand rock. They mistakenly believed the music could be molded to *kitsch* conventions because they did not comprehend it as an idiom which was distinct from popular art. In a period of changing values, the majors were slow to adjust; to them, folk music sounded crude and primitive instead of powerful and authentic.

This distinction in musical styles is apparent immediately in a comparison of the Chords' version of "Sh-Boom" with that of the Crew Cuts—as it is apparent in a comparison of nearly all of the early rock originals with their covers by Pop musicians. The Chords' version contains a rich blend between the vocal and instrumental portions of the song. In the Crew Cuts' version, the instrumental background is clearly separated from the lyrics; it is subordinated to the lyrics while they are being sung and it enters only to fill spaces when the lyrics stop. The Chords put everything together, and they used fragmentary words or words which had no logical relation to the literary content of the song. They used the voice like an additional musical instrument—as jazz vocalists had done in the late forties—and thereby emphasized the close relationship between the vocal and instrumental elements. In the rock songs, the lyrics often consisted of oohs and aahs, dip-dips, and dom-be-do-bes. And there was the suggestion that the singers were creating lines as they went along and using them to express immediate feelings. In this, the rock artists aligned themselves with the folk tradition.

These features made the Chords' record distinctive. It

projected a fabric of sound in which everything struck the
listener at once—instrumental sound, lyrics, fragmentary
or improvised lyrics, and all with a powerful incessant
beat. By comparison, the "proto-rock" song of 1954, the
Crows' "Gee," started out with the same density of combined elements, but after two vocal choruses broke into an
electric guitar section that sounded more like a popularized jazz riff than an intuitive folk gesture. This section
contradicted the driving beat of the rest of the song, and it
prevented the record from having the totality of impact
that "Sh-Boom" had.

This immediate totality of impact was probably why
"Sh-Boom" sounded strange to many listeners in the popular audience in 1954. They were accustomed to a cleaner
kind of music in which the separate parts were more easily
perceptible, where lyrics were distinctly enunciated,
where voices were either individualized or precisely unified, and where vocal and instrumental sections did not
impose on one another. The Crew Cuts "cleaned up" "Sh-
Boom," and that is what the Pop groups generally did
when they produced cover versions of the early rock songs.
In doing so, they radically altered the stylistic character of
the music: They may have preserved a faint echo of the
original beat, but they lost its totality of impact by strip-
ping it of its folk spontaneity.

Early Rock: Style and Content

The preceding sections of this discussion might give the
impression that rock began when a number of records orig-
inating in the Rhythm and Blues field gained acceptance
with the Pop audience and its musicians, and that the
rock style took its character solely from the Rhythm and
Blues tradition. However, many other factors were involved in the genesis and meaning of the new music.

While rock took its style from the Rhythm and Blues tradition, it took its subject matter from the Pop field. It was a music that belonged essentially to young people, that described in immediate terms the realities with which they were concerned, and that used a hard-driving vocabulary to voice their feelings about the world. In a sense, rock was from the start a protest art. For the first decade of its existence, admittedly, it did not describe its protest in literal terms. It did not speak of social injustice, of war, of crumbling establishments, or of the older generation and its value systems. The literal enunciation of such concerns came later, when the artists and the audience of rock had become far more sophisticated and publicly frustrated than they were in the early and middle fifties. Nevertheless, that is what rock meant, even in its early history: a protest against the music of the past and of an older generation, and against the values of that generation as they were expressed by the artificiality of *kitsch*. In this deepest sense of responding to reality in terms of art—but without being conscious of art—rock revealed itself as a folk medium.

Much of the subject matter of rock came, as I suggested, from the traditions of Pop music. In combination with a Rhythm and Blues beat, these subjects produced a new kind of idiom within the larger history of either popular or folk music. In the music industry itself, the mixture of Pop and Rhythm and Blues elements was noted as "producing a strange group of songs and records, material which eschews the primitive, folk-derived quality of true Rhythm and Blues and concerns itself in lyrics, with such essentially pop song concepts as angels, Paradise, weddings, eternal love, heaven, etc."* An enormous number of records reflect this tendency: "Earth Angel," "Teen An-

* Paul Ackerman, "Tin Pan Alley Days Fade on Pop Music Broader Horizons," *Billboard*, October 15, 1955, pp. 1, 16.

gel," "Altar of Love," "To the Aisle," "The Book of Love,"
"Ten Commandments of Love," "Heaven and Paradise,"
"The Chapel of Love," "Heavenly Father," "Angel Baby,"
and "Down the Aisle of Love" are a few. Within the tradition of Rhythm and Blues lyrics, such subjects and the concerns they represented were new. For Rhythm and Blues
had traditionally expressed itself in lyrics which were directed to earthy, tangible realities: the love of a woman,
finding or losing a woman, getting a job, not having
enough money. The blues existed not only as a particular
musical structure, but also as the vehicle of an artist's feelings—generally about an immediate and pressing reality.

The more ethereal or make-believe world which rock
tended to substitute for the earthy world of Rhythm and
Blues gave the new music a romantic flavor. When today's
youth, including today's rock artists and critics, look back
at such tendencies, they sometimes express a certain embarrassment, as if they were seeing a blatant escapism on
the part of the artists of the early and middle fifties. In
distinguishing today's rock from its earlier phases, they
often refer to the greater realism of the current music,
meaning it includes those subjects of the everyday world
which were missing in the rock of a decade ago. Critics
have frequently leveled this distinction at the popular arts,
and they have occasionally used it to separate the Rhythm
and Blues and the Pop traditions in music.* In the context
of rock as a folk idiom, however, the distinction becomes
problematic; that is, we become less certain about what is
real and what is unreal. If we talk about subject matter
alone, we can say that tangible, factual material is real
and that mental concepts and fantasies are unreal. But

---

* See, for instance, S. I. Hayakawa, "Popular Songs vs. the Facts
of Life," in *Mass Culture: The Popular Arts In America,* ed. Bernard
Rosenberg and David Manning White, paperback edition (London:
The Free Press, 1964), pp. 393-403.

works of art never consist of subject matter alone. The subject matter of rock has generally become more "realistic,"
just as its overall style has become generally less romantic.
But the music has always constituted the experience of reality, despite the particular character of the subjects with
which its lyrics have dealt. While those lyrics came
largely from the sentimental Pop tradition, rock gave
them reality.

For the total folk function of rock, the rhythm of the
music has always had as much meaning as its subject matter, for it has given the subject matter a real *immediacy*.
In rock's early phases, this rhythm had a primitive and
"funky" sound which almost disappeared during the music's later development. Through the early and middle fifties, however, these qualities persisted. They were generally emphasized by a pounding piano or saxophone and
were reinforced, as I have said, by a vocal manner which,
in effect, provided additional raw instrumentation. These
elements came from the Rhythm and Blues tradition, and
rock built upon their foundation. In other words, the new
music can be said to have found greater significance in
the rhythm of Rhythm and Blues than in its blues. This
Rhythm and Blues contribution to the rock style was more
apparent during the early and middle 1950's than it was
toward the end of the decade—but then, as I will describe
later, the music of the sixties altered this pattern by re-
viving the entire Rhythm and Blues heritage.

Early Rock: The Contribution of Bill Haley

Bill Haley and his Comets occupy an important position in
the early development of rock. Haley was the first artist
from the Pop field to produce a distinctly rock style—com-

pared to the diluted cover versions of rock material which
were recorded by the Crew Cuts, the McGuire Sisters, and
other Pop favorites. Haley did cover recordings, especially
during the early years of his career, but his records were
oriented toward the new aesthetic instead of toward the
Tin Pan Alley tradition of the past. His work demonstrated the real stylistic integration of Pop and Rhythm
and Blues elements which accounted for the beginning of
rock, and he produced one of the first classics of the idiom
—a record that announced the new music not only to the
music business but across the country at large: "Rock
Around the Clock." It was the first rock record to reach the
number one position in the Pop charts, and it carried the
new music to England by going to the top of the English
charts as well.

Haley and his group were originally styled Country and
Western, and they called themselves the Saddlemen. By
1953, they had become Bill Haley and his Comets, and
they were producing in the style of Rhythm and Blues
such recordings as "Crazy Man Crazy." Their cover version of Joe Turner's "Shake, Rattle and Roll," a tremendous success in the Rhythm and Blues field, became one of
the best-selling records in the Pop field during 1954. But,
somewhat curiously, "Rock Around the Clock," which was
also released in 1954 and which was also a cover of a
Rhythm and Blues original—a commercially unsuccessful
one by Sonny Dae—never reached the national charts in
that year. In 1955, the group's popularity continued to increase with the issue of "Dim Dim the Lights." The distinctive feature of this last record was that it broke into
the national charts of the best-selling Rhythm and Blues
records. This was the first time that a recording from the
Pop field had achieved such a distinction, and it proved to
be a harbinger of the effect rock would have on chart patterns during the 1950's. Haley was the first of the white

Courtesy Columbia Pictures. From the film Don't Knock the Rock

Bill Haley and His Comets

rock artists to enjoy such a success, and it reflected the fact
that the music he produced contained a rhythmic quality
which was distinctly different from—and, because of its
folk orientation, more authentic than—the covers being
produced by Pop musicians. The records by the Crew Cuts
and the McGuire Sisters, for instance, had never penetrated the Rhythm and Blues market. Haley's "Shake,
Rattle and Roll" did not penetrate it either, since his version
of that song faced the competition of a much higher quality
original recording than either "Dim Dim the Lights" or
"Rock Around the Clock."

While Haley's records enjoyed considerable success during 1954 and into 1955, none of them created the phenomenal excitement that is associated with "Rock Around the
Clock." When the record was reissued, in connection with
the release of the film *Blackboard Jungle*, it went immediately to the top of the Pop charts, and it went considerably
higher in the Rhythm and Blues charts than had "Dim
Dim the Lights." In England, it became the first rock song
to top the English charts of best-selling popular records.

Needless to say, the association of "Rock Around the
Clock" with *Blackboard Jungle* was largely responsible
for the record's extraordinary success. The combination of
the image of rebellious youth with the raucous and driving
sound of rock spelled out an interpretation which was already implicit in the popular imagination: This was rebellious music. In this particular case, the content of the
film reinforced the appeal of the music. In the best Hollywood tradition, the film presented a young man who, as
the Shangri-Las say in a record which is ten years younger
than the film, is "good-bad, but he's not evil." This was
the character of rock too: foreign, perhaps, and strangely
rebellious, but sensuous and exciting with its youthful vitality. When "Rock Around the Clock" inspired a riot on
the Princeton University campus late in the spring of

1955, a newspaper article described the event, appropriately, as "feverish though harmless."*

Actually, there was something revolutionary in "Rock Around the Clock" and in Haley's music generally, even though it was probably not the thing which the national audience consciously considered: his style. Haley created a sound which was similar to the other early rock songs I have described. He tended to shout his lyrics rather than cleanly "vocalizing" them, and he let his rhythm section of guitars and saxophones into the foreground of the total arrangement. An important distinction between Haley's music and other early rock records, however, was in his stronger insistence on guitars, and also in the hint of a Country and Western twang that persisted in nearly all his songs. This is especially apparent in the instrumental sections of his records—in "Rock Around the Clock," for instance—which feature rapid and seemingly complicated guitar riffs, the kind that audiences are expected to applaud on variety shows.

Haley's later records are in no way as significant as these early ones. By 1956, he had issued "See You Later Alligator," "Rockin' Through the Rye," and "Saints Rock and Roll," but in these he seems to have simply capitalized on his own image as a rock artist and to have produced popularized versions or mere imitations of his own best music. Haley's later productions clearly demonstrate that a folk artist can become a popular artist. Nevertheless, this does not detract from his general importance in the earlier development of rock. As I have said, he was the first of the Pop-based artists to produce a distinctive rock style and, because of his popularity, he was responsible for spreading an image of the new music: into films (not only *Blackboard Jungle*, but *Rock Around the Clock* and *Don't Knock*

---

* The newspaper was the *Philadelphia Inquirer*; the item was subsequently reported in *Billboard*, May 28, 1955, p. 35.

the Rock in which he appeared along with other rock artists) and into other countries (in England he was received with enormous enthusiasm as late as 1957). Finally, the character of Haley's group was a significant factor in his historical importance. It was a small unit—usually consisting of five or six musicians—that was, for the most part, musically autonomous. Certain recording techniques helped to account for its sound—a fact which caused some disappointment during in-person performances—but the group sang, and also provided its own instrumental accompaniment. This meant that rock music could be produced easily. A large orchestra and a chorus of voices were unnecessary, because a minimum of elements sufficed to evoke a mood. Bill Haley and his Comets symbolized the immediacy and the availability of rock, and they started a trend which has continued to gain momentum through the entire history of the music.

Early Rock: The Contribution of Elvis Presley

Elvis Presley is the most important individual rock artist to emerge during the music's early development between 1954 and 1956. His extraordinary popularity surpassed that of any artist who appeared in those years, and it remained as a standard for almost a decade—until the Beatles and other young artists appeared toward the middle of the 1960's. Not all of Presley's records from those years have the historical significance or the aesthetic impact of his early work, but the mere fact that he stayed in the spotlight for so long makes him a special case within the larger history of the music. For the music industry, Presley was "king" for almost ten years. He was the first rock artist to establish a continuing and independent motion picture career, the first to have a whole series of mil-

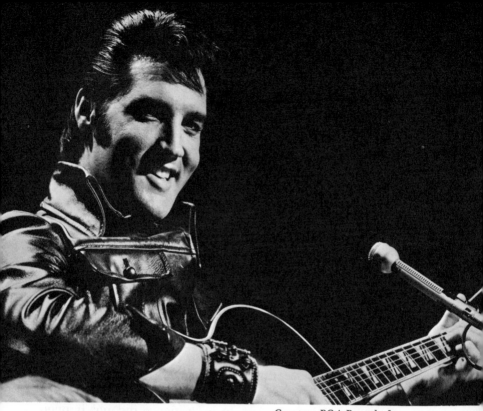

Elvis Presley

lion-selling single records—before 1960 he had eighteen—
and the first to dominate consistently the tastes of the foreign record market, especially in England, where popularity polls listed him among the top favorites for each
year until the arrival of the Beatles.

For the history of rock, Presley's importance lay primarily in his releases of 1956. Beginning with "Heartbreak Hotel," his records for RCA spread across all of the
fields of the popular music market and confirmed the in-
tegrating pattern which the music had already begun during 1954 and 1955. Presley, however, was the first of the
new artists to emerge from the Country and Western field.
This background was clearly evident, much more than the
hint of Country and Western that lingered in Bill Haley's
music. This new stylistic ingredient has persisted generally
in rock, but it was only after Presley defined it that the
Everly Brothers, Buddy Holly and the Crickets, Jerry Lee
Lewis, and other Country and Western-based artists
brought their own individual contributions to rock music.

Of course, Presley's rise to prominence did not happen
in quite the overnight fashion that we tend to associate
with his career. After signing a contract with RCA at the
end of 1955, he did become suddenly popular—by means
of television appearances, particularly on the Ed Sullivan
show, coverage by the press, and some extraordinary record sales—but these national successes were preceded by
two years of work in and around his home town of Memphis where he was under contract to Sun records. Presley's
career with Sun was more ordinary than it has been since,
and it consisted of his gradual establishment in the Country and Western field. His first two records for Sun—
"That's All Right"/"Blue Moon Of Kentucky" and "Good
Rockin' Tonight"/"I Don't Care If the Sun Don't Shine"—
were both merely local hits which appeared sporadically
on the Memphis charts. The significance of these early

records, however, is their stylistic range. In both cases, Presley brought a rock interpretation to a song from the more conventional Country and Western idiom. Both sides of his first records were popular, and this anticipated the range of the appeal he would have when he became nationally known.

In 1955, Presley began to make an impression on a much larger Country and Western market. His second and third Sun recordings both reached the national charts of best-selling Country and Western songs: "You're Right, I'm Left, She's Gone"/"Baby Let's Play House" and "I Forgot To Remember To Forget"/"Mystery Train." By this time, Presley had also become one of the featured artists of the *Louisiana Hayride* show which continually toured the Country and Western circuit. His growing significance was indicated by the *Billboard* disk jockey poll of 1955, in which he was voted the number one "Up and Coming" Country and Western artist. A year before, the same poll listed him in the number eight position. These activities brought Presley to the attention of RCA representative Steve Sholes, and the company purchased his Sun contract—as well as his unreleased masters and all rights to the songwriting and publishing activities connected with his records—for $40,000 in December of 1955.

Presley's first release for RCA was "Heartbreak Hotel." It appeared in February, 1956, and quickly rose to the number one position in the Pop and Country and Western charts and to the top five of the Rhythm and Blues charts. Such wide-ranging appeal was extraordinary but not entirely unique: Carl Perkins's "Blue Suede Shoes"—released originally in the Country and Western field at about the same time as "Heartbreak Hotel"—also swept across all three fields of the popular music market. "Blue Suede Shoes" was an enormous success. However, it never reached as high in any of the charts as did "Heartbreak Hotel," and Presley

was able to repeat his first success—not once or twice, but
with a long series of single records and albums. In 1956,
"I Want You, I Need You, I Love You," "Don't Be Cruel,"
"Hound Dog," and "Love Me Tender" all stimulated the
sweeping success of "Heartbreak Hotel." In Elvis Presley
rock possessed its first consistently spectacular artist as opposed to its occasionally spectacular records.

The success of Presley's records was closely linked to his
image as a personality. He became an idol whose public
appearances were documented by the press, and whose
audience constantly thirsted for details regarding his life,
his daily activities, his background, his tastes, his romantic
interests—anything which might reveal more about the
"real" Elvis Presley. This phenomenal devotion was new
to the realm of rock artists, and it enabled the producers of
mass media—of teen magazines and newspapers—to capitalize upon an audience's desire to "know" the personalities behind the most popular records. During the 1950's,
the practice applied primarily to white artists from the
Pop or Country and Western fields; in the sixties, however,
Negro artists from the Rhythm and Blues field began to
enjoy comparable publicity. But in either case, the trend
revealed that rock is experienced as a folk genre. Its audience has always bought more than records: They have
bought fragments of "real" personalities. Since Elvis Presley, this factor has become increasingly important in un-
derscoring rock's function as a total way of life.

Presley's records from 1956 show clearly his contribution to the rock style. The most distinctive facet of that
contribution is the expressive range of Presley's voice. In
"Heartbreak Hotel," the voice strikes the first sound on
the record and quickly ranges from a wailing blues to a
textured, almost spoken growl; in "I Want You, I Need
You, I Love You," it virtually cries; and in "Love Me
Tender," it is throaty and sensual. The voice is the most

powerful feature in all of these records; as an expressive vehicle, it shifts from high to low notes, it groans, it slurs, and it produces breathless changes of rhythm. To many listeners, Presley's voice may have seemed crude, but its folk immediacy resided in this crudeness. His vocals directly conveyed a restless tension, suggesting that the lyrics were strongly felt, but that the feelings were also restrained—as if the moaning could have been deeper or the wailing more frenetic. This combination of tension and spontaneity formed the real appeal of Presley's rock style.

In his early records, Presley's vocal strength was occasionally accompanied by an equally strong electric guitar style—in "Heartbreak Hotel," for instance, or "I Got A Woman," which was included in his first RCA album. But the majority of his records did not feature significant instrumental accompaniment. Generally, that accompaniment merely formed a background for the vocal, and its popularized country style failed to duplicate the heavy impact of Presley's extraordinary voice. In Presley's later records, the qualitative distinction between vocal and instrumental became less accentuated, but in an aesthetically unfortunate way. When RCA added the harmonizing background voices of the Jordanaires to his records, for instance, the individuality of Presley's own voice was increasingly undermined, and his music became more sweet. Like Bill Haley, Elvis Presley slowly gravitated toward popular art. Unlike Bill Haley, Presley periodically showed that he could recapture the folk authenticity of his original style: The 1962 record, "His Latest Flame," is reminiscent of his first RCA releases, and his 1968 television special, while largely a popular art production, nevertheless contained moments of Presley's initial folk inspiration.

In his early career especially, Elvis Presley forcefully presented the image of a singer with his guitar. Like his folk predecessors, and like Bill Haley and his Comets, he was a symbol of the autonomous musician. More than his contemporaries, however, Presley expressed the sensuous vitality of the new rock music. As he sang, he also danced —in a raucous and sexy manner which inspired his well-known nickname, "Elvis the Pelvis." Presley's long hair, sideburns, and suggestive dancing provoked criticisms of his music and of rock generally. To conservative adults in the 1950's, the new music appeared to be an expression of hostile, rebellious youth. To his enthusiastic audience, Presley's spontaneous dancing was a visual counterpart to the feelings which his singing inspired.

Throughout his career, Presley's style has reflected his Country and Western sources. His films—*Jailhouse Rock*, *Love Me Tender*, *King Creole*, and *Kissin' Cousins*, among others—generally present him as a "country boy." In his music, the country background is reflected in his constant production of Christmas and religious albums—which have always been a traditional part of the Country and Western field, but in which rock artists have rarely been interested. Like his first album for RCA, which contained "I'll Never Let You Go, Little Darlin' " and "I'm Counting On You," Presley's regular albums have always contained several traditional Country and Western songs which he did not interpret in a rock style. Despite these persistent country connections, however, and despite his leadership in uniting the country and rock styles, Presley now has an ironic relationship to the Country and Western field, because that field has ceased to include him. After his return from military service, Presley's records gradually dropped off the country charts. This fact reveals the peculiar exclusiveness of the Country and Western field—an exclusiveness based less upon artistic style than upon spiritual allegiance. In these terms, Elvis Presley probably seemed like a Hollywood "star" instead of a faithful member of the country field. Such a distinction may reflect the change in Presley's personal image, but it does not negate his historical contribution to an earlier phase of authentic folk music.

Radio as a Rock Medium

When rock emerged in the middle of the 1950's, it was accompanied by important changes in the style of radio programming and by a new relationship between the disk jockey and the music he played. Because of its incessant rhythm, rock forced the radio medium to accelerate its presentation and the disk jockeys who became most popular were those who could maintain the music's excited pace. News, weather, advertisements, and public information were all announced in the hectic style which characterized the music, and a radio show—frequently an entire station —became a unified experience of forced excitement.

Rock was inherently suited to the radio medium, because the music was generally oriented toward records rather than live performances. Because the majority of rock songs made their first impressions via radio, and because both records and radio were relatively mechanical, impersonal media, the music did not sacrifice much of its impact. On the contrary, the early rock artists frequently lost their aesthetic impact when they performed in live concert situations which could not duplicate the mechanical effects of the recording studio, and which forced them to compete with the mental images that their own records had created. Certainly, not all rock artists were faced with this problem; Chuck Berry, Fats Domino, and Elvis Presley each possessed a live-performance style which compensated for the difference between records and concerts by providing the latter with a theatrical content of their own. Generally, however, the sounds produced in the recording studio did not accompany the artists in the concert hall. Interestingly, the spontaneous bedlam which prevailed at most rock concerts helped to compensate for the loss. The total effect of the live situation became more important than the fact that the original sound of an artist's hit record was not being duplicated.

Rock's radio and record orientation is critical in distinguishing the music as a folk idiom. Although rock was not the first folk music style to *use* records and radio, it was the first to express itself *primarily* through these mechanical, impersonal media. Before rock, popular records and radio shows were inspired by live situations—Broadway shows, nightclub performances, and other personal appearances of a group or individual. Radio tried to duplicate these situations; Pop disk jockeys like Al Jarvis and Martin Block described "make-believe ballrooms" which created the atmosphere of a large dance hall, and in which songs were experienced as if a particular musician were performing in person instead of on records. Similarly, folk music traditionally emerged from live situations—from groups sharing a common experience of work or play, or from an individual singing to his people. With rock, however, records became the primary, common bond among artists and listeners, and radio shows provided the primary, common situation in which the music was experienced. Without consciously describing a hootenanny or trying to elicit the atmosphere of one, the rock radio show generated the experience of a folk gathering. The unique feature of this experience was that it existed only in the mind and emotion of the individual listener; he did not pretend that the records he heard were anything but records, because the sounds he absorbed were realities in themselves.

The rock disk jockey played an instrumental role in this experiential folk reality. Because he spontaneously participated in the event—rather than structuring it and separating it from himself by assuming the role of a detached "master of ceremonies"—he encouraged the listeners to react in equally spontaneous and personal ways. Moreover, when the disk jockey audibly hammered the beat to one of his favorite songs, or sang a few of its lyrics, and when he breathlessly read the news, weather and sports, he gave the radio show a pace which—to listeners accustomed to an older radio style—caused everything to blend indiscriminately together. But this style also surrounded the show with a total atmosphere that was typical of rock. In the dense fabric of sounds which characterized the radio event, the records assumed the imprint of performances and the show assumed the immediacy—although not the illusion—of a live folk gathering.

With rock, the radio and record media assumed lives of their own. They became ends in themselves instead of means to other ends. This may help to explain why television shows like the *Hit Parade* gradually died when rock became prominent. Stylistically, Snooky Lanson and the *Hit Parade* cast were unsympathetic to the new music, and they misunderstood its basic folk identity. More important, however, they failed to realize that rock was essentially an experiential phenomenon which involved hearing more than seeing. The *Hit Parade* cast could translate older songs into a television show because the Tin Pan Alley musicians they imitated were similarly oriented toward in-person performances. But rock existed primarily on records and radio, and the impact these media projected could not be duplicated by the *Hit Parade* personalities or by live performance. Significantly, when rock artists "performed" their own songs on television, as they frequently did on the *American Bandstand* show, they generally "lipped" the song while the record was played. In these instances, which only appeared after the advent of rock, the live personalities can perhaps be said to have "imitated" records or radio.

To many listeners and viewers—to Ed Sullivan, for instance, who does not permit these events on his television show—the lipped performance is disturbing because it is partly dishonest. That is, it enables an individual merely to *act* as though he is performing, when, in fact, he is not performing at all. In the 1950's, this "dishonesty" was frequently cited to substantiate the feeling that rock was not music, or not very good music, because its artists could not "really" sing (such arguments are reminiscent of the claims that abstract painters are not painters, or not very good painters, unless they can draw illusionistically). But I wish to suggest a different explanation for the disturbing quality of the lipped performance, one which concerns our expectations about original works of art and their reproductions in the mass media. My feeling with regard to rock is that records generally constitute the originals and that the live performances which follow them are actually reproductions. Lipped performances unconsciously admit this: They transform the singer to an imitative status. These events are disturbing, however, because of our uncertainty about what that imitative status consists of: Is the singer imitating a record or is he imitating himself? To the extent that the primary experience of rock is connected with records, I would argue that he is imitating a record.

Misunderstandings about the expressiveness of rock in different media persisted in the 1960's. They have been accentuated because many current groups, particularly San Francisco groups like the Jefferson Airplane and the Grateful Dead, have developed their music through concert performances instead of orienting it primarily to radio or records. As a result, their records frequently lack the aesthetic impact and the immediacy of their personal ap-

pearances. Bill Graham, promoter at the Fillmore West
and the Fillmore East has suggested that the discrepancy
is caused by record producers—especially the older ones—
who do not understand the latest rock music.* He feels
that younger, more sympathetic producers will gradually
close the aesthetic gap between records and concerts. In
other words, Graham envisions records as having an imitative function. The history of rock, however, suggests an
alternative explanation. As I have said, it reveals that the
music made its strongest impact by unconsciously recognizing that radio and records were not imitative.

The Role of the Disk Jockey: Alan Freed

In the relationship which was established between rock
and radio, the disk jockey occupied a crucial position. He
did not merely become an important "personality," because disk jockeys had enjoyed that distinction before. He
became a type of folk artist himself. He became directly
linked with the music, with the style of his radio program,
and with the impact which both made upon his audience.
An important question, however, concerns the extent to
which he was able to influence the tastes of that audience.
During the early years of the rock development—when
the music was viewed with skepticism, and when it was
often associated with juvenile delinquency—the attitude
of the disk jockey was frequently cited as the primary reason for the music's growing popularity. At the time of the
payola hearings in 1959 and 1960, disk jockeys became
open targets for the suspicion that they played rock simply
because record companies had financially coerced them into
doing so. The disk jockey was felt to be the focus of an
illegal situation which had produced a biased promotion
of rock and a dictation of tastes in its favor.

* Personal interview, San Francisco, April 1966.

While payola practices existed in connection with rock, they did not insure the success of the new music. Certainly, the rock disk jockey's excitement could help to promote a new record, but it could not guarantee sales. By far the most important fact concerning disk jockeys and early rock is that they resisted the new music as enthusiastically as they supported it. With the emergence of rock, radio became increasingly competitive; individual disk jockeys and entire radio stations were absorbed in a struggle to gain large portions of a growing audience. This competition generally focused on rock and a station's decision to play, or not to play, the new music. The decision *not* to play rock was generally accompanied by the most theatrical anti-promotion practices: Rock records were destroyed *en masse*, and disk jockeys vowed to play only "good music." But rock persisted in its development, which is astonishing if one assumes that disk jockeys could dictate public taste—unless, of course, one assumes that only *rock* disk jockeys could dictate public taste. The history of radio competition in the 1950's contradicts such assumptions and it suggests that disk jockeys were as much affected by the new music as they affected it.

The shifting image of the rock disk jockey—ranging from public acclaim to severe public criticism—is dramatically expressed in the career of Alan Freed. He was the self-appointed, generally accepted "Father of Rock and Roll," and he enjoyed more than ten years of close association with the music, as disk jockey, artist, song writer, promoter, and "personality." Freed's varied activities paralleled the hectic expansion of rock during the 1950's, they reached a climax at the end of the decade, and they rapidly disintegrated from the time of the payola hearings until his death in 1965 at the age of 43.

Freed became famous as a disk jockey in New York, where he worked for WINS and later for WABC. Before

1954, when he came to WINS, Freed was associated with
station WJW in Cleveland; before that he worked for
WAKR in Akron, and he began his career with WKST in
Newcastle, Pennsylvania, where he played classical music.
Freed first used the term "Rock and Roll" in 1951.* Thus,
he had had a long association with the music, even though
his greatest national recognition as a rock personality
came after he moved to New York City, and after he became affiliated with the far-reaching Pop stations there.
Through the fifties, Freed strengthened his relation to
rock by promoting large-scale concerts which generally
attracted huge crowds. He presented these shows in Akron,
Cleveland, New York, and elsewhere in the east, and they
invariably had the most important artists of the period as
their musical climax: in the early fifties, Billy Ward and
the Dominos or the Clovers, and later Fats Domino or
Chuck Berry. These concerts showed cross sections of the
expanding rock style, including groups, individuals, and
bands which represented all areas of the new music.

Freed's involvements with rock went beyond his activities as a disk jockey and concert promoter. By 1956 he was
credited as the author or co-author of fifteen songs including "Sincerely," "Most of All," "Maybellene," and "Na-
dine," all of which were nationally popular. In 1956, he
also organized his own band, and signed a contract with
Coral records to create a series of rock albums which were
suitable for teenage dance parties. He also appeared in the
film *Rock Around the Clock*, which featured Bill Haley
and his Comets, Little Richard, Chuck Berry, and other
rock artists. Throughout the period of the middle 1950's,
Freed's name constantly appeared in the news of both the
music business and the popular press. In some cases these
reports were favorable, in others they were not; together,

* Freed made this claim on the album notes for the record, *Alan
Freed's Top 15* (End).

however, they reflect the chaotic nature of his career. Before he signed with Coral to record albums, for instance, *Billboard* first reported that he was joining the company as an A&R (artist and repertoire) man and a free-lance scout for new talent and songs; a second report mentioned that he would act as an artist rather than an A&R man; and a third report announced that his prospective association with Coral had been cancelled because of Freed's extensive prior commitments. Some of Freed's most favorable publicity accompanied his appearance on an Eric Severeid CBS television show in 1956 when he was asked to defend rock against a series of criticisms which had been published in the *New York Daily News*. Some of his most damaging publicity accompanied a riot in Boston in May, 1958: The riot erupted after one of Freed's concerts, and he was accused of having incited it. Generally, Freed's career survived the public notoriety which his activities generated, but it did not survive the payola investigations of 1959-60* or an indictment for income tax evasion which took place at the same time.

The lamentable conclusion of Freed's career does not negate his contribution to the rise of rock. As a writer, he was responsible for some of the music's first classics. As a concert promoter, he did more to make the music a nationally recognized phenomenon than any other individual. And as a disk jockey, he forcefully expressed the vitality of the music because he allowed it to inspire a new style of radio programming.

Rock and the Record Industry

I have already mentioned some of the changes in the music industry which accompanied the development of rock: the expansion of independent record companies, the

* See below, pp. 109-16.

integration of the traditionally separate fields of popular music, and the evolution of a new style of radio programming. Another significant change which happened between 1954 and 1956 concerns the 45 rpm record. In the total sales of single records, 45s first surpassed 78s in these years, and this shift was directly related to the growing popularity of rock music.

Forty-five rpm records were not new in 1954; they had been introduced by RCA in 1949 and their new vinyl composition had been developed during World War II when the federal government drastically monopolized the supply of shellac—the material which had previously been used in record manufacture. But the 45 medium was not accepted immediately because radio stations and individual consumers were reluctant to purchase the new record-playing equipment which the 45 demanded. The situation gradually changed, however, particularly when RCA introduced a relatively low-priced record player, and when optional centers became standard, so that the new records could fit conventional spindles. In 1954, moreover, several of the major record companies, including RCA and Mercury, announced that they would send 45s instead of 78s to disk jockeys. This decision increased pressure on the radio stations, and it provoked arguments about "change-of-speed" policies which were waged throughout the year. These arguments, and the resistance to the 45 which they reflected, were essentially based upon economic considerations. This is also reflected by the fact that 45s penetrated last into the Rhythm and Blues market. Although they first surpassed 78s in the Pop market sales in 1954, they were outsold by 78s, by a 3 to 1 margin, in the Rhythm and Blues field as late as 1956. The explanation for this is obvious: The generally less privileged Negro communities in the south and in the northern or western urban areas were the last to experience the growing national affluence of the decade.

Despite resistance by radio stations and individual consumers, the replacement of 78s by 45s persisted and was
complete in all fields of the popular music business by
1957. The change took place most dramatically between
1954 and 1956—that is, the period in which rock first
achieved national significance. In the record industry and
in the popular imagination, 45s were associated with rock.
This relationship was not coincidental; rather, it was
based on the fact that the records and the music possessed
a common meaning.

While its speed was slower, in all of its other features,
the 45 constituted a speeding-up process. This was true
for everyone connected with the records: manufacturers,
distributors, shop owners, disk jockeys, and individual
buyers. The lightness, ease of handling, and physical resil-
ience of the 45 sharply distinguished it from the cumber-
some 78. It was easily manufactured, due to the development of automatic injection and compression systems in
record production which obviated the older hand compression molds still in use for many 78s in 1954. For distributors and manufacturers, the new records presented fewer
shipping problems, because they could be sent by air or by
first class mail instead of by the slower fourth class rate
necessitated by the protective packaging of the fragile 78s.
The lightness of 45s, coupled with their doughnut shape
and the large spindle of 45 players, also produced faster,
easier listening. The "search" for the small hole in the
center of the 78 was eliminated, and a listener could
quickly skim through a large group of records, playing or
rejecting them at a moment's notice. The process of playing records therefore became more casual, and there was
a more immediate relationship between listener and record than had been possible with the heavy and breakable
78s. With these qualities, 45s offered distinct advantages
over 78s; but the advantages became most obvious when

the music on the records complemented the function of the records as a medium. Rock provided this complement.

In the 1950's, 45s became the medium for youth and for their music. As the 78 died, the 33 rpm record—which became popular along with the 45—assumed the functions of the adult medium. This broad generalization is hard to substantiate, and its validity has certainly been undermined during the sixties, particularly as young people have been able to afford the more expensive LPs, and as rock material has gravitated increasingly toward the 33 medium. As late as 1963, however, the publisher of *Billboard*, Hal Cook, wrote, ". . . the general public identifies the 33 as 'good' music, while it classifies the 45 with the black leather jacket and motorcycle set."*

Forty-fives are as distinct from 33s as they were from 78s. When rock emerged, little of the music was issued on LPs; the 33 medium instead became linked with classical music or with traditional Pop music. This separation was encouraged by the style of the 33. In comparison to 45s, LPs demanded a long-range decision—to hear twenty or twenty-five minutes of the same artist—and they resisted the spontaneous selection which was characteristic of the smaller records. Of course, listeners could nullify these demands by selecting one or two songs from an LP, but this contradicted the design of the record. The 33 medium implied a seriousness of purpose which, before the later 1960's, seemed foreign both to the casualness of the 45 and to the folk immediacy of rock. This evaluation is reinforced by the story of the defunct 33 rpm, seven-inch single. In an effort to standardize record speeds, major companies—including RCA, Columbia and Capitol—planned to issue singles in this new format. The proposal was suggested several times during 1960 and 1961, but it was never accepted. The cost of new machinery provoked re-

* *Billboard*, July 20, 1963, p. 3.

sistance throughout the music industry, particularly on
the part of juke box operators. Significantly, the same resistance had been expressed during the shift from 78s to
45s, but it had been overcome. In other words, the 33 single may have failed because it was not accompanied by a
complementary musical style.

As rock has changed, the implications of the different
record speeds have also changed. During the late 1960's,
rock groups have used the LP to record long improvisatory
sessions, very much as jazz musicians have done ever since
the late 1940's. In doing so, they have not negated the
meaning which the 33 formerly had; rather, they have
added to it. On the one hand, rock's shift to LPs suggests
that LPs no longer belong exclusively to adults; on the
other, it suggests a growing artistic seriousness within rock
music itself. In its larger development, rock has not denied
the 45, but has grown beyond it.

Public Response to Rock

Whole books could be written about the public response
to rock during its development. Periods of concern, censorship, and enthusiasm have constantly followed one another in the mass media, and interest has focused on the
artists, the songs, the disk jockeys, and the audience of
rock. In the 1950's, Elvis Presley was criticized for his
suggestive dancing; in the 1960's, records have been
burned because John Lennon announced that the Beatles
were more popular than Christ. When rock emerged, its
lyrics were called "smutty," and "clean-up" campaigns
discovered unsavory messages in all types of popular music. In recent years, similar campaigns have searched for
"hidden" references to marijuana, LSD, and other drugs.
Disk jockeys have periodically been accused of illegal pro-

motion of the music, and the rock audience has often been labeled "socially irresponsible."

Discussion of all this belongs more to the sociology of art than to the history of art. It is concerned with the social effects of artistic change rather than the change itself. Nevertheless, these effects can provide evidence about the character of art. The public response to rock obviously reflected the revolutionary character of the music, but it also reflected the music's folk orientation. The layman, for instance, is not generally concerned about fine art. It occasionally provokes headlines, but usually for non-artistic reasons—the high prices at an auction, the uncovering of a forgery, or the large crowds which visit a special exhibition. With folk art, however, the situation is different. Folk art arises directly from the people, and it provokes an immediate response from the layman. He can express this without feeling that he must first have the specialized training which is demanded by fine art. Opinions therefore flow easily and publicly regarding folk art, as they have with rock.*

Between 1954 and 1956, public response to rock was primarily directed to censorship issues. The label of "smut" was applied to numerous records which contained references to sex, especially to records which originated in the

---

* I am suggesting that folk art contains and elicits *feeling*. Fine art, of course, also contains and elicits feeling, but it exists in a different context of experience. The self-defining process of modernist fine art, particularly painting and sculpture, constitutes such a context. In a sense, painting and sculpture have developed their own *languages*, and it is through these languages that they express themselves. Until the spectator understands the language, he is blocked, so to speak, from the experience contained in a particular work. That is, he is blocked from feeling. Popular art, by comparison, contains and elicits not feeling, but sentiment. The distinction is a tricky one, and I had better rely now for confirmation simply on the individual spectator's (or listener's) examination of his own responses to these different types of artistic expression.

Rhythm and Blues field. The Midnighters' "Work With
Me Annie" and "Annie Had a Baby," and Clyde Mc-
Phatter's "Such a Night" and "Honey Love" were all cited
in this connection. The lyrics of these songs were absolutely traditional Rhythm and Blues lyrics and had never
before provoked public indignity. An article in *Billboard*
by Bill Simon made this point in 1956: 'In the old days,
most blues were concerned with money or love problems,
usually loss or lack thereof. And since these recordings received little or no air play, double or single entendre was
employed as frequently as not."* Rock brought these songs
to national attention, so they no longer enjoyed the protec-
tion of exclusiveness.

The censorship which was initially directed at Rhythm
and Blues spread to other musical traditions during the
1954-56 period. There were "witch-hunts" and there were
several highly amusing incidents. On ABC radio, Martin
Block refused to play Rosemary Clooney's "Italiano
Mambo" when he learned that it offended portions of his
Italian-American audience.** Webb Pierce's "There
Stands the Glass," a best-selling record in the Country and
Western field in 1954, was criticized because it described
an alcoholic who was never punished.† In the Pop field,
Cole Porter's "Let's Do It" and "All of You" were felt to be
in "bad taste" because of their suggestive lyrics. But sex
was not the only taboo subject for the self-conscious pro-
tectors of public dignity. The term "darkies" was carefully
avoided, as were other colloquialisms which had racial
overtones. As a result, even "Carry Me Back to Old Vir-
ginia" had to be reworded for radio play.‡ The most extraordinary accusation of this period, however, was made

---

* *Billboard*, February 4, 1956, p. 55.
** *Ibid.*, November 20, 1954, p. 16.
† *Ibid.*, January 30, 1954, p. 22.
‡ *Ibid.*, June 9, 1956, pp. 1, 18.

by Peter Potter, master of ceremonies on the Hollywood *Juke Box Jury*, who said, "All Rhythm and Blues records are dirty and as bad for kids as dope."[*]

Needless to say, the level of critical intelligence which was expressed in these censorship incidents was uniformly low. In the style of the critical attacks on it, however, rock became distinguished from other music. Out of all the music which provoked public indignation, that is, rock inspired the most virulent criticism. Words like "smut" became common in the news, while civic or religious groups talked of "waging campaigns" against it. Social response is, as I have said, really outside the concern of the present study. At the same time, I do wish to make one point about the problem of so-called "dirty" art: In folk art and in fine art, an artist creates with the material which is most immediate and meaningful to him—whether it is sex, or LSD, or heaven and paradise.

[*] *Ibid.*, March 26, 1955, p. 20.

The Expansion of the Rock Style:
1957 through 1963

Introduction

Between 1957 and 1963, rock continued to expand enormously. Unknown artists entered the music business and became popular with their first or second record. The record companies searched frantically for new material and new styles. As a result, rock reflected influences from a variety of sources—calypso and Hawaiian trends, English folk traditions, quasi-classical Pop conventions, and the work of numerous individual artists in the Country and Western field. These influences followed one another with unprecedented speed. Rock had shattered the conservative pattern of the Tin Pan Alley tradition. By the later fifties, the music industry had been transformed into a volatile, unpredictable business. Amidst the chaos, record companies constantly tried to anticipate a new direction which the field would take. The market offered music for every type of taste. But nearly all of the new material possessed the beat of rock. Rock's ability to maintain this beat, while changing superficially to absorb new influences, enabled it to grow through the 1950's, and it continued to grow in the 1960's.

The expansion of the rock style is not the only important characteristic of the 1957-1963 period. Rock dances including the Twist, the Stroll, and the Loco-Motion, became popular in these years; television shows featuring rock gained national recognition; and "Oldies But Goodies" became a standard part of radio programs and the record market. These developments brought rock right into the lives of its audience. Rock became a way of life, complete with its own literature, its own traditions, and its own media of expression. When specific life-styles, the "surfer" for instance, blossomed in the 1960's, they were rooted in the previous decade, and they merely required a set of accoutrements to give them particular meaning.

The payola hearings took place in the middle of this period. The scandal disrupted numerous individual careers in the music business, and, for many listeners, it "proved" that rock was "bad" music. But rock survived this crisis just as it previously survived the accusation that it was pornographic and smutty. In fact, the music did more than survive, for these fertile years produced many of the greatest records in rock history. Here I shall cite a few of my own candidates, as I will not have the opportunity for such an indulgence elsewhere: "Shop Around" by Smokey Robinson and the Miracles, "What's Your Name?" by Don and Juan, "Stay" by Maurice Williams and the Zodiacs, "Johnny B. Goode" by Chuck Berry, "Twist and Shout" by the Isley Brothers, "So Fine" by the Fiestas, "The Mountain's High" by Dick and Dee Dee, "Baby, It's You" by the Shirelles, "Mother-in-Law" by Ernie K. Doe, and "Money" by Barrett Strong.

Chuck Berry: Folk Poet of the Fifties

Few artists in the history of rock have been able to produce high-quality records over a long period of time. The ma-

jority have been "one-shots" who disappear after their first
or second hit record. There are notable exceptions: Fats
Domino and Chuck Berry in the 1950's; or the Beach Boys,
the Beatles, and the Rolling Stones in the 1960's. All of
these artists produced music of a high quality for a relatively long period. Others—Elvis Presley, for instance, or
the Supremes—have remained popular for an extended
period, although the quality of their music has diminished.

Chuck Berry has not at the time of writing produced a
top-selling record since "It Goes To Show You Never Can
Tell," which appeared in the spring of 1964. Before that,
however, he produced a string of hits which spanned almost a decade. Many of these—"School Day," "Sweet
Little Sixteen," "Rock and Roll Music," "Johnny B.
Goode," "Carol," and "Almost Grown," among others—
originated in the years between 1957 and 1963. All of
them, including the earlier "Maybellene," "Too Much
Monkey Business" and "Roll Over Beethoven," are as powerful and immediate today as they were when they first
appeared. But an interesting feature of these records is
that they do not reflect stylistic change. Chuck Berry's
style in 1964 was essentially the same as it was in 1955
and, from the evidence of his recent personal appearances,
it is exactly the same today. Few artists have so consistently resisted the self-consciousness brought about by popular success.

Chuck Berry epitomizes the folk artist of the rock idiom.
His style did not change because it did not have to; from
the beginning it unconsciously expressed the responses of
the artist and his audience to the ordinary realities of their
world: to cars, girls, growing up, school, or music. An in-
genuous vitality pervades all of his songs. His subjects are
never treated self-consciously, and his lyrics reveal no effort to find special "meaning" or "significance" in the activities they describe. The keynote of Chuck Berry's style

Chuck Berry

is its open endorsement of happiness, fun, and good times: "School Day," for instance, describes the "burden" of being in class, the excitement which accompanies the three o'clock bell, and the pleasure of arriving at the "juke joint;" "Roll Over Beethoven" encourages the listener—and Beethoven—to feel the music, to "reel and rock" to its vital rhythm. The frankness, honesty, and naïveté of Chuck Berry's songs give them a continuing significance. The fact that their subject matter may be less immediate now than it was is irrelevant to the aesthetic experience of the records. Their attitude is their content. Its meaning is in the spontaneous, vital pleasure of creating music.

The lyrics of Chuck Berry's songs constitute some of the most exciting folk poetry in the rock field. They represent the folk artist's unconsciousness of art—particularly in his innocent notion that poetry should rhyme and that all rhythmic spaces should be filled, even if filling them necessitates the slicing of words or the creation of new ones. In "Too Much Monkey Business," for example, every verse rhymes, and, when words cannot fill the existing spaces, the artist fills them with a flexible "aah." Of course, the poetry in this song is *sung* poetry. Its quality cannot be duplicated by reading it or by writing it down. In Chuck Berry's breathless presentation, the "aahs" which conclude each verse change each time they are verbalized. In one case they imply a sigh of disgust and, in another, a type of sultry indignation. But the language of Chuck Berry's poetry is always ordinary. He employs it naturally and without sophistication. The impact of the Chuck Berry records suggests that naturalness came unconsciously to his music. Younger rock artists, Bob Dylan for instance, have been able to learn it. They have been conscious of alternative types of language and they have deliberately chosen to give their songs the flavor of the natural. But Chuck Berry did not make that choice because he was not aware of the alternatives. As a traditional folk artist, he created art unconsciously.

An important aspect of Chuck Berry's artistic power, one which enhances his relevance to the current rock scene, is his guitar style. His records are generally characterized by a piercing electric guitar which is played by Berry himself, and which is occasionally accompanied by drums and piano. In contrast to the majority of Rhythm and Blues artists of the 1950's, Chuck Berry did not rely upon the support of saxophones. Like Elvis Presley, he was "a man with his guitar." More than Presley, however, Chuck Berry played the guitar with a vitality that constituted an important element in the total effect of his records.

Here too, Chuck Berry's attitude was that of the folk artist. His songs repeatedly use an identical introductory phrase on the guitar, or a slight variation of it, and they rely internally on similar "favorite" guitar melodies and combinations. These elements hardly changed in a decade of record production. The artist intuited their aesthetic rightness, and he continued to use them because they remained expressively functional. His folk artistry, perhaps his genius, lay in the fact that he never tried to change them; he never felt the need to keep up with stylistic innovations, because he was never conscious of style itself.

Chuck Berry's relation to his guitar is intimate and loving, and this is evident in both musical and visual terms. Musically, the guitar penetrates the lyrics and frequently responds to one or two lines of a given verse, so that voice and guitar account equally for the total impact of the sound. Visually, the same close relationship is emphasized, between the entire person of the artist and his instrument. When Chuck Berry performs, he cuddles and caresses his guitar; he playfully teases notes from it, and he dances with it in the process. This display involves more than a virtuoso technique: it emanates from a folk convention that the guitar is human: Like a woman, whose body it obviously resembles, it must be loved before it will radiate its absorbing music.

Chuck Berry composed and wrote nearly all of the songs he recorded. In this, he further epitomized the traditional folk artist who, in comparison to popular art singers, created his own material instead of having it written for him. During the 1950's, the practice exemplified by Chuck Berry gradually became common, and it marked a major difference between rock and other musical styles which made up the Pop field. Like Berry, Fats Domino, Little Richard, and Ray Charles—as well as the more traditional blues artists like B. B. King—almost invariably wrote the music and lyrics of the songs they recorded. In the 1960's, this practice became even more characteristic of rock music. It has now become a standard feature of the most creative groups.

In the late 1960's, Chuck Berry has enjoyed a comeback. During 1967, his personal appearances in London and San Francisco were greeted with enthusiastic appreciation and standing ovations, reportedly to the amazement of the artist himself. This response is the consequence of the growing sophistication of rock artists and audiences, the emergence of a sub-style called "folk-rock," and a revival of the Rhythm and Blues tradition in both England and the United States. Rock has become aware of its past. In view of Chuck Berry's quality, this awareness is welcome. But it is also ironic, because he has only recently been recognized as the folk artist he has always been.

The Spread of Country and Western Music: Rockabilly

After the sweeping success of Elvis Presley in 1956, a growing number of country artists began to penetrate the

Fats Domino

Pop field. The trend was strongest between 1957 and 1960; after that, only occasional country records appealed to the larger national audience.

The country music which became popular in the Pop field during the later 1950's was not always rock. It was generally called "rockabilly," but it was played by Pop musicians, such as Jimmie Rogers or Ricky Nelson; by some pure Country and Western artists, including Johnny Cash and Bobby Helms; and by rock performers, such as the Everly Brothers, Jerry Lee Lewis, and Buddy Holly. The elements of country folk music steadily penetrated the broader rock style, and they became increasingly familiar to the national audience. This growing familiarization provided an important background for the popular folk style which developed at the end of the 1950's and the early 1960's and was exemplified by the Kingston Trio and Peter, Paul and Mary. The background sensitized younger artists to the historical material which their own music sought to revive.

The interest in Country and Western music during the later fifties was not unprecedented. In the first half of the decade, "Tennessee Waltz," "High Noon," and "The Yellow Rose Of Texas" sold extensively in the Pop field and piqued a taste for the rustic style of country music. The most popular of these earlier songs was the "Ballad of Davy Crockett"; in the spring of 1955, it inspired three different versions all of which were in the top ten of the Pop charts—by Fess Parker, Tennessee Ernie Ford, and Bill Hayes. But the "Ballad of Davy Crockett" involved more than record sales in spreading the image of country music. The Davy Crockett craze began with a Walt Disney film and it later included toys, games, coonskin hats, and other trappings which recalled the folk hero. Because of all this, the song achieved a phenomenal success. In 1955 it sold over 7,000,000 records on more than twenty differ-

Courtesy Okeh Records, Inc.

Little Richard

ent labels. In the history of the music business, this success was comparable to that of "Rudolph the Red-Nosed
Reindeer," which was one of the most popular songs of all
time and had then sold over 18,000,000 records in more
than eighty different versions.

A less commercial expression of country music also
gained recognition at this time: "16 Tons." The song was
written by folk balladeer Merle Travis in the late 1940's,
and Tennessee Ernie Ford's version of it became a national
success in 1955. It went to the top of the Pop charts in
three weeks, which meant that it was the fastest-selling
record in the history of that field. Ford's pleasant interpretation of the song undoubtedly contributed to its enormous
success. Like Ford's television shows, the record eschewed
the raw hillbilly elements of the country tradition and
converted the song's folk character into a more palatable,
popular statement. Most television Westerns similarly
transformed folk subjects into popular art, and their growing success in these years was closely linked with the sensibility manifested by "16 Tons." Along with these popular
art trends, however, other types of country music began
to achieve recognition. The *Grand Ole Opry*, for instance,
became available on national television and began to sensi-
tize the American public to a more authentic style of
Country and Western expression.

For the history of rock, the rockabilly artists are more
important than the individuals who, like Johnny Cash,
had occasional songs in the Pop field, but generally remained faithful to the traditional Country and Western
style. Between 1957 and 1960, rockabilly persisted within
the larger rock idiom, and it featured numerous high-
quality records. The style was softer and more pleasant
than the Rhythm and Blues music which had penetrated
the Pop field around 1954, largely because it eschewed
the pounding Rhythm and Blues saxophone. The softening

Courtesy ABC Records, Inc.

Ray Charles

of this type of rock paralleled a broader trend of the music during the second half of the decade. Artists from the Rhythm and Blues field also turned toward a sweeter, more elegant style: for instance, the Shirelles and Little Anthony and the Imperials, both of whom employed strings and other orchestral sections in their recordings. These elements sharply distinguished their music from the heavy, small-group sound of Little Richard, Fats Domino, and Elvis Presley. The best rockabilly artists, the Everly Brothers and Buddy Holly and the Crickets, were also small groups, but their music never had that heavy sound. Rockabilly records by the Everly Brothers and Buddy Holly emphasized a rock beat while retaining the twanging guitar and the high-pitched, whining drawl of the country vocal. In place of the traditional Country and Western subjects, however, they substituted casual, Pop-based concerns: "Wake Up, Little Susie," "Bird Dog," "Cathy's Clown," "Maybe Baby," "Peggy Sue," "Oh Boy," and others. These replaced songs emphasizing moral feeling and subjects such as God, the afterlife, cheating and lying, true and false love, and nature. But the rock beat somehow gave validity to any new subject matter. In its rockabilly phase, then, the new music created its own realities, just as it did when it drew from Rhythm and Blues sources.

Rockabilly's impact on the national audience was reflected by popular imitations of the style which appeared as late as 1960. Johnny Horton's "Battle Of New Orleans" and Stonewall Jackson's "Waterloo," both from the summer of 1959, represent Tin Pan Alley versions of the country tradition. Like the Tin Pan Alley versions of earlier rock, they provide only an appearance of folk subjects and style. From 1960, Connie Francis's "Everybody's Somebody's Fool" and Pat Boone's "I'm Walkin' The Floor Over You," belong in the same popular art category. By 1960,

Jerry Lee Lewis

however, the authentic rockabilly style had largely been
absorbed by the broader rock development, and national attention had already shifted to the self-conscious, historiciz-
ing folk music of the Kingston Trio.

Popular Folk Music

The Kingston Trio appeared on the national scene of
popular music in 1958. Their first top-selling record was
an LP, *From the Hungry i.* "Tom Dooley," their first important single, was included in the album. It was a new
version of a nineteenth-century ballad about the hanging
of Tom Dula in Statesville, North Carolina in 1868. This
song marked the beginning of a popularized, self-conscious
folk trend which lasted into the 1960's. It remains as one
type of popular music today, but it reached its peak of recognition in 1963. After that it was eclipsed by the extraordinary popularity of the Beatles and other new groups,
and also by the resurgent interest in Rhythm and Blues.
As a movement, however, it provides valuable insights into
the changing popular conception of folk music; by default,
it helps to clarify the character of authentic folk music.

The popular folk style of the Kingston Trio was anticipated by several developments which took place earlier in
the decade in the Pop field. I have already mentioned the
Country and Western folk songs which gained national attention between 1950 and 1955 and the broader rockabilly
trend which began in 1957. Of equal importance were the
Weavers, who had a long background in traditional folk
music. Although the Weavers could not be regarded as a
popular music group, several of their records had achieved
popular acceptance in the early 1950's. During 1950 and
1951, "Goodnight Irene," "Tzena, Tzena," and "On Top
Of Old Smokey" reached the top of the Pop charts. In
1956, their Vanguard album, *The Weavers at Carnegie*

Courtesy Warner Brothers—Seven Arts Records, Inc.

The Everly Brothers

Hall, also became a commercial success. All of these records were traditional folk music with a rich regional and
ethnic flavor. The broad welcome that they received indicated that the Weavers' style was one of the more important sounds in American popular music in the first half of
the decade. It might have remained important if accusa-
tions of Communist sympathies had not damaged the
group's public image.

Several other trends sharpened the country's appetite for
traditional folk music before 1958. In 1956, Lonnie Donegan's "Rock Island Line" began a short-lived trend which
was called "skiffle" music. The style was also exemplified
by Bob Cort, Clyde McDevitt, and Nancy Wiskey, whose
recording of "Freight Train" became popular in 1957.
Like Donegan, most of the skiffle artists came from England, where the trend coincided with a revival of Hank
Williams's songs in the middle 1950's.* The most distinctive features of the style were its use of narrative songs and
the acoustic guitar. The songs told a story, but telling the
story was more important than feeling it. Skiffle records
generally had a skipping beat instead of a rocking beat; a
guitar provided rhythm, but it never impinged upon the
vocal. This approach was radically different from rock's
treatment of narrative, traditional folk songs. "Stagger
Lee," for example, was an old folk song which Lloyd Price
recorded in 1958, and the same was true for Chuck Willis's
"C. C. Rider," which appeared in 1956. But these artists
gave the traditional material a heavy beat that sometimes
obscured the lyrics, and they did not try to duplicate the
songs as they had originally been sung. Skiffle, like the
popular folk music which followed it, was partly artificial
because it sought to preserve the past instead of interpret-
ing it with spontaneous, personal feeling.

* This was reported in an interview with Clyde McDevitt, in *Billboard*, July 8, 1957, p. 56.

Courtesy Coral Records, Inc.

Buddy Holly

A more exotic type of traditional folk music also gained recognition in 1957: the calypso style of the West Indies. Harry Belafonte was the most popular of the calypso musicians although the Tarriers and Terry Gilkyson strengthened the trend within the Pop field. Belafonte's "Jamaica Farewell," "Mama Look-a-Booboo," and "Day-O" were among the top-selling calypso records during 1957, but Nat Cole's "When Rock and Roll Comes To Trinidad," from the same year, was a more direct expression of the style's impact. As the title suggests, the song reflected the Pop field's uncertainty about the new trend replacing rock. Of course, calypso did not replace rock, but its distinctive sound helped to condition the national audience to a more traditional folk music. Calypso employed acoustic guitars and various bongo drums; like skiffle music, it did not rely upon the special effects of recording studios, an aspect of rock which the audience of traditional folk music always regarded as dishonest. Calypso songs were narratives, and this gave the music a dignity of content which rock supposedly lacked. Finally, the structure of calypso, based on a vocal and chorus, encouraged listeners to join the music and experience it as part of a hootenanny. These elements became essential to the style of the Kingston Trio and other popular groups. For the most part, however, calypso was adult music. In America it was heard in nightclubs and it appealed to upper middle-class audiences who periodically toured the West Indies.* Youth remained on the periphery of the calypso trend. The Kingston Trio, however, came into the colleges and the coffee houses. It was a part of the youth world in a way that the calypso musicians never were.

With the Kingston Trio, popular folk music clearly shifted its audience orientation. Most of its following and many of its musicians came from colleges and universities.

* *Billboard*, April 29, 1957, pp. 1, 21.

The Kingston Trio

This was not generally true at that time for rock. In the popular imagination if not in fact, rock belonged to teenagers in high school, even to "juvenile delinquents"; but folk music belonged to young adults who were pursuing higher education and developing a sense of "purpose." These attitudes gave popular folk music an aura of seriousness which became increasingly apparent as the movement developed. The trend did not deny pleasure or spontaneity, but it tended to standardize them, to put them, so to speak, "in their place." The hootenanny television shows of the early 1960's reflected this: As the artists performed, the camera scanned the audience and revealed faces which were uniformly solemn as they studied the music and concentrated on the "pleasure" of hearing it. This self-consciousness was reflected by the artists as well: Their involvement with the songs was invariably shown by rapt and furrowed expressions which indicated that the music had a "message."

The early style of the folk movement was also manifested in the dress and appearance of the Kingston Trio. The group had a tailored, Ivy League look which made them eminently acceptable to college audiences during the late 1950's. Moreover, their appearance did not offend adults. As a result, neither the artists nor the music of this folk trend provoked the public indignation which rock did. In fact, its acceptance by adults was signaled in 1960 by a Mitch Miller album entitled *Folk Songs Sing Along With Mitch*. Miller's many "sing-along" records dominated the popular adult market at that time, but none of these contained rock songs.

From its beginning, the popular folk trend relied on the LP market. The Kingston Trio's "Tom Dooley" was issued as a single *after* it had appeared in an album. The group later released other singles—the most popular was "MTA" —but their regular sales were of albums released between

1958 and 1962. The same pattern was true for other folk groups and individuals. The Chad Mitchell Trio, the Limelighters, Peter, Paul and Mary, and Joan Baez, among others, issued occasional singles but concentrated primarily on LPs. Bob Dylan started his career in this way, but he later became the first of the folk-based artists to penetrate the singles market on a steady, large-scale basis.

This connection between the folk trend and the 33 medium is interesting. Since 33s were generally an adult medium, it reveals that the folk movement was not only acceptable to adults but actually aspired to adult values, a conclusion which is substantiated by the forced "seriousness" of the music. At the same time the connection existed unconsciously, just as rock's allegiance to the 45 medium existed unconsciously. In recent years, beginning around 1964, this situation has changed: Rock music has continued the LP orientation begun by the popular folk movement, but its artists and audience have forcefully declared their independence from adult values.

In 1958, the meaning and the direction of the folk movement were largely undefined. The Kingston Trio's progress provided an outline for the movement but its internal directions did not become clear for several years. For instance, many of the Kingston Trio's records were based on revised or revived historical folk songs. Later groups and individuals, especially Peter, Paul and Mary, Joan Baez, and Bob Dylan, similarly used historical material, but they directed their music more and more to current issues and events, and the folk movement gradually assumed a definite socio-political dimension.

This added awareness underscored the sophistication of the folk movement. Early rock was not consciously interested in these matters, although both were implicit in the meaning of rock music. Popular folk music brought them to the attention of the national audience. In doing so, the style provoked an awareness of older musical traditions, of the cultures of other countries, and of artists who had been producing folk songs for many years. Collectors and students of folk music, John and Alan Lomax for instance, had documented this material before the late 1950's, and it was available in numerous books and record anthologies. But the folk trend made some of this music history readily available; it obviated the task of searching for the past in book stacks and record libraries. It was itself educative. As the style evolved, moreover, it taught not only about the past, but about the present as well. The music's involvement with social problems and political events at once enlightened its audience and expressed their growing awareness of realities which were unknown to youth in the earlier 1950's. These issues were felt by rock after their initial expression in popular folk music, that is, in the middle 1960's, after national interest in popular folk music had declined.

The sophistication of the folk music trend was meaningful in some ways, but it was misleading and artificial in other ways. The concentration on historical songs and sociopolitical subjects implied that "real" folk music had been dead during the 1950's; that is, it undermined the folk function which rock had performed in that period, and it misrepresented the deepest meaning of folk art in general. Paradoxically, the folk *trend* never fully understood folk *art:* it appreciated historical styles, but it mistakenly tried to impose those styles on current experiences and sensibilities. It encouraged a rigid, standardized style which could not encompass the richness and variety of contemporary realities. For female vocalists, the standard folk style was equated with an elegant, clear-throated trill. For groups, it consisted of wholesome, spirited unison. The common stylistic element for both groups and individuals, however, lay in the tastefulness of their music. It admitted its sources more openly than the *kitsch* music of Frank Sinatra or Dean Martin, but it was *kitsch* nevertheless.

As I pointed out, the folk movement was centered among college students and other young adults. *Billboard* periodically conducts polls of the college audiences in order to learn who are their favorite artists. The results generally show the limitations of their sophistication. In 1965, for instance, Andy Williams and Barbra Streisand were the favorite male and female vocalists; the Beatles were the favorite vocal group—followed by the Four Freshmen, the Letterman, and the Four Seasons; while Harry Belafonte, Bob Dylan, and Joan Baez were the favorite folk singers. This represented a transition in taste and sensibility—a gravitation in the college audience away from the folk trend but with no wholehearted shift toward another type of music. The distinctions I have been making between popular art, folk art, and fine art did not matter much to these audiences, as they had not mattered much to the artists and audiences of early rock. But the term "folk" music was being used now, and the distinctions were clearly meaning something to popular folk musicians and audiences. This was important in the larger history of rock, because it showed a growing, albeit partial awareness of the different *kinds* of music that comprised popular music.

That the popular folk trend could create confusion about folk art is understandable. That it could extend this confusion, even unconsciously, into a restricting morality is more disturbing. Nevertheless, this is what happened in the movement during the early 1960's. The first album released by Peter, Paul and Mary is an example. The record appeared in 1962 and contained the following notes:

> Peter, Paul and Mary sing folk music. In your hands you hold their first album. But to be more accurate, you

hold a bouquet of song still fresh as the earth, and strong
with the perfume of sincerity. For Peter, Paul and Mary
sing! There is nothing apologetic about their work. No
ineptitude disguised as charm. No uninspired profes-
sionalism passed off as authenticity. Whatever they have
thus far undertaken, Peter, Paul and Mary have done
well, and with flair. And, obviously, with their whole
hearts. The temptation is to run on in a riot of superla-
tives. Probably, you're either reading this instead of
listening, or else, reading and trying to listen at the same
time. Either way, it's a mistake. The *Truth* is on the
record. It deserves your exclusive attention. No dancing,
please. Just look at their faces, listen to their songs, and
hope that you have a chance to hear (and see) them in
person.

. . . There seems to be something optimistic, something
encouraging about this whole musical experience. Peter,
Paul and Mary's first album is bright with enthusiasm.
No gimmicks. There is just something *Good* about it all.
Good in the sense of virtue, that is. And the news that
something this *Good* can be as popular as this can fill
you with a new kind of optimism. Maybe everything's
going to be all right. Maybe mediocrity has had it.
Maybe hysteria is on the way out. One thing is for sure
in any case: Honesty is back. Tell your neighbor.*

The stress of this sermon is on honesty and sincerity
and on the importance of "authenticity." But the folk
movement's conception of authenticity was as uncertain
as its understanding of folk art. Consider how the image
of authenticity changed betwen 1958 and 1963. In the late
fifties, the Kingston Trio seemed to be an authentic, vital
folk group. But Peter, Paul and Mary—with a more intense style and a more casual appearance—made the
Kingston Trio appear commercialized and artificial. The
austerity of Joan Baez, in turn, made Peter, Paul and

* *Peter, Paul and Mary*, Warner Bros. Records, Inc., 1962 (WS
1449). With permission.

Peter, Paul, and Mary

Mary seem like spurious "folkniks." A *Time Magazine* article in 1962 described the type of authenticity which pervaded Joan Baez's style:

> Her voice is as clear as air in the autumn, a vibrant, strong, untrained and thrilling soprano. She wears no makeup, and her long black hair hangs like a drapery, parted around her long almond face. In performance she comes on, walks straight to the microphone, and begins to sing. No patter. No show business. She usually wears a sweater and skirt or a simple dress. Occasionally she affects something semi-Oriental that seems to have been hand-sewn out of burlap. The purity of her voice suggests purity of approach. She is only 21 and palpably nubile. But there is little sex in that clear flow of sound. It is haunted and plaintive, a mother's voice, and it has in it distant reminders of black women wailing in the night, of detached madrigal singers performing calmly at court, and of saddened gypsies trying to charm death into leaving their Spanish caves.*

These statements concentrated on the appearance of the folk artists and the seriousness of their music. They tacitly assumed that the music was folk music. Their descriptions, however, contradicted the meaning of folk art—at least as I have tried to describe it. Listeners were discouraged from participating in the musical experience; they were told that it was a "mistake" to listen and read at the same time; they were advised not to dance; and, finally, they were informed that "patter" and "show business" would conflict with the folk experience. By insisting on the conditions of aesthetic experience, the folk trend undermined the spontaneity of real folk music.

By 1963, the popular folk movement had become a nationally recognized phenomenon. Concerts in Carnegie Hall and the Hollywood Bowl attracted enormous crowds;

* *Time*, November 23, 1962, p. 54.

the Newport Folk Festival became an annual mecca for folk artists and audiences; ABC television offered a weekly *Hootenanny*; *Billboard* devoted special sections to the music; and "We Shall Overcome" became the theme of a giant freedom march on Washington. In the music business, the folk movement was compared to the explosive emergence of rock which had taken place almost ten years earlier. But the popular folk movement suddenly evaporated after 1963, and folk songs appeared only sporadically on the charts of best-selling albums or single records.

The decline of the folk movement had numerous and complex causes, the unravelling of which is beyond the scope of this study. One of the most important factors, however, was the arrival of the Beatles. When records by the English group appeared in 1964, they generated more excitement than any music in the history of rock. Personal appearances by the group stimulated an enthusiasm which was even more phenomenal. These events dramatically denied that rock was exhausted as a musical style, and that "hysteria [was] on the way out." In other words, the Beatles destroyed the folk movement's assumptions about rock. They accomplished this, furthermore, through the high quality of their music: In a sense, their records convinced everyone, even the folk audience who had previously felt that rock was meaningless.

The popular folk movement assumed that songs could change the world. Its social and political "messages" were intended to provoke thought, concern, and action. For individual listeners, the songs may have accomplished this. But they did not accomplish it for "society." On the contrary, bitter experience suggested that this type of art could certainly not change society. Their folk movement was based upon sincere but unrealistic values. When the national audience recognized this, the movement lost its power.

Oldies But Goodies

At the end of the 1950's, rock became aware of its own history. "Oldies But Goodies" appeared. These were records which had been hits in the past; they were also called "super oldies," "golden oldies," "golden goodies," and other names. The revival of old rock records began in the record industry, but it spread into radio programming before the end of the decade. In the record industry, the trend continued during the 1960's, and it gradually showed increasing selectivity among stylistic categories. The first albums of oldies generally contained a mixture of rock, pure Rhythm and Blues, and semi-Pop songs; later releases concentrated on one or another of these traditions. On the radio, the oldies have become a standard feature for most stations. One or two are played each hour, and on weekends they are usually played alternately with the current hits.

Oldies But Goodies provided an awareness of the rock tradition, and reflected the growing independence of rock from its original sources in the Pop, Rhythm and Blues, and Country and Western traditions. The awareness of a rock tradition had been expressed by certain rock records which preceded the Oldies But Goodies trend. Larry Williams's "Short Fat Fanny," for instance, contained numerous references to earlier rock songs and personalities, among them, "Bony Marony," "Long Tall Sally," and "Blue Suede Shoes." More recently, Chris Kenner's "Land Of A Thousand Dances" recalled the specialized dances of the late fifties and the early sixties. In these songs, the subjects of rock were perpetuated like folk heroes, and the music generated its own mythology.

The myth-making function of the oldies clarifies the similarities and differences between rock and traditional folk music, and also between rock and the popular folk trend of the late fifties. Like traditional folk songs, rock records survived because they continued to have meaning for a large group of people. As the term Oldies But Goodies indicates, their survival was based on quality. In addition, the oldies made the personalities of rock lyrics into folk heroes: "Long Tall Sally" became the "Darlin' Cory" of the fifties, and the "Duke Of Earl" assumed the role of "John Henry." These images persisted when the rock style changed. Their revival as oldies did not result from historical study; they *happened* to be old, but they remained meaningful. Their quality did not depend on age, as the popular folk movement had implied, but on an aesthetic impact that seemed timeless. This timeless quality is inadvertantly reflected by the fact that disk jockeys rarely mention the date when an oldie first appeared. Even albums generally ignore such information. When listeners *are* told the date of an oldie, they are frequently surprised because the song sounds fresh and new.

The following album notes were written by disk jockey Art Laboe for volume three of the *Oldies But Goodies* series:

> At a party with friends, have a ball!—ROCK!—to the rock side OR . . . listen to the dreamy side with your "special person" . . . It will bring you closer together . . . For some of us, the 'Dreamy' side means just memories . . . so there in the loneliness of your room, with just this little album, remember—and maybe even cry a little—about a love gone wrong, long ago—Whoever you are . . . Wherever you are . . . the 'Oldies But Goodies' are with you and they seem to understand. . . .*

This in itself is folk literature. And the listener is expected similarly not to be concerned with art, or tradition, or

* Original Sound Sales Corp., 1966 (OSR-LPM-5004). Reprinted by permission.

history itself, but with the present reality of the music on the records. In fact, the records are so real that they assume human presence: They "understand."

The Twist and Other Dances

Since the late 1950's, rock has been accompanied by a whole series of changing dances. When the music began, the dancing which accompanied it was called either the Lindy or the Jitterbug. The former had survived since the late 1920's, while the latter was inherited as a jazz dancing style from the 1940's. In the middle fifties, Elvis Presley was largely responsible for adding greater eroticism to these dances, and the prevailing style became known as the Bop. The Bop style was loosely defined, and it permitted a variety of interpretations by dancing couples. And its links to the Lindy and the Jitterbug were clearly in evidence, particularly in the emphasis on physical gymnastics and virtuoso footwork.

Rock revolutionized dancing styles by the time the movement was three years old. The Jitterbug had survived for a decade, but rock dances changed overnight. Knowing each new dance became important for the audiences of the new music, as shown by the Contours' record, which asked, "Do you love me, now that I can *dance?*" With its dances, rock developed its own type of *avant garde*. The question of old dances versus new dances became a central issue in determining which listeners were most up-to-date. Significantly, however, these were folk concerns: It was not the particular style of the music which concerned the rock audience so much as the physical responses to it.

Rock dances differed from earlier dances in requiring particular varieties of execution. While the Bop and the Lindy could take several, but similar, forms, rock dancers insisted on distinguishing between the Duck and the Pony, the Dog and the Fly, and other new dances. Several of these dances were inspired by records in which the lyrics provided directions for their performance—for instance, the Popeye and the Madison. Others were merely associated with song titles: the Mashed Potato, the Watusi, the Loco-Motion, and the Twist. But the majority of the dances originated spontaneously among the rock audience, and young people learned them by watching one another. They were folk inventions. Although each new dance was characterized by specialized movements, others were invented so quickly that no particular style became standard.

The most important general feature of the rock dances involved the interrelation of the dancers. While doing the Bop or the Lindy, the bodies of the partners met and moved through various stages of contact, sometimes close and occasionally at arm's length. With the rock dances, partners casually faced one another without making physical contact. This gave the dancing a visible coolness and an impersonal tone, because neither partner exhibited outward concern for what the other was doing. However, the dancers showed great individual involvement with the act of dancing and with the music which provided its inspiration. Each dancer became absorbed in a world of intense, personal experience. Visually, a rock dance provided the counterpart of the way rock music was otherwise most typically experienced—that is, by transistor radios which allowed a massive audience to share the same experience, but to feel it individually. The bond among the dancers resided in the music they heard, but their physical separation showed that the bond was privately felt. In the panorama of a rock dance, one could not determine who was dancing with whom; rather, everyone seemed to dance with everyone else. In the so-called line dances—the Popeye or the Hitch Hike—this impression was formalized:

All of the dancers separated into two parallel lines, they faced one another, and they performed a single, total dance. The scene resembled a folk chorus line because it unconsciously expressed the sense of group unity elicited by rock.

The number of dances which were invented during the 1950's and 1960's staggers the imagination. The following list is partial: the Harlem Shuffle, the Limbo, the Swim, the Fly, the Wiggle Wobble, the Duck, the Boogaloo, the Shingaling, the Funky Broadway, the Bristol Stomp, the Cool Jerk, the Freddie, the Fish, the Mashed Potato, the Watusi, the Loco-Motion, the Twist, the Madison, the Hitch Hike, the Popeye, the Frug, the Jerk, the Surfer Stomp, the Monkey, the Boston Monkey, the Chicken, the Shake, the Temptation Walk, the Pony, the Skate, the Bounce, the Philly Jerk, the Batman, the Hully Gully, the Waddle, the Walk, the Stomp, and the Dip. The majority of these styles emerged from Negro audiences, among whom dancing has generally retained its expressive folk character. Among whites, dancing has frequently become a type of popular entertainment, particularly for those individuals who cannot master the steps and movements. To a nonparticipant, these dances may have looked identical; but to the performers, each one incorporated subtle changes and refinements, and each one assumed a different meaning. Moreover, their total number reflects the extraordinary variety of the physical and emotional responses which rock music has inspired.

Of all the rock dances, the Twist received the most enthusiastic popular attention. Generally, the success of the Twist in 1961 meant that rock music and dancing had gained acceptance within the adult market, even with the cultural "elite." The clearest demonstration of this acceptance took place at the Peppermint Lounge, and its special character has been brilliantly expressed by Tom Wolfe:

The Peppermint Lounge! You know about the Peppermint Lounge. One week in October, 1961, a few socialites, riding hard under the crop of a couple of New York columnists, discovered the Peppermint Lounge and by the next week all of Jet Set New York was discovering the Twist, after the manner of the first 900 decorators who ever laid hands on an African mask. Great Garbo, Elsa Maxwell, Countess Bernadotte, Noel Coward, Tennessee Williams and the Duke of Bedford—everybody was there, and the hindmost were laying fives, tens and twenty-dollar bills on cops, doormen and a couple of sets of maitre d's to get within sight of the bandstand and a dance floor the size of somebody's kitchen. By November, Joey Dee, twenty-two, the bandleader at the Peppermint Lounge, was playing the Twist at the $100-a-plate Party of the Year at the Metropolitan Museum of Art.*

Adults were enjoying rock culture, but that did not mean that older audiences had actually caught up with teenage dance innovations. By the time adult America was doing the Twist, youth had already invented newer styles of dancing, and they were amused by the popular notion that their parents had become "hip." The fact was that the Twist had initially been popular more than a year before it arrived at the Peppermint Lounge. The original recording of "The Twist," by Hank Ballard and the Midnighters, appeared in the spring of 1959, but it never sold extensively in the Pop field. In the summer of 1960, Chubby Checker's version of the song was released, and it reached the top of the best-selling Pop charts. It did not provoke special interest. The record was a commercial success, but it was merely an addition to the growing list of dance-oriented songs.

The Twist craze started about a year after the Chubby

* *The Kandy-Kolored Tangerine-Flake Streamline Baby* (New York, Noonday Press, 1966), pp. 53-54.

Checker record had been a best seller. It was stimulated by
the artist's appearance on the Ed Sullivan show in October, 1961, after which the Twist quickly became a national phenomenon. Chubby Checker's version went to the
top of the Pop charts for a second time, and other Twist
recordings flooded the popular market. Their range was
amusing: from a Sammy Kaye version to one by a group
called Tubby Chess and the Chessmen. The Twist was
taught in dance studios, and it inspired films—one of
which, *Twist All Night*, starred nightclub performer Louis
Prima and appeared as late in the craze as 1962. Amidst
the exploitation of the Twist, several good records were
created, such as "The Peppermint Twist" by Joey Dee and
the Starliters and "Twistin' The Night Away" by Sam
Cooke. The best Twist record was "Twist And Shout" by
the Isley Brothers, and its quality has kept the trend from
becoming a mere historical anecdote.

The Twist and the Peppermint Lounge began a popularization of rock dancing. By the mid-sixties, the discotheque, a nightclub where one danced to records, replaced
such places as the Peppermint Lounge in serving to ini-
tiate adults into youth culture. After the Twist, discotheque
girls and nightclub chorus lines constantly transformed
each new dance into popular entertainment. In doing so,
they stripped the styles of their folk spontaneity and they
showed that dances were no more immune from popular
art than were rock artists or songs. In a sense, the rock
audience has battled this trend by inventing new dances
at an accelerated pace. But the resistance is unconscious;
like rock dancing, it is a folk response.

The Surfing Scene and Its Music

I have already suggested that rock is almost as much a
way of life as it is a musical style. As the rock development

persisted into the 1960's, this became increasingly apparent, particularly in the Southern California "surf scene" and its music. The close links between the music, its subject matter, and the activities of its artists and audiences showed that rock had assumed a complex meaning by the turn of the present decade.

Popular notions about the surf scene and surf music are usually derived from the Beach Boys' best-selling singles and albums. In the early sixties, their personal image drew on the California sun cult, surf boards, hot rods, casual dress, girls, and all the pleasures of the beach world. Their records described this world in detail: "Surfin' USA," "Surfer Girl," "Catch A Wave," "Warmth Of The Sun," "Little Deuce Coupe," "This Car Of Mine," and "Keep An Eye On Summer." Since the middle sixties, the surfing image of the Beach Boys has become less important than it was when they appeared in 1962. At the same time, the creative abilities of their acknowledged leader, Brian Wilson, have increasingly gained attention. From the Beach Boys' beginning, Wilson has provided most of their song writing and arranging energies, and his talent has been responsible for the group's continuing importance in the rock development.

The Beach Boys emerged at an early stage in the surf trend, and they propelled it into a national phenomenon. But they were not alone in giving the style its early definition. Important prototypes were established by Jan and Dean and by Dick Dale and the Deltones. In both cases, the artists possessed Southern California backgrounds, and they had regional audiences before they became nationally known. For Jan and Dean, national recognition came gradually over a four-year period, reaching its climax in 1963 with their most popular record, "Surf City." Dick Dale, by comparison, received one of the most ambitious promotional campaigns of the early sixties, but never became popular on a nationwide scale. When he signed a contract with Capitol Records, in February 1963, the accompanying publicity gave the impression that Dick Dale was as distinctive as Elvis Presley and that his records and personal appearances would similarly captivate the national audience. But Dick Dale failed to fulfill the promise of his publicity, and today his name is almost forgotten. The style of his music has also been forgotten. Although it differed from the style both of Jan and Dean and of the Beach Boys, it nevertheless represented the surf sound—in California, that is—at the beginning of the 1960's.

There were two important reasons for Dick Dale's failure to win a national audience. In the first place, his music did not follow the general trend of rock in the early sixties. The Dick Dale sound had a heavy, crashing quality; it was dominated by a strong bass guitar and a blaring saxophone. This combination of elements gave the music its surf character. It simulated the incessant pounding of waves on a beach, and it evoked the robust vitality of the surfing sport. Dale's vocals possessed a harshness which was similar to the early style of Elvis Presley; moreover, his overall aesthetic was probably inspired by the raw Presley manner. By the early sixties, however, this style sounded more like a revival than a relevant, current trend. The saxophone was becoming uncommon as a primary sustaining element in the rock sound, and the majority of best-selling records either ignored the instrument or softened its impact with elegant string sections. Rock had become refined but the Dick Dale style had not. His music was successful in the concert hall, but not on records.

In 1960, Dick Dale established a reputation in Southern California as the "Pied Piper of Balboa." At the Rendezvous Ballroom there, he attracted large and enthusiastic audiences for his performances at weekend dances. By 1962, his records, including "Peppermint Man," "Miserlou," and an album entitled *Surfer's Choice*, reached the top of the Southern California charts. This success eventually brought him to the attention of the major record companies. But the major companies failed to realize that Dick Dale's popularity was based upon his live performances. These were electrifying, but their quality was not successfully transferred to his records. Capitol Records misinterpreted Dale's Southern California record sales, which were based upon memories of live situations.

The Jan and Dean records never suffered from associations with live performances. On the contrary, their concerts generally had less impact than their records, because their style consistently involved recording-room manipulations. They developed this style between 1959, the date of "Baby Talk," and 1963, when "Surf City" was issued. During that period, their records became increasingly complex and intricate, but all of them were smoother and lighter than the Dick Dale style, and this probably enhanced their popularity and sense of relevance. By 1963, Jan and Dean had capitalized on the growing lore of the surfing world, particularly in the remarkable record, "Surf City."

The image and jargon of the surf scene were as important as the music in transforming the trend into a national craze. With the trappings of wetsuits and woodies, baggies and bikinis, any individual could join the surf cult, because, absurd as it may seem, the surf itself had been obviated as an essential ingredient. By 1963, the craze spread to Philadelphia, New York, Chicago, and other cities where big waves were at a premium. A Denver group called the Astronauts also released a surfing album, thereby combining the best of all possible worlds available at that time. For the original surfers who had participated in the sport since the 1950's, this national fad undoubtedly represented a commercialization of their way of life. But neither the Beach Boys nor Jan and Dean were wholly responsible. Hollywood had begun the exploitation of the Southern California surf world with a series of beach films. *Gidget* was the first of these; it appeared in 1959 starring Sandra Dee, James Darren, and Cliff Robertson and gave the impression that the "Lonely Surfer" was merely on a temporary vacation from a lucrative and respectable middle-class job. This interpretation conflicted radically with the early surfers' image of the demanding skills of the sport and its challenging confrontation of the natural elements. With real surf many miles away, however, America's popular audience was less interested in the rough realities of the sport than in its superficial trappings.

The Beach Boys contributed as much to the definition of surfing music as they did to the definition of the surfing world. When the group entered the Pop field in 1962, the style of surfing music was largely undefined. It contained the narrative, instrumental approach of Dick Dale on the one hand, and the more elegant, abstract approach of Jan and Dean on the other. But the consistently high quality of the Beach Boys' records gradually established their music as *the* popularly-recognized surf style. Still, their dominance was never absolute. For instance, the earlier, instrumental-based surf style was continued into 1963 by the Surfaris' "Wipe Out," a record whose popularity coincided with the Beach Boys' "Surfin' USA."

The Beach Boys' control of the surfing market was helped by their general stylistic development and by the extensiveness and authority of their subject range. For Brian Wilson especially, the surf world represented more than an occasional inspiration or a subject on which merely to capitalize as a writer. The Beach Boys' singles and albums outline the total world of surfing activities, and they do the same for hot rods and for many of the concerns of

The Beach Boys

youth in general, as in "Fun, Fun, Fun," "In My Room," "Wendy," and "When I Grow Up." The casual, conventional subjects of these records contradicted the popular folk movement's tendency to concentrate on songs with social or political content. Through 1968, however, the group continued to give conventional subjects an unconventional impact. One of the best records of the decade, "Good Vibrations," from 1966, begins with these lines:

> I love the go-go clothes she wears,
> And the way the sunlight plays upon her hair. . . .*

In 1968, "Do It Again" describes a wish to return to the surfing world, parties, and people of earlier experiences. Against the background of "serious" subjects which have dominated rock in the 1960's, the Beach Boys' records seem anachronistic, like a revival of the romanticism of the 1950's. But the lyrics alone give this impression. The high quality and the total sound of "Good Vibrations" and "Do It Again" lend real vitality to the lyrics and underscore the fact that rock is not defined by subject matter alone.

"Good Vibrations" and "Do It Again" were the climax of the Beach Boys' stylistic development since 1962. From the beginning, their style was based on recording studio techniques utilizing electronics and multiple tapes. Careful manipulation of these elements, usually directed by Brian Wilson, transformed five voices into a full chorus and a handful of instruments into a complete orchestra. Like twentieth-century madrigals, the Beach Boys' songs have a complex delicacy and a ringing ethereality which are unprecedented in rock history. At the same time, their intertwining of voices and instruments represents an extension of the original rock aesthetic of simultaneity. The Beach Boys' music is linked to the past, but it marks a new

* Lyrics quoted by permission of Brian Wilson, Sea of Tunes Publishing Company.

level in folk sophistication; and its high quality demonstrates that surf music consisted of more than a popular fad.

Television Shows and Rock

In 1954, an unknown singer named Joan Weber appeared in a CBS television drama and sang a song called "Let Me Go, Lover." The show was part of the *Studio One* series, and its story dealt with a disk jockey. The song had existed in a different version entitled "Let Me Go, Devil," and a record of it had been issued about a year before. Joan Weber's recording of "Let Me Go. Lover" had appeared several weeks before its television exposure, and it had stimulated very little activity in terms of Pop sales. In fact, *Billboard* had given it a "60" rating, thereby predicting that it would enjoy only limited popularity. On the day after the television show, however, the record suddenly began to sell. It literally became an overnight sensation; it reached the top of the Pop charts, and it was covered by numerous Pop vocalists, including Peggy Lee, Patti Page, Teresa Brewer, and Sunny Gale.

Joan Weber never issued another hit record, but "Let Me Go, Lover" remained as a stunning example of the promotion power of the television medium. The same power also turned Tommy Sands's "Teenage Crush" into an overnight success after he appeared on NBC's *Kraft Theater* in February, 1957. Because of incidents like these, major networks and individual producers realized that there was a place for popular music and for rock music on TV. Yet, finding that place has proved to be a tricky enterprise because it has necessitated an understanding of both the television medium and the music. For popular singers—Perry Como, Dean Martin or Andy Williams, for instance—this problem has not been too acute. Their pleasing brand of entertainment has continually satisfied the tastes of the larger television audience. Each of these artists has starred in weekly or special variety shows, and each possesses a large, faithful audience. In other words, the commercial appeal of popular music has remained generally predictable. But television shows devoted to rock have been more problematic in terms of their commercial appeal. Rock programs have quickly originated and just as quickly disappeared. Few shows have been able to sustain an interest across the nation. At the same time, this pattern helps to illuminate the character of rock and the ways in which its style has changed during the past decade.

Of all the television shows that have dealt with rock, one classic has survived: *American Bandstand*. It was first seen nationally in 1957, at the most popular weekday viewing hours for teenagers, 3 to 5 P.M. It continues today, although it is limited to one day per week and one hour, generally on Saturday afternoons. *American Bandstand* presently emanates from Hollywood, and its host is the same Dick Clark who has been associated with the show for more than ten years. However, it originated in Philadelphia at the astonishingly early date of 1952. At that time it was simply called *Bandstand*, and its master of ceremonies was Bob Horn. When its national telecasts began, the show adopted a new title, and Dick Clark became a nationally recognized personality. Before that he had been merely a Philadelphia disk jockey, and he had been with *Bandstand* about a year before its network recognition.

American Bandstand was a deceptively simple show. With Dick Clark it retained the format that it had had with Bob Horn: that is, it was a teenage dance which happened to be on television. Records were played and the audience danced, and this pattern was periodically broken by the visit of a guest performer, the formation of a panel which judged new releases, and very short interviews in which the teenagers filed past the microphone, introduced themselves, and named the schools they attended. The ingredients were few, but the program became a national success which Clark parlayed into additional shows and into an extensive personal business.

The appeal of *American Bandstand* lay in its very simplicity. The program made no positive effort to "entertain" the television audience. It existed primarily for the pleasure of the audience within the television studio, as it had since its inception. In 1952, *Bandstand* consisted of a record show in which filmed performances accompanied each song and provided visual appeal. An audience of teenagers was present in the studio, and they spontaneously began dancing when the records were played. As this phenomenon persisted, the entire show unexpectedly evolved into a dance party. Ultimately, this gave the program its meaning: It was a life situation which anyone was allowed to observe. If one viewed it often enough, one became familiar with the "regulars"—that is, the kids who attended the dance four or five days a week. One knew who was dating whom, or going steady, as well as other personal details about the individuals in the audience. The folk, in other words, were the real stars of *American Bandstand*. Of course most of them remained anonymous, but their lifelike situation was immediately accessible to the television viewer. In this type of setting, rock music unconsciously performed its function: The dance was a living drama, and, although the music generally remained in the background, it nevertheless unified the audience and provided their *raison d'être*. Instead of being transformed into popular entertainment, it was permitted to maintain its inherent folk identity.

In the passive medium of television, *American Bandstand* provided an absorbing and intimate experience to which Dick Clark's personal style was perfectly suited.

Clark's manner was consistently relaxed, controlled, and quiet. Unlike his radio counterparts, he introduced records with relative casualness. In his relation to the audience, he never imposed himself on the teenagers or sought to assume their dress, vocabulary or attitudes. His image was that of an attractive older brother or father; that is, a distinguished personality who understood and sympathized with teenagers, enjoyed their music, but did not assume their way of life. Dick Clark's mild style accounted for his appeal: He receded behind the music and permitted the dancing of the teenagers to describe rock's vitality and impact.

In the 1950's, Dick Clark became an idol for teenagers and a symbol of their aspirations. Like the young man described by Chuck Berry's "Too Much Monkey Business," Dick Clark married, bought a home, settled down, and wrote a book. Later he was divorced, and in 1959 and 1960 his name became unfavorably connected with the payola hearings. They publicly revealed the extraordinary breadth of Clark's commercial enterprises and showed that he was a super-entrepreneur as well as a mild-mannered disk jockey. His distinctiveness, however, has resided in his ability to balance these different roles against one another without sacrificing the rewards of either. He still conducts *American Bandstand*, for instance, although his presence on the show constitutes a tradition more than it provides a relevant insight into current television rock shows. Clark's other program, *Where The Action Is*, reflected more clearly his image during the 1960's. He rarely appeared in the half-hour show, not because its structure could not accommodate him, but because he probably realized that his style was not as meaningful to teenagers in 1967 as it had been a decade earlier.

The significance of Clark's *American Bandstand* becomes clearer when the program is compared to a more recent version of the same idea, the *Lloyd Thaxton Show*. It too was a televised dance for teenagers, featuring records, visits from guest stars, and brief conversations with members of the audience. But the distinctive feature of the *Lloyd Thaxton Show* lay in its stylization of elements which had arisen spontaneously in *American Bandstand*. Through various manipulations of the records and the audience, it transformed a folk situation into popular art. Thaxton, for instance, performed as an entertainer: He frequently mimed the lyrics of a record while it was being played, or feigned an organ or trumpet performance during the instrumental sections. Likewise, the audience became entertainers. A group of teenagers periodically mimed a current song in the Thaxton manner or entered a contest in which they actually sang with a record and had to continue its beat and lyrics when the song was unexpectedly halted. Dancing also became popular art instead of folk expression. Contests required dancers to hold their positions, like statues, when the music was interrupted; any subsequent movement automatically eliminated a couple from the competition. Even the non-contest dances possessed an aura of popular entertainment, as when a couple danced behind a screen on which the silhouettes of their bodies were projected, like lantern-slide reproductions of paintings. Because of these gimmicks and contests, the meaning of the *Lloyd Thaxton Show* became radically different from Dick Clark's *American Bandstand*. The show willfully molded the audience into a core of entertainers instead of allowing them to entertain unconsciously by being themselves; in addition, it showed less respect for the music, because it constantly interrupted records in order to force them into the structures of a contest. While the results were often amusing, they were neither as spontaneous nor as expressive as the events which characterized *American Bandstand*. In fact, they changed

American Bandstand in the way that the Peppermint
Lounge changed rock dancing, that RCA changed Elvis
Presley, and that the Crew Cuts changed "Sh-Boom."

The thrust toward stylization and popular art typified
most of the television rock shows of the 1960's. Both *Shindig* and *Hullabaloo* exemplified this tendency. *Shindig*
originated in 1964 and lasted about one year; *Hullabaloo*
quickly followed *Shindig* but survived into 1966, largely
because it gradually broadened its format to include artists
who were popular with adult audiences. *Shindig* performers had been more exclusively teen-oriented. Both programs initially generated an enthusiastic response within
the television audience, but the response was not sustained,
probably because the programs ignored the life context of
American Bandstand and created a variety-show atmosphere instead. The programs invariably consisted of appearances by currently popular groups and individuals
who performed their hit records. As they did, they were
accompanied by a troop of professional dancers who did
the Jerk, the Monkey, or whichever dance was best known
at the time. Although these dancers performed with extraordinary enthusiasm this did not conceal their resemblance to popular art chorus lines. That is, they standardized dances and made them academic, retaining only a
superficial appearance of folk excitement and involvement. Moreover, the presence of famous artists did not
insure the programs' commercial success. Although a keen
excitement accompanied the first appearance of a particular group or individual, this response dissipated when the
audience became familiar with the new faces. The decline
in interest was accentuated by the fact that neither show
permitted viewer participation or empathy. The rock artists and music were merely projected at the television audience in an entertainment package that excluded the
viewer's world of experience. Both *Shindig* and *Hullabaloo*

failed to grasp the essential folk function of the rock music they promoted. They took their inspiration from television variety shows like Ed Sullivan's. While perennially helping to popularize rock among adult audiences, however, Ed Sullivan has always maintained a balance between rock and other kinds of entertainment. *Shindig* and *Hullabaloo* never achieved this balance. In following the variety show format, moreover, they overlooked the crucial connections between rock and the life situations from which it originates and in terms of which it ultimately has meaning.

Several television shows of the late sixties attempted to present rock music in a more lifelike context. *Where The Action Is* and *Malibu U.*, for instance, both made effective use of video tape, extending the television medium in a way which seemed to defy the viewer's ability to separate the actual world from the world of film reproductions. *Where The Action Is* was particularly subtle in capitalizing on this ambiguity. In many ways, the show employed the same format as *Shindig* or *Hullabaloo*: Current groups performed their hit records and were accompanied by the program's own dance troupe, the "Action Kids." Instead of the television studio, however, the out-of-doors provided the setting for each record play. The scenes varied from the beach at Santa Monica to a ski resort in the Colorado Rockies, and from the San Francisco Bay to the Boston Harbor. Within the space of one show, rock music jumped from coast to coast and border to border, and video tape transformed the whole into a disarmingly immediate experience. But *Where The Action Is* seemed to operate on the assumption that rock involves pleasure exclusively: Since, however, pleasure represents only one side of the complex meaning of rock, the show was unduly restrictive. Like *Shindig* and *Hullabaloo*, *Where The Action Is* made folk art into popular entertainment.

Malibu U. was a short-lived adaptation of *Where The Action Is.* When the show appeared in 1967, it was described as a mythical university whose courses were conducted by Ricky Nelson and other popular stars. The university and its courses ostensibly provided a life situation for the music. Actually, the show consisted of a television beach film, and its only tie with the life situation of a university lay in the introduction of such performers as "our next drop-in," and "our professor of marine biology." *Malibu U.* was simply popular art. It not only standardized the music by forcing it into the categories of college courses, but it standardized fun as well. The show was crowded with bikini-clad girls who, as they scampered through forests and across beaches, were reminiscent of stale nineteenth-century paintings by French academicians such as Bouguereau, paintings which disguised a restricting aesthetic in the cloak of a supposedly natural vitality.

Television's transformation of rock into popular art reached a climax with *The Monkees*, which survived two years of network viewing before being removed in the 1968-69 season. The program was extraordinary, however, in the overtness of its commerciality. Each element of the Monkees' style was carefully and blatantly culled from existing rock groups, particularly from the Beatles. The ingredients were welded together into an image of youthful exuberance and well-meaning rebellion. The resulting style was polished and seductive, an acme of popular art perfection. But the style appealed primarily to subteens, children between the ages of six and twelve who had never seen *American Bandstand*. For older viewers, the program was too obviously an artificial pastiche. Through many years of viewing, years which began with *American Bandstand* and culminated with *The Monkees*, the rock audience had gradually become more sophisticated.

The Payola Hearings

The most scandalous event in the history of rock concerned the payola hearings of 1959 and 1960. In the aftermath of the TV quiz scandals, the House of Representatives Special Subcommittee on Legislative Oversight questioned numerous individuals from the music industry in order to investigate promotion practices for songs and records. Oren Harris presided over the hearings, and the results are contained in over 1600 pages of documentation entitled *Responsibilities of Broadcasting Licensees and Station Personnel.*

A primary target of the payola hearings was the radio disk jockey. He was charged with accepting material bribes from record producers, manufacturers, and distributors in return for "plugging" certain records, and, therefore, with the illegal limiting of business competition and with dictating public taste. But the impetus behind these hearings was undeniably related to an assumption that rock was "bad" music, that it encouraged juvenile delinquency, and that it could only have been forced on the public by illegal business activities. Examples of rock songs and artists were constantly cited by the House Committee to make these points. As a result, the discussions between committee members and testifiers frequently wandered from issues of legality and entered the domain of aesthetics. As much as any fact in rock history, this demonstrated that the music had made a profound and revolutionary impact on the American public. For the payola hearings would never have taken place if rock had been aesthetically pleasing to the popular music audience or, to put it another way, if rock had been popular art instead of authentic folk art.

The discussions of aesthetics which took place during the payola hearings were often as amusing as they were revealing. The following exchange took place between Representative Steven Derounian and Dick Clark:

MR. DEROUNIAN   What do you think of John Crosby of the Herald Tribune as a critic? Does he call his shots impartially, or did I say a bad word to you?

MR. CLARK   I don't know.

MR. DEROUNIAN   Here is what he had to say about your Fabian: "Reeling like a top, snapping his fingers and jerking his eyeballs, with hair like something Medusa had sent back, and a voice that was enormously improved by total unintelligibility." And Mitch Miller—

MR. CLARK   Wishes he had him.

MR. DEROUNIAN   No.

MR. CLARK   Excuse me; I'm sorry.

MR. DEROUNIAN   He said:
"You would not invite those unwashed kids into your living room to meet your family, why thrust them into the living rooms of your audience?"
Mr. Clark, I think what you are saying is this: the singer appears on your program physically—and apparently this is your format, you get a big hunk of young man who has got a lot of cheesecake to him and the kids are thrilled by this on the television program —and then you play his records, but you don't have him sing too often. That is the way you sell records and that is a pretty cute way to do it.
And all I want you to do, if that is the case, is to admit that the singing part of his talent is not the all-important part, but his physical appearance plays a great part in whether or not you are going to let him appear on your show.

MR. CLARK   No, it is not factual.

MR. DEROUNIAN   You would then have an ugly person appear on your show?

MR. CLARK   Mr. Derounian, do you want me to say I have had a lot of ugly people appear on my program?

MR. DEROUNIAN   Attractive to teenagers?

MR. CLARK   Mr. Derounian, all things and all different kinds of people are attracted to different types of people. Beauty—

MR. DEROUNIAN   Beauty is relative. I know that.*

This discussion is typical of the confusion which has surrounded rock. Like most of the adult public in the 1950's, Steven Derounian tacitly assumed that rock was popular art, that "cheesecake" was being sold to the public in the guise of music. He never questioned this assumption about the music's identity; instead, he blithely cited the remarks of a critic who agreed with his aesthetic responses. This practice pervaded the payola hearings. Members of the government committee never questioned the identity of the music they were dealing with, so they never questioned the validity of their responses to it. Ironically, they were as unconscious of the distinctions between fine art, folk art, and popular art as the music itself was. Of course, consciousness of these distinctions would not have insured an enjoyment of rock; it would only have prohibited expectations that the music should function in a manner foreign to it.

To many people in the national audience, payola could not be separated from rock at the time of the federal hearings. This identification was unfortunate. Payola did not originate with rock. The history of payola, the forms it took and the areas where it thrived, became evident during the hearings, particularly through the testimony of Paul Ackerman, the music editor of *Billboard*. Ackerman's statement to the House Committee was a highlight of the

* *Responsibilities of Broadcasting Licensees and Station Personnel.* Hearings Before a Subcommittee of the Committee on Interstate and Foreign Commerce. House of Representatives, Eighty-sixth Congress, Second Session on Payola and Other Deceptive Practices in the Broadcasting Field. United States Government Printing Office, 1960, Part 2, p. 1342.

hearings, because it established a perspective with which
to view the whole phenomenon of payola.

Ackerman pointed out that payola was an extension of
the traditional practice of song plugging, of persuading a
band leader, a singer, or a disk jockey to perform or play
a song or record. This provided exposure for the music and
obviously helped to insure its commercial success. As Ackerman mentioned, song plugging could frequently be
honest and legal. Increased competition, however, periodically stretched song plugging into payola. According to
Ackerman:

> In the late 1930's, when the record business was rela-
> tively small compared to what it is today, and when the
> disk jockey was unimportant in comparison to his status
> today, payola already was rampant, but had not yet be-
> come of such general importance because music had not
> yet become a major part of radio station programming.
>
> Use of records on stations was relatively minor. Some
> labels even frowned upon such use—feeling that it hurt
> sales in retail stores.
>
> Where was the payola evil of the 1930's centered? It
> was centered where it always is, at the primary source
> of exposure, at that time: dance bands, whose per-
> formances at hotels and ballrooms throughout the coun-
> try were broadcast via remote wire over network and
> independent radio stations.*

During the 1930's, attempts to restrict payola activities
failed. At that time, sheet music provided the major source
of income for song writers and publishers, and most publishers felt that payola was a "necessary evil" in their
effort to survive commercially. The same feeling prevailed
throughout the 1940's and the 1950's when records became
the major source of income, and when radio assumed the
function formerly occupied by vaudeville or band per-

* *Ibid.*, p. 900.

formances. Of course, as radio became the primary center for music exposure, the disk jockey became a focus for payola practices. Yet, he was not the only focus. As Ackerman's statement pointed out:

> One of the banes of the record business, and this laps over into radio, is the abundance of product. About 130 single records and about 100 long-play records are released weekly.
>
> Competition for exposure is extreme, for, without wide public exposure, the potential buyer would never hear of most of these records. This is true not only at the broadcast level, where payola enters into play, but also at the retail level, where payola again enters into play. We are familiar with aspects of payola at the broadcast level.
>
> At the retail level, it often takes the form of free records furnished by distributors to dealers. The dealers are expected to "push" labels which are generous with free merchandise. Dealer cooperation often takes the form of listing certain records on so-called popularity lists of radio stations and trade papers.
>
> Many of these listings are therefore invalid and, inasmuch as they are used as programming and buying guides, they serve to subvert the airways and mislead the consumer public.*

The "abundance of product" as Ackerman called it, was directly linked to the development of rock, particularly to the music's rebellion against Tin Pan Alley's control of the Pop field.

> In the rock-and-roll era, there was a tremendous increase in the number of record firms with publishing subsidiaries. This came about in a natural way. Rock and roll drew from the specialty fields known as country music and rhythm and blues. Much of this music was

* *Ibid.*, pp. 903-4.

unavailable through traditional Broadway or Tin Pan
Alley channels.

Unlike the product of so-called professional song-
writers, this material is folk oriented in the sense that
the performing artist is often the writer. A record label
in the country field, or in the rhythm and blues field,
therefore, did not seek song material from New York's
Tin Pan Alley. It relied on the song product of its own
artists, and published and recorded the material itself.*

Ackerman also made an interesting general point about
the relation between single records and albums:

Much of the investigation of the music industry has
centered around the so-called singles record business,
which is a very small part of the total record business.
The singles business is a declining one and in December
represented only 20 percent of the industry's dollar volume. The industry's annual dollar volume is over $400
million at the retail level based upon list price. Longplay
records currently account for approximately 80 percent
of the total dollar volume.

It is estimated that jukeboxes, of which there are about
500,000, account for 45 percent of single records sold in
this country.

Although the programming of long-play records by
radio stations is increasing, it is interesting to note that
the major part of station programming still is drawn
from singles—or, in other words, from a product which
today is aimed essentially at the teenage market.**

This implies that the general public's image of payola
activities was somewhat distorted, especially with regard
to the disk jockey. According to Ackerman, radio was primarily oriented to a relatively small portion of the total

* *Ibid.*, p. 902.
** *Ibid.*, p. 904.

record industry, but payola was rife throughout the *whole* of the record industry. To assume that the disk jockey was the root of payola evil was therefore unrealistic. Nevertheless the public—and the House Committee—generally made that assumption. And they did, I suggest, because the style of the rock disk jockey provoked an aesthetic response that was as profound and revolutionary as the response provoked by rock music.

The effects of the payola hearings on the music industry were considerable. As I mentioned earlier, the career of Alan Freed was virtually ended in 1960. On the other hand, Dick Clark was never convicted of having accepted payola. The hearings revealed the extraordinary extent of his commercial enterprises, however, and his employer, ABC television, demanded that Clark divest himself of those which represented a conflict of interest. Such aspects of the music industry are outside the scope of this study, however. In the present context, the question is: did payola account for the development and popularity of rock? The evidence of the hearings suggested that it did not. Certainly payola existed in the 1950's, as it probably exists today; but it also existed long before rock. Because rock stimulated a phenomenal increase in competition for record sales, it undoubtedly heightened payola practices. But this conclusion implies that rock brought about an increase in payola, not that payola created the popularity of rock. Such a conclusion may not reflect favorably on the music as a whole. Still, the social *uses* of the music cannot necessarily be equated with the meaning of the music. Some of the highest quality paintings in the history of art have occasionally been involved in tax evasions, false value estimates, and other illegal activities, none of which affect the aesthetic significance of the work. The quality and significance of rock is neither greater nor less than the music itself. The payola hearings did not "prove" its artistic shortcomings any more than its artistic merit is "proved" by the fact that it is studied in college or university symposia.

Radio Programming

While the payola hearings did not inhibit the development of rock, they did affect the radio programming through which the music gained exposure, generally by reinforcing a trend that had already begun in the 1950's—"Top 40" programming.

When rock became established in the middle of the 1950's, criticisms of its "smutty" or "pornographic" content gradually eased. Within the radio industry, they were replaced by questions of programming technique. Competition for listener ratings was waged between rock programs and "good music" programs, and one station in San Francisco issued bumper stickers saying "I kicked the junk music habit by listening to KSFR."* Amidst this competition, Top 40 programming became popular with radio stations and listeners. The Top 40 program was based on the notion that, despite the extraordinary number of records available at a given moment, most listeners were interested in hearing only a fraction of the total number. Each station therefore composed a list of the forty most popular songs on a week-to-week basis and these were played regularly. The list was generally compiled by a station manager after he had consulted local record stores or national popularity charts in the trade periodicals. The use of these lists meant that the selection of records for radio play became increasingly standardized and correspondingly removed from the taste of the individual disk jockey. Thus, the opportunities for payola were minimized.

* *Billboard*, April 21, 1958, p. 1.

In the 1960's, Top 40 radio has gained increasing acceptance. Most stations feature a group of "good guys," disk jockeys who conform to a frenetic style of record presentation, but who are rarely singled out as the creators of a distinctive show. There are exceptions to this pattern, for instance "Cousin" Bruce Marrow in New York or Russ Syracuse in San Francisco. But the majority of disk jockeys sound uniformly anonymous, and this is probably their appeal: They do not impose on the music itself. The anonymous "good guy" conforms to the aesthetic pattern of the music but does not distract from it. Similarly, radio advertisements have adjusted to the music, and the most appealing ones frequently sound like rock songs.

The most significant recent development in the radio programming of rock music has concerned FM stations. Since about 1966, major cities across the country have begun to offer one or two rock programs on FM bands, and they have done so in reaction to the restrictiveness of the Top 40 format. Instead of merely playing singles, the FM programs feature entire albums, and they frequently provide exposure for rock groups who are not oriented toward the Pop field. This development has extraordinary significance within the history of rock. Like the increasing album-orientation of rock artists, it reflects a growing seriousness and sophistication within the music, and it also means that rock has made inroads into areas of expression which formerly belonged to adults. At the same time, and to the extent that FM radio has traditionally been associated with classical music, the development suggests that rock has begun to jettison its folk background.

The Maturity of Rock:
1964 through 1968

Introduction

Since 1964, rock has become a total cultural movement whose scope exceeds any of the sub-trends which had previously composed its history. Rock presently commands the attention of a truly international audience, and it more openly manifests a way of life than it did at any point in its earlier development.

The phenomenal impact of rock during the late 1960's is directly related to the impact of one group, the Beatles. This group by itself has generated more public enthusiasm and more activity in the music industry than any individual or group in rock history, more even than Elvis Presley generated when he appeared in 1956. But the Beatles have not been alone in molding the character of rock in these years. The current style has also been profoundly influenced by Bob Dylan, whose audience in many ways is just as keenly committed as that of the Beatles. Another major development involves the nationwide revival of Rhythm and Blues and the adoption of the "soul" style in connection with it. This trend constitutes a way of life for the Negro community just as the Beatles' or Dylan's music constitutes a way of life for white audiences. A final element characterizes the current period: the growing popularity of dances in which bands perform live. The center of this activity was originally San Francisco, but it has quickly spread to New York, Boston, Los Angeles, and other cities throughout the country.

Together these developments have had an appreciable effect on the style of rock. The music has revealed a growing sophistication—an awareness which did not exist during the 1950's. This sophistication has been manifested in the broadened range in the subject matter of rock lyrics and in the increasing concern with rock's own artistic tradition. The latter, of course, represents the major interest of this study, and its growing momentum carries crucial implications regarding the fundamental character of rock. As its consciousness of art evolves, the identity of rock necessarily changes: It may aspire to the status of fine art, but it may also fail, merely displaying self-consciousness. Much rock is presently in this transitional state. Thus, it defies categorization as *either* folk art *or* fine art. Rock's growing awareness of art means that it has begun to elicit comparisons with the contemporary fine arts, not only music, but poetry, painting, and theater. While the music remained an essentially folk expression, it did not encourage these comparisons. As rock continues to incline toward art consciousness, however, it must be judged by the criteria of the fine arts.

At the present time, rock also elicits a specific comparison with jazz, particularly with one development which modern jazz manifested during the 1950's. In the years in which rock emerged, jazz was enjoying an increased popularity among white audiences in the United States, especially among young people either in college or of college age. College jazz concerts became common during the early and middle fifties. Among the most popular attractions were the rather cerebral Dave Brubeck, Gerry Mulli-

gan, and Modern Jazz quartets. These groups were inclin-
ing toward a fine art approach characterized by complex,
intricate and often fugue-like exchanges of arranged and
improvised solos. The Modern Jazz Quartet was, and is, a
prime example of this extremely "cool" and sophisticated
tendency, whose products often sound like a chamber music version of jazz.

A similar shift currently exists within the rock scene. In
their live concerts especially, groups such as the Cream
show a penchant for explorative, extended improvisation
and for developing a communicative language that is
purely musical, although they maintain the heavy rock
beat. The connection between rock and jazz at this time is
emphasized by the appearance of groups which are clearly
jazz-based, like Charles Lloyd's, at numerous rock concerts.

The English Scene: Background

The Beatles' music appeared in the United States in 1964
and its overwhelming success staggered the record market.
The furor surpassed any excitement being generated by
American music at the time, and it made previous imports
from England seem ordinary by comparison.

English records had filtered into the American market
before the arrival of the Beatles. I have already mentioned
Bob Cort, Lonnie Donegan, and other skiffle artists who
achieved a temporary popularity in America in 1957. In
the years before 1964, Laurie London, Cliff Richard, the
Tornados, and the Chris Barber jazz band also gained nationwide acclaim in the American Pop field. Laurie London's "He's Got The Whole World In His Hands," for instance, became a best seller in 1958, and "Telestar," by the
Tornados, reached the top of the charts in 1962. Generally,
however, the flow of rock music on an international level
went *from* the United States *to* England and other coun-

tries. Most English artists who were popular abroad seemed like imitations of American rock singers when they appeared in this country. Tommy Steele, for instance, was considered the "Elvis of Great Britain" around 1957, but he never became popular with listeners in the United States. Cliff Richard stimulated an enthusiastic following in England before 1964, but he too failed to make a strong impact on the American market.

Before 1964, if English records became popular in America, the fact that they were English did not lend them any distinctiveness. In the case of the Beatles, however, the group's English origin was clearly recognized by the American audience; it represented an important facet of their image even before their records became available here. Moreover, this recognition attended other English groups and individuals who followed the Beatles into the American market during 1964. Together, they constituted an English "scene"—a total world which did not exist for American audiences before 1964, but subsequently distinguished the Beatles and their compatriots from any of the English artists who had preceded them.

American enthusiasm for the English scene was justified by the large number of high-quality artists who entered the rock picture in 1964. Besides the Beatles, there were the Rolling Stones, Gerry and the Pacemakers, Herman and His Hermits, the Dave Clark Five, and many others whose presence added solidity to the image of the English movement. Further reinforcement was provided by the common background and development of many of the English groups. Like the Beatles, many of them had gained their first recognition at the Cavern Club in Liverpool. This was the *locus classicus* for the English trend, and it possessed associative, historical meaning for outside audiences. The Cavern's legendary function was reflected by the fact that American teen newspapers such as *The Beat* featured weekly columns on the club's activities until it closed in March, 1966.

The English scene inspired a fad in the United States. Like any fad, its popularity probably enabled certain English artists to become successful solely because of their origin—Noel Harrison with his *kitsch* style, for instance, or Freddie and the Dreamers. For about a year, the fad was so consuming that some American groups were thought to be British, particularly if their style exhibited the unified smoothness that had become known as the Liverpool or Mersey sound. The Beau Brummels, from San Francisco, were a case in point: On hearing their first records, east coast listeners assumed that the group was English.

But the most significant effect of the English fad was that it provoked a general consciousness of the national or regional origin of a group or individual. This was the first time in the history of rock that such a consciousness had emerged, and it quickly manifested itself in the expression of stylistic "schools" within the music's new international scope. To the Mersey or the Liverpool sound, American audiences added the west coast sound, the surfing sound, the Detroit sound, and the Nashville sound. Since 1964, the list has continued to expand, with the San Francisco sound and the Boston sound. Insofar as they represented conscious and critical evaluation of artistic style, these distinctions revealed the growing sophistication of rock artists and audiences. However, the sophisticated practice of distinguishing stylistic schools was not entirely divorced from the older folk approach to rock music. Each school was characterized by its own clothes, vocabulary, and other life elements as much as it was characterized by artistic elements. To put it another way, the abstract method of discussing style in the fine arts, of separating artists from works of art, was never grasped with full consciousness by the rock audience. Rather, the folk desire

to concentrate on immediate, tangible realities, and to in-
sist·upon a link between the artist and his work persisted.

The life associations which American listeners made
with British music were not based on fantasies. By the
time English music reached the United States, England
possessed a fully developed rock scene of its own. The
shows *Juke Box Jury* and *Ready, Steady, Go* had been
bringing the music to a large English audience. The popularity of the Beatles, the Rolling Stones, the Dave Clark
Five, and other groups had grown steadily during 1962
and 1963 and reached a peak of frenzy just before the
start of 1964. Moreover, the English scene contained numerous life accoutrements, particularly "mod" clothes and
hair styles. These were relatively unknown to Americans
before 1964, and they provoked a kind of cultural shock
when they reached America, one which corresponded to
and reinforced the excitement about English rock. English
rock had not developed overnight or in isolation from
other cultural phenomena, although a large portion of the
American audience certainly held this impression. Rather,
English rock was part of a larger creative explosion which
had begun in the early sixties, and it reflected the generally relaxed atmosphere of the time. Factors which accounted for this atmosphere included English Pop Art; a
burgeoning theatrical scene rivalling that of the first Eliz-
abethan age; the defiant heroes and anti-heroes with regional (definitely not upper-class) accents in many excellent movies; the election of a Labour government; the ir-
reverent satire of the magazine *Private Eye*, the review
Beyond the Fringe, the club The Establishment, and the
BBC Television show *That Was the Week That Was*; the
presence of new universities to challenge the authority of
the more established ones; and fashions such as mini-skirts
and bizarre uniforms among the more affluent urban
youth.

A distinctive aspect of the English scene was that its records simply sounded new to American audiences. Although many of the English groups had been musically educated by artists from America, the latter were no longer in the national spotlight. Chuck Berry, Bo Diddley, and Buddy Holly, for instance, each inspired English groups, but they had achieved their greatest American success around 1957 and 1958, and they were generally forgotten by 1964. The most popular national trend in the United States at that time consisted of surfing and hot rod songs, and these were considerably different from the rock music of the 1950's. Moreover, the British groups were strongly influenced by certain Negro artists such as Muddy Waters and Howlin' Wolf whose music was not well-known among white American listeners. Through the 1950's, and before, their blues style existed almost exclusively within the Negro market, and it became popular with whites only after the English craze had gained momentum. So English music entered an atmosphere that was receptive to a distinct sound, even though it was based on music which was not very old or whose popularity had been partially eclipsed by other trends. Admittedly, Oldies But Goodies kept some of the music of older rock or blues artists alive for audiences in this country, but they did so in terms of remembered life experiences and not in terms of artistic style.

The English groups did not provoke thoughts of earlier styles when they first appeared, and they gave no suggestion of constituting a musical revival. The impact of their personal styles was most important and their audiences were primarily interested in its immediacy rather than its background or history. The revival of early rock sources came later, after the English artists had openly praised their predecessors, and after repeated listening to the new music provoked a natural curiosity about its background.

A fascinating aspect of the English groups lay in the fact that their singing generally revealed no trace of an English accent. Instead, they sounded like any other rock artists, and their Britishness only became apparent during radio and television interviews. In these situations the accent became noticeable, and it seemed to lend an aura of dignity to the new group of rock personalities, since Americans have traditionally felt that a British accent is a symbol of culture and intelligence. The Beatles, of course, were able to reinforce this image through their quick wit and their engaging quips to American interviewers, and one English artist, Peter Noone, the leader of Herman and His Hermits, incorporated it into his records. In "Henry The Eighth," Herman sang about a cornerstone of popular English history, and he did so in a characteristically British style: "I'm 'enry the Eighth, I am." But in most of the English records, the speaking accent was absent, which suggested the rock had an international language and had become the common bond between artists and audiences of all countries.

The consciousness of the British scene's dignified Britishness in 1964 and 1965 had some interesting parallels in the larger history of American taste and sensibility. It was reminiscent, for instance, of this country's colonial artists and patrons who felt a constant need to travel to England and to collect English art in order to keep abreast of the most advanced aesthetic trends. Several of America's best eighteenth-century painters, among them John Singleton Copley and Benjamin West, left their native environment to live and work in what they believed was the more civilized atmosphere of the London Academy. This practice persisted into the nineteenth century and it was not until after the Civil War that American artists began to question the assumption that English or European culture was superior to their own. By comparison, the audience and artists of rock learned more quickly that the national origin of a work of art does not guarantee its quality. After two years, the English fad began to fade. High quality records continued to originate in England, but they were accepted more cautiously, on musical grounds and not merely because they were English. This idea that a work of art must stand on its own instead of on its life associations, was again part of rock's movement away from a folk context and toward that of the fine arts.

The English Scene: The Beatles

The special significance of the Beatles is not simply a matter of their Britishness, nor of their ability to define the stylistic scope of English rock. The uniqueness of their contribution to the history of rock resides in the quality of their music: Its authority surpasses that of any group or individual who has worked, or is working in the rock idiom.

It has become commonplace to point out that the Beatles brought an atmosphere of fun and happiness to a rock style which had previously been filled with mourning and self-pity. Their carefree enthusiasm constantly informed their records and their personal appearances, and later it gave special quality to their films. In contrast to the anxious rock songs about a dying girlfriend or an unfaithful lover, the Beatles' music reflected an exuberant embracing of life and an ability to accept it casually on its own terms.

By 1964, however, this image was not entirely new to either English or American culture. The United States, for instance, had engaged in youthful frivolity when the Twist craze swept the country in 1961. Moreover, English and American artists in the fine arts had begun to display

The Beatles

an interest in humor when the Pop Art movement first emerged in the early sixties. Pop Art openly admitted that its inspirations were comic books, billboards, magazine advertisements, and other anti-intellectual aspects of the mass culture. The movement's endorsement of pleasure therefore anticipated the carefree spirit which came to be nationally expressed on the arrival of the Beatles. At the beginning of 1964, the American public was experiencing a lingering gloom over the assassination of John Kennedy. It is hard to substantiate, but it can be suggested that the Beatles' arrival provided an escape from that gloom. Similar incidents had occurred before in the music business: The Twist craze, for instance, followed a general uneasiness about atomic fallout in the early 1960's.

The Beatles offered not only happiness and frivolity to the national audience, but youth and love as well. Of course, youthful idols were common in the world of rock, but their publicity generally stressed that they were young adults rather than teenagers. This was especially true for white rock personalities—Ricky Nelson, Frankie Avalon, and Gene Pitney, for instance. They were symbols for teenagers to emulate, since they were supposedly more mature than the young members of their fan clubs. But the Beatles overtly shunned adult values and adult behavior. They treated interviews with amusement and they ridiculed newsmen's efforts to ask serious or "important" questions. This approach gave them a unique image. They flatly confessed that they were primarly interested in commercial success but their disdainful, witty attitude suggested that commercial success constituted an absurd goal. Because the Beatles mocked their own achievements, they remained on the same level as their fans. They were millionaires, but they had conquered the adult world without submitting to it. With the Beatles, the message of youthfulness, implicit in rock since its beginning, erupted as a dramatically explicit declaration. Since 1964, it has gained increasing momentum in the national consciousness, and it reached a climax in 1967 when *Time* magazine named youth "the man of the year."

The Beatles' first visit to New York City took place in February, 1964. A *Billboard* headline summarized the event by declaring: "Beatles Bring Love To NY." The accompanying story suggested that "love has seldom been put on a more public display."* Like the image of youth, the image of love has expanded in the years since 1964— into the "love generation," the "hippies," and the "flower children" of San Francisco and other American cities. The character and meaning of this new kind of love, however, were already in evidence when the Beatles appeared in America.

To many people, the Beatles' reception was merely a craze in which teenagers dissolved in hysterical rapture at the sight of their idols, as teenagers of earlier generations had with Frank Sinatra and Elvis Presley. But the mad enthusiasm which surrounded the Beatles differed from earlier public demonstrations in several important ways. In the first place, its scope was broader than any previous craze. In their numbers and in their hysteria, the Beatles' audiences surpassed any earlier group of fans. In addition, they openly displayed their love for the English artists, and they did so on a national scale. With earlier rock stars, love may have been reflected in the audience response, but it was admitted with embarrassment. In the Beatles' case, love became so real and consuming that it was publicly declared. To adults, this type of love appeared shallow and artificial because it was not based on any actual contact with the individuals involved. In this sense, it resembled the stylistic changes that had taken place in dancing. When the dances began, they seemed narcissistic

* *Billboard*, February 22, 1964, pp. 1, 38.

because partners did not touch one another; only by observing them and participating in them did one realize that physical detachment could elicit heightened subjective involvement with the dance itself and with another person. Love for the Beatles, like love among the "love generation," was a real and absorbing experience.

The Beatles' impact on the music business paralleled their impact on the American listening public. Beginning with their first release, "I Want To Hold Your Hand," their records achieved an unprecedented commercial success. Within ten days of its issue, "I Want To Hold Your Hand" had received orders for over one million copies. It entered the national chart of best-selling records at number 45, and rose to the number one position in only two weeks. This marked it as one of the fastest selling records in the history of the business, comparable to "16 Tons." It also surpassed the largest selling single in the history of the English market, the Tornados' "Telstar."

The fact that "I Want To Hold Your Hand" sold so quickly was extraordinary, but it was not without precedent. The unique aspect of the Beatles' commercial impact lay in their ability continually to repeat their initial success. Before their first record had been in circulation for two weeks, new releases began to flood the market. By the beginning of April, there were twelve Beatle records on the list of the 100 best sellers in the country, and, astonishingly, five of these held the top five positions. "Can't Buy Me Love" was number one, while "Twist and Shout," "She Loves You," "I Want To Hold Your Hand," and "Please Please Me" occupied the next four positions. Overwhelmed by this activity, the music industry estimated that the Beatles' records actually accounted for 60 per cent of the entire singles business during the first three months of 1964.*

* *Ibid.*, March 14, 1964, p. 3.

With their albums, the Beatles also broke existing precedents for commercial success. When the LP, *Beatles 65*, was released in January 1965, it soared from number 98 to number one in the national charts after one week. This achievement repeated the success of their first album, *Meet the Beatles*, as well as their other two LPs from 1964, *The Beatles' Second Album* and *Hard Day's Night*, all of which had similarly reached the top of the album listings. Phenomenally, *Hard Day's Night* sold enough copies to cover the production costs of the film on which the album was based—before the film ever premiered. Like so many events connected with the Beatles, this had not happened in the history of the movies.*

Most rock groups who create records at a steady pace issue them gradually. Singles are spaced out over many months, and LPs are usually timed to follow the impact of a successful 45 release. The uniqueness of the Beatles during 1964, however, lay in the fact that they released an enormous number of records within a relatively short time. More extraordinary was the fact that each one was commercially successful. This production was possible because the Beatles, particularly through the energies of John Lennon and Paul McCartney, were more creative than any of their predecessors or contemporaries in the rock field. The presence of concurrent 45s resulted from a rare situation in which the group's songs were initially available on a variety of labels, including Vee Jay, Atco, and Swan, as well as Capitol. Since 1964, Capitol has held the American rights for the Beatles' records, and the releases have followed a relatively ordered pattern. But early in 1964, when the Beatles were spreading love through the country, heated arguments among record companies were spreading through courtrooms. Swan, Capitol and Vee Jay each contended priority rights to the Beatles, and accusa-

* *Ibid.*, July 25, 1964, p. 1.

tions were common that certain distributors had received records from Canada where prices and profits differed from those in the American market. In Chicago, a disk jockey obtained a copy of the Beatles' version of "Roll Over Beethoven," played it on the radio, and created a furor among record stores because none of them knew where the record originated or where it could be purchased.* By the end of the year, most of this industrial chaos had subsided and Capitol Records restored order to the Beatles' American market. Capitol's problems did not end though; public complaints continued to arise, especially when the Beatles' English albums leaked into this country and consumers found that they included more songs than the American-released albums. This commercial confusion, of course, has little or no bearing on the Beatles' music; nevertheless, it shows the group's distinctiveness in the history of the music business.

It is of course the artistic uniqueness of the Beatles which accounts for the extraordinary statistics. Their accomplishments in the rock idiom have completely altered the course of the music's development, and their songs have provoked critical issues from which rock was formerly immune. The Beatles have never undermined the essential folk function of rock, but they have enhanced it and expanded it in a way that is completely unprecedented and is unparalled still.

The Beatles' significance is primarily a matter of the amazing development of their personal style. The group's more recent records—for instance, the 1967 album, *Sgt. Pepper's Lonely Hearts Club Band*—are radically different from their first releases. But their 1967 style did evolve from the style of their earlier songs. The best and the most important examples of the early style are "Can't Buy Me Love," "She Loves You," and "I Want To Hold Your

* *Ibid.*, February 22, 1964, p. 1.

Hand." Each of these exhibits a wildness and excitement, especially in the vocals which invariably dominate the accompanying guitars or drums. Yet the excitement of the Beatles' style on these records is always controlled. In comparison to the raucous and funky rock of the 1950's, the Beatles' music has always been clearer, smoother, and more sophisticated. Moreover, they have used the guitar as a unifying element, instead of permitting it to break out of a particular song structure as it does, for instance, in many of Chuck Berry's pieces. This was the essential character of the Beatles' first songs, and it constituted the basis on which their later music was built.

During the first year and a half of their international recognition, the Beatles' records followed a relatively normal course of development. Essentially, their work in this period revealed them as masters of the overall rock style, since their repertory included almost every variant of the music that existed at the time. Together with the songs they personally created, the Beatles' albums and singles from 1964 and 1965 represented a compendium of rock sources and directions: In the Rhythm and Blues style they did "Roll Over Beethoven," "Money," "She's A Woman," and "Long Tall Sally"; in the Country and Western or rockabilly style, there was "I've Just Seen A Face" and "Words of Love"; the popular folk idiom was exemplified by "I'll Follow the Sun"; and, finally, a traditional ballad style was reflected in "And I Love Her," "If I Fell," and "Till There Was You." The range of these songs indicated that the Beatles were thoroughly schooled in every kind of rock music, although their strongest artistic sympathies were with the mainstream of the best rock music. Chuck Berry, Little Richard, the Isley Brothers, the Shirelles, Larry Williams, and Buddy Holly had each influenced the English group, as shown by the Beatles' versions of earlier hits, for instance "Twist and Shout," "Baby

It's You," and "Dizzy Miss Lizzy." While the variety of
these sources naturally included several raucous styles,
particularly Little Richard's, this type of rock was a relatively minor influence on the Beatles' personal style. Several early vocals by John Lennon showed a penchant for
this type of rock, such as "Bad Boy," "Dizzy Miss Lizzy,"
and "She's A Woman," but it was generally a smoother,
more unified and quietly intricate music which became
characteristic of the Beatles and which proved to be the
most fruitful source for their further artistic development.
Still, the group has never discarded early rock: In 1968,
they overtly returned to the past, but they did so from a
point of view that was radically different from their point
of view in 1964 or 1965.

A significant aspect of the Beatles' records during 1964
and 1965 is that they never repeated themselves and never
regressed to imitating their own most successful songs.
Mannered self-imitations are a common phenomenon in
the history of rock, as discussed earlier, but each new Beatles record had a distinct and convincing impact in comparison to their previous releases. As I have mentioned already, this inventiveness resulted from the wide range of
the Beatles sources, and also from the writing abilities of
John Lennon and Paul McCartney, who created each song
as a distinct statement. The Lennon-McCartney songwriting style will be considered later; in the present context,
however, it must be pointed out that their unique talents
have been instrumental in effecting the group's constant
artistic growth.

In the summer of 1965 the Beatles released "Yesterday."
Sung by Paul McCartney, the record quickly reached the
top of the national charts and inspired the same kind of
special enthusiasm that had accompanied the group's first
releases. "Yesterday," however, was a more elegant and
refined ballad than any the Beatles had produced up to

that time and it was unique in terms of the history of the whole Pop field. The distinctive quality of the record lay in the fact that a cello accompanied McCartney's solo voice, giving the song a special sound from the world of classical music. String sections had been used by plenty of other groups before the Beatles, but "Yesterday" was different in that it emphasized the discipline and intricacy of the cello itself. The record's simplicity, along with its sense of internal restraint, gave an impression of chamber music that was unprecedented in rock. Its refinement, furthermore, was more consciously "classical," more specifically aware of the sound of traditional classical music, than any song by the Beatles or any other group, and this awareness marked a new stylistic direction for the Beatles to explore.

With the appearance of the *Rubber Soul* album in December 1965, the Beatles demonstrated that "Yesterday" was not an isolated tangent to a high-quality, but otherwise ordinary development. The album, which marked a turning point in the group's career, continued the exploration of the uses of classical music within rock. One of the songs, "In My Life," included an instrumental passage that sounded overtly like a baroque harpsichord (it was actually achieved by accelerating the tape of George Martin's piano playing). And in all of the songs there was a new complexity and richness which had been merely implicit in the Beatles' earlier creations. That this richness had classical music overtones, and that it was implied in all of the Beatles' songs, was perhaps reflected by an album called the *Baroque Beatles Songbook* which was released about the same time that *Rubber Soul* appeared. The LP was created by Joshua Rifkin, conductor of a group of New York musicians called the Merseyside Kammermusikgesellschaft. It consisted of baroque arrangements of many of the Beatles' records, including "I Want To Hold

Your Hand," "Ticket To Ride," "Please Please Me," "Hard Day's Night" and "She Loves You."

The significance of *Rubber Soul* was not merely in its inclusion of several passages reminiscent of classical music. With "Michelle," "Norwegian Wood," and "Think For Yourself," the Beatles included foreign languages, foreign instruments, and foreign culture generally. The use of new instruments, however, was probably the album's most specific contribution to rock history, since other rock groups have been strongly influenced by this. During the late sixties, the Indian sitar became especially popular and its extensive use paralleled a growing interest in Indian culture within the rock scene, an interest specifically and publicly shown by Beatle George Harrison who studied the sitar under its famous virtuoso practitioner, Ravi Shankar. The album generally revealed the Beatles' creative restlessness and their insistent desire to penetrate untested types of expression. Since 1965, these values constantly informed the Beatles' music and culminated most brilliantly in the group's 1968 album.

The Beatles' post-1965 productions have continued to fulfill the artistic promise of their earlier records. This has been accomplished especially on their albums, rather than on their single releases, a distinction which was first signaled by the breadth of *Rubber Soul*, and which has become increasingly characteristic of the rock scene as a whole. Through albums, the Beatles and other groups have been afforded more space in which to experiment with new types of sounds and electronic effects. The meaning of the LP has gradually changed. Before the emergence of the Beatles, rock albums existed to capitalize on a 45 rpm success; that is, they usually contained ten or twelve songs that were merely stylistic imitations of a popular single. The Beatles, however, like the better current groups, devote most of their creative energy to the production of a

whole new album from which their single releases are subsequently selected. This procedure constitutes a reversal of
the traditional production pattern for rock songs, and it
reflects a growing sophistication within the music and its
artists. The music has increasingly become an end in itself,
an artistic reality which rock groups are conscious of and
which they can explore more fully in albums than in 45s.
This is one of the ways in which present-day rock has aspired to, although not necessarily attained, the status of
fine art.

The albums which showed most clearly the Beatles'
growing experimentalist tendencies are *Revolver*, issued
during the summer of 1966, and *Sgt. Pepper's Lonely
Hearts Club Band*, released in the spring of 1967. The most
radical of the LPs is their 1968 album, *The Beatles*.

The Beatles' 1968 album, called the "White Album," is
even more self-conscious than *Sgt. Pepper*. At the time of
its release, the album provoked extensive controversy. It
was said to be a "put-down," a "put-on," and to represent
the group's way of "dropping out" of the rock picture.
These judgments were inspired by the fact that the album
contains references to the over-all history of rock—to the
Beach Boys, Chuck Berry, Bob Dylan, and the Beatles' own
past, and to trends such as Country and Western, Rhythm
and Blues, popular folk, folk rock, acid rock, psychedelic
rock, and others that appeared during the 1960's.

To many listeners, these references to the past were disturbing because they envisioned the Beatles as rock's *avant
garde*, as the signal for each new direction in the music.
For these listeners, the Beatles had suddenly "dropped out"
of the rock evolution. Moreover, the Beatles invariably
were viewed as the most sophisticated rock group. Their return to the music of earlier periods seemed inconsistent
with their previous development away from it. Because of
this seeming inconsistency, listeners concluded that the

Beatles were either "putting down" earlier rock or "putting on" their audience, joking with them about the muscial fads of the past. Support for these conclusions was provided by other records which did satirize fifties' rock—for instance, *Cruising With Ruben And The Jets* by Frank Zappa and the Mothers of Invention. Rather than a parody, however the White Album is first of all an expression of musical consciousness; without direct reference to things in the world, it presents the experience of music as music.

The record's consciousness of itself is shown in many ways. In the first place, the variety of its songs presents a singular, unified subject: rock music as it has existed and changed since the early 1950's. More precisely, the subject of the record is rock history as experienced by the Beatles. What is their attitude toward rock on this record? The evidence, admittedly aesthetic, suggests that the Beatles have a profound respect for the music which provides their subject matter. Each song, that is, implies respect for its subject because each is a fine interpretation of one or another example from the spectrum of rock sub-styles. Songs derived from the Beach Boys have an elegant harmony; the Chuck Berry inspirations are rocking, explosive, and humorous; the Rhythm and Blues examples have a direct and heavy beat; and the Beatle-type ballads are tender and restrained. The songs isolate and emphasize the best musical aspects of their subjects. They do not imply that their musical subject matter is inane, insignificant, or in any way embarrassing.

In *Revolver*, certain songs retain the baroque elements of *Rubber Soul*, particularly "Eleanor Rigby" with its staccato strings, and "For No One" with a harpsichord-like piano and a horn passage. Residual "classical" elements persist in *Sgt. Pepper*, especially in "She's Leaving Home" and "Lucy In The Sky With Diamonds." But by 1967 the Beatles apparently sensed the difference between using such motifs unconsciously and using them to create fine art music. The *Sgt. Pepper* album poses this distinction. "Gimmicks," as they might be called, are used liberally; they include crowd noises and barnyard sounds, as well as the offbeat and "campy" music of combs and kazoos. But the point is that these elements are used consciously, in a manner which draws explicit attention to the fact that they are gimmicks. This consciousness tinges the gimmicks with humor, but it also gives them the potential of functioning as sounds in themselves, as music. As a whole, the album seems to ask: What kind of sounds constitute music? This question pervades the entire record and provides its unity. Along with the "gimmicks," then, electronic sounds are used repeatedly, climaxing in the album's last song, "A Day In The Life," which features two electronic explosions and a coda that lasts for 45 seconds. Because sound variety is stressed throughout the album, *Sgt. Pepper* has the effect of a rock symphony. But at its conclusion, the meaning of the symphony—at least with regard to its folk art or fine art identity—remains unresolved. Certainly, the record consciously achieves a totality of sound impact that transcends any of the individual songs. This totality is clearly underscored by the album's lyrics. The theme of the Sgt. Pepper band is stated at the outset of the record and given a reprise before the last song. Lyric unity is emphasized in the title song, which closes with the introduction of "Billy Shears" and is followed by Ringo Starr's vocal, "A Little Help From My Friends." There is no gap of silence between these two songs, and there is none between the last three parts of the album's second side, "Good Morning, Good Morning," the title reprise, and "A Day In The Life." Sound continuity and lyric continuity are intertwined throughout the record and emphasize its self-contained symphonic unity. But the question remains: Is this symphonic unity, and its implicit art-consciousness, insisted upon by the record, or are these aspects only urged? My conclusion is that they are only urged. The music consciousness elicited by the use of gimmick sounds and electronic sounds does not demand to be experienced. Both types question what constitutes music, but they do not answer that question with authority or decisiveness. The electronic sounds at first seem abstract, like pure sound, but they also function narratively, as nonverbal descriptions of the lyrics' literal content. This is especially true of "A Day In The Life" in which the electronic sounds provide a metaphor for the "mind-blowing," "dream fantasy" experiences that are described by the lyrics. Similarly, the gimmick sounds also create an image of a performing band, for instance, and a barnyard. They do not exist solely as the sounds of music. Without question, the *Sgt. Pepper album* strives for a sound experience that is conscious of itself and independent of immediate reference to the world of nonmusical realities. But those realities are present in the experience of the record, in all of the ways in which the record makes direct statements *about* the world. Because they are present, the record precariously shares the identities of both folk art and fine art; its consciousness of art is undeniable, but it is not convincingly realized. This is not to say that the record is an aesthetic failure. On the contrary, it is one of the most ambitious and one of the finest achievements in the history of rock.

Consistency between the Beatles' 1968 album and their earlier records is evident in several ways. Like *Rubber Soul*, *Revolver*, and particularly *Sgt. Pepper*, the White Album has an extraordinary range and extraordinary inventiveness. Lyrically, the songs shift from the straightforward "Julia," "I Will," or "Dear Prudence," to the elusive and quasi-surrealistic "Glass Onion" and "Happiness Is A Warm Gun"; the lyrics also range from simple narrative in

"Rocky Raccoon" to virtual anti-narrative in "Why Don't We Do It In The Road," which consists merely of three lines, two of which are identical; in addition, they include numerous expressions of humor as in "Back In The U.S.S.R.," "Ob-La-Di, Ob-La-Da," and "The Continuing Story of Bungalow Bill"; and, in George Harrison's "Piggies," social commentary. The range of writing in the White Album is unprecedented in either past or present rock history.

In this album, the Beatles go back over musical territory which they have already covered, which they already know, and which they have left. The consciousness with which they look back is significant for the history of rock because it has been transformed into artistic content. In part, the transformation is achieved by the overtness with which the past is used. In comparison to the White Album, an awareness of Chuck Berry, the Beach Boys, and other rock artists was never the *content* of the Beatles' earlier songs. Those artists were simply influences on them. In the 1968 album, they are recognized *as* influences, and this recognition or consciousness openly pervades the entire record and becomes its content. Moreover, because the White Album is aware of itself, it cannot be regarded as a revival of the past or an imitation of it. As a musical statement, the album clearly belongs to the Beatles; its over-all style is consistent with the group's previous development, although it extends that development beyond folk naïveté.

The nature of the Beatles' development is unique in the history of rock. The music of other groups has changed, but the changes have been predictable, often in the direction of superficial complexity or mannerism. But the Beatles' development is charged with different implications. They have imposed a new standard of quality on the rock field, particularly in their ability really to grow as musicians. No previous or current group has shown such a

distinctive achievement, and none has offered such a
clear challenge to its contemporaries. The Beatles' music
constitutes a qualitative measure for the past, the present,
and also the future of rock.

An exception within the Beatles' overall stylistic development is provided by the songs of George Harrison, particularly by his interest in Indian music since 1965. In
"Norwegian Wood" from the *Rubber Soul* album, Harrison performed on the sitar, but he treated the instrument
like a western guitar. In the *Revolver* and *Sgt. Pepper* albums, he tried to develop a more authentic Indian sound
within his personal compositions, especially in "Love To
You" and "Within You Without You." But these songs
were rather self-conscious; their effort to sound authentically Indian outweighed the impact of the music itself.
However sincere, the songs were less important than their
inspirational motive, for which they were merely vehicles.
By comparison, the Lennon-McCartney compositions have
never been self-conscious. On the contrary, an aura of ef-
fortlessness characterizes the musical development I have
been tracing. While George Harrison's personal search for
identity and meaning is clearly linked with Indian music,
then, his own recent compositions—including an album
released in 1969—have not been good enough to endow
that search with anything more than biographical significance.

The lyrics created by John Lennon and Paul McCartney
have revealed the distinctiveness of the Beatles with as
much authority as has the group's musical sound. The
Lennon-McCartney team has written an overwhelming
majority of the songs recorded by the Beatles; in addition,
they have written songs for other groups, resulting in a
total production that surpasses that of any composers currently active. Moreover, their range of material is unique
in the history of rock. They have written tender ballads

("If I Fell," "Michelle," "Here, There And Everywhere," and "Yesterday"), hard rock songs ("She Loves You," "I Want To Hold Your Hand," and "Can't Buy Me Love"), novelty songs ("Yellow Submarine"), and social commentaries ("Nowhere Man" and "Eleanor Rigby" and "She's Leaving Home"). Their lyrics cover nearly every subject that has ever been treated in rock, with the exception of Christmas trees and reindeer.

The Lennon-McCartney repertory has constantly displayed an intelligence and wit that are unparalleled in the rock tradition. Many of their songs seem to toy with the popular image of the Beatles. They sang "I'm Not What I Appear To Be" in the midst of confusion about what their individual members were "really" like; they recorded "I'm Down" while they were at the height of their concert-movie-record-interview successes; "When I'm Sixty-Four" was released before any of the Beatles had reached thirty; and Ringo sang "A Little Help From My Friends" as a humorous reference to his image as an "outsider" within the group.

Lennon's and McCartney's sensitivity to language has also contributed to the lighthearted tenor of the Beatles' music. Their songs frequently juxtapose word images, for instance black and blue in "Baby's In Black," or red and blue in "Yes It Is." The writing of John Lennon has provoked additional curiosity about the language of many of the Beatles' songs; his two books, *In His Own Write* and *A Spaniard In the Works*, contain a rich assortment of brilliant and imaginative linguistic manipulations. The vocabulary of the Beatles' songs, of course, is not as unconventional as it is in Lennon's books, but the same word-consciousness informs them. Like the music-consciousness of the Beatles, their word-consciousness may come about intuitively, but it compels recognition nevertheless. With the singular exception of Bob Dylan, whose word-consciousness occasionally matches that of the Beatles, it shows the distinctiveness of the group's position within the rock scene.

The carefree image projected by the Lennon-McCartney songs parallels the Beatles' public image of youthful vitality. But this is not the only aspect of their lyric art. For each of the autobiographical connections that the songs inspire, and for each of the personal meanings that Beatle fans try to discover in the lyrics, the songs ultimately defy literalist interpretations. As a whole, the lyrics are open-ended. The casualness of "Lovely Rita" and of "When I'm Sixty-Four," for instance, must be contrasted to the penetrating "She Said She Said," which openly questions verbal communication and vascillates lyrically from "she said" to "I said" to "she said," and concludes with "I don't understand what she said." Likewise, the intellectual intricacies of "Here, There And Everywhere," are countered by "Tomorrow Never Knows," which advises the listener to turn off his mind and relax. The Lennon-McCartney lyrics do not possess a literal or absolute meaning, and they cannot be linked to the writers' personalities. In a sense, Lennon and McCartney are impersonal writers by comparison to the great majority of past and present folk artists. However elusive, their songs elicit meaning objectively and this meaning is grasped in our experience of the songs, not by relating it to the artists or their lives.

As I pointed out in relation to their musical style, the Beatles' art-consciousness is encouraged but not demanded by their lyrics. That is, it is not demanded by their pre-1968 music. Before 1968, their songs elicit a folk response at the same time that they imply art-consciousness. This delicate balancing of folk art and fine art sensibilities probably accounts for the confused interpretations of the Beatles' music. Adult critics have generally discovered complex and intricate meanings in the Lennon-McCartney songs, while the teenage audience merely exclaimed that the Beatles constitute a revolutionary way of life. Each critical camp felt that its opposition was misunderstanding the Beatles' music. But I want to argue that, before the 1968 album, the music inherently functioned on both levels and its high quality legitimately compelled the convictions of each camp.

The Beatles' social commentaries clearly reveal the dual function of their art. The group has not been particularly interested in this aspect of rock, although it has represented a growing trend during the past three or four years. The best-known pre-1968 social commentaries by the Beatles are "Nowhere Man," "Eleanor Rigby," and "She's Leaving Home." "Nowhere Man" describes an anonymous and listless "everyman" who has the world at his command, but possesses no point of view and no personal direction. "Eleanor Rigby" presents two faceless creatures who belong to the proverbial "lonely crowd" of the twentieth century, and "She's Leaving Home" tells of a girl who leaves the parents who gave her "everything." All three songs question the meaning of modern society and the identity of the individuals who compose it. This questioning has become common among sociologists, psychologists, writers, and film makers during the 1950's and 1960's and, as testified by rock, among youth generally in the 1960's. "Nowhere Man," "Eleanor Rigby" and "She's Leaving Home" were sympathetically received when they appeared in 1965 and 1966. In both records, at the same time, the Beatles went beyond a simple folk response. "Nowhere Man," for instance, does not merely aim its criticism at the apathy of the impersonal "other guy"; it asks if "nowhere man" is not like "you and me." In comparison, lower quality records—the Monkees' "Pleasant Valley Sunday" or the Kinks' "Well-Respected Man"—invariably maintain that the "other guy" is at fault because their lyrics never refer to the "I" self. The majority of social commentaries enable the listener to feel that he is immune from the social disease cited. The distinctive feature of the Beatles' artistic intelligence lies in their avoidance of this type of fallacy. "Eleanor Rigby" is similarly intelligent—not only because of its considered viewpoint, but also because of the incisiveness of its imagery. The song describes a woman who leads a lonely fantasy existence and wears a face "that she keeps in a jar." This image is haunting and powerful, almost surrealistic; its inspired inventiveness is remarkable in the history of rock lyrics.

The Beatles' songs about love and human relationships have also demonstrated the new level of quality that they have brought to the lyrics of rock music. Certainly, the majority of Lennon-McCartney songs have been devoted to these traditional subjects, from "I Want To Hold Your Hand" and "She Loves You" to their recent singles, "Love, Love, Love" and "Hey Jude." The songs reveal a constantly growing insight into their subjects. This growth, like the growth of their musical style, has kept the Beatles from repeating themselves and from becoming lyrically static. At the same time, there are threads of consistent meaning in the Lennon-McCartney writing, especially in their overall viewpoint about love. They treat the subject with a distinct coolness and objectivity; to sensibilities of an older romanticism, these qualities occasionally appear impersonal, but they nevertheless constitute the relevance of the Beatles' songs for the young generation.

The earliest songs, those which preceded *Rubber Soul*, are relatively innocent. "She Loves You," for instance, describes a typical situation of losing love, finding love, and declaring love. The situation is uncomplicated and, literally, "it can't be bad." In "I Saw Her Standing There," the attitude is similarly uncomplicated, and the overall vision is refreshing and naïve: The world is young; it consists of dancing and holding hands. The casual simplicity of these songs characterizes the Beatles' early period. Together, they offered a meaningful spiritual alternative to the anxious love-until-death sensibility which had developed in rock during the 1950's, and which persisted in 1964, for instance in J. Frank Wilson's "The Last Kiss," which describes an automobile accident, the death of a young girl, and a hero who will see her again in heaven. The light-hearted honesty of the Beatles' songs also offered a clear alternative to the self-consciousness of the popular folk movement, to the melancholia of Joan Baez's "All My Sorrows," and Peter, Paul and Mary's "Where Have All The Flowers Gone." To this seriousness, the Beatles responded with "I Want To Hold Your Hand," "I Feel Fine," "All My Loving," and other songs which exuberantly offered a message of love and pleasure to the world.

Rubber Soul revealed a new depth of insight in the Lennon-McCartney writing, paralleling the advanced musical experimentation of the album. In particular, "It's Only Love," "Girl," and "I'm Looking Through You" expressed a more sophisticated awareness of the complexities of human relations than had the Beatles' first songs. A hint of disenchantment, even sadness, pervades these newer songs. "I'm Looking Through You" poignantly concentrates on the elusiveness of love, the way it changes and disappears, the way words lose their meaning, the way misunderstanding and doubt replace honesty and trust. Similarly, "It's Only Love" stresses the difficulty and the uncertainty of love. If love is accompanied by sadness, however, its uniqueness is reaffirmed by "Girl," in which the vocal insists "you don't regret a single day." In these songs, the Beatles decisively eclipsed the so-called "moon-June-spoon" tradition of Tin Pan Alley writing. They realistically expressed both the fluctuations and difficulties of human relations as well as their beauty and pleasure.

Moreover, the sheer elegance of the *Rubber Soul* music provided a brilliant counterpart to the elegance of its lyrics. In 1966, the Beatles' new level of seriousness was further developed by "For No One," "Here, There And Everywhere," and other songs in their new album, *Revolver*. Once more, these stressed the joy as well as the disappointment of love, and they departed from the casualness of the Beatles' early statements dealing with dancing or holding hands. But the new seriousness of the Beatles' music never excluded the humor for which the group was known from the beginning. *Revolver* contains the amusing "Got To Get You Into My Life," suggesting that, while there might be an inclination for love, there might not be time or space. Similarly, the 1967 album, *Sgt. Pepper*, includes the carefree "Lovely Rita" and "When I'm Sixty-Four," both of which treat love with a playful attitude.

The Beatles' cool, impersonal attitude toward love emerges in a variety of ways. For instance, the Lennon-McCartney songs rarely make a direct statement of "I love you." "She Loves You" is based upon indirect discourse: One person talks *about* another, and *about* love, but the individuals in love never actually confront one another. Similarly, "And I Love Her" talks *about* the loved one rather than *to* her, and the same approach is also used in "Girl." The love is publicly announced to an anonymous third person, but, as a confession of feeling, it remains highly personal.

"Do You Want To Know A Secret" contains one of the Beatles' few direct declarations of love. Amusingly, this is described as a secret, about which "nobody will know." For the most part, however, the Beatles' songs reveal a hesitancy about openly and directly admitting love to the loved one. For instance, "If I Fell" qualifies its entire statement with an emphatic "if." When a direct confrontation of lovers does take place, in "I'm Looking Through You," for instance and "It's Only Love," it usually takes the form of the more realistic and problematic statements that I have already described.

Through the rich texture of the Lennon-McCartney lyrics then, the notion emerges that love is an all-pervasive and special force in the world, possibly an ultimate force, but it must be filtered through the complex fabric of events that is called reality. As the songs evolve, this filtering process is undertaken with reserve and intelligence, in fact with a maturity that is truly extraordinary in the history of rock. One of the songs which shows this reserve most clearly, and which exemplifies the detachment of the Lennon-McCartney approach is "In My Life," from the *Rubber Soul* album. With a worldly objectivity, it tells of knowing and loving many places and people; but it also admits that most of these become forgotten, that they eventually lose their meaning, and that nothing compares with the one who is most deeply loved. The song's unpretentious quality is achieved by understating the scope of its message, and is reinforced by the quiet and melodic phrasing of the music. By comparison, George Harrison's "Within You Without You," which also expresses the experience of all-pervasive love, is self-conscious. The song forces and insists upon a message rather than compelling conviction in it. The lines are sincere, yet the song itself does not make them meaningful. With few exceptions—"Love, Love, Love" is one—the Lennon-McCartney writing has rarely suffered from this confusion between consciousness and self-consciousness. Their art has gradually achieved maturity, but it has done so naturally, not artificially.

The coolness of the Lennon-McCartney style is crucial if we are to understand the meaning of love for youth in the 1960's. This meaning is clearly stated in "The Word," which introduces the concept of freedom. The song does not assume that love involves an undying or eternal commitment to another person. True, the Beatles' concept of love in this song is different in kind from that described in the 1950's in such songs as "The Ten Commandments Of Love" or "The Book Of Love." The new style involves greater objectivity: The Beatles sing *about* the loved one and describe their feelings to an unknown listener. They sing that one is free to love independently, to love everyone, but also to experience love in an intensely personal and intimate way. Love unites the world, but each person seeks his own meaning within it and within himself.

In concluding this discussion, I want to mention one feature of the Beatles' career which is not centrally relevant to their music, but which has nevertheless distinguished the group within the larger history of rock: that is, their association with personalities outside of their own quartet. In itself, this is not extraordinary, since the artistic production of any high-quality group or individual is invariably linked with other personalities, most of whom generally remain anonymous. The development of the Beatles, however, has been marked by an unusual ability to select associates who have become well-known for their personal contributions to the total image of the Beatles. The films of Richard Lester, for instance, broke the conventional pattern in which popular singing stars made awkward and artificial appearances in the movies. *Hard Day's Night* and *Help!* are good films in their own right, and both helped considerably in spreading an awareness of the Beatles' quality among adult audiences. George Martin, the Beatles' musical producer, has obviously played a significant role in the technical and artistic advances of the group's albums. Between 1961 and 1967, finally, Brian Epstein managed the Beatles' public image with a brilliant sense of timing and insight that constantly kept them in the center of international recognition.

The different contributions to the group's achievements cannot be pinpointed absolutely. When he first saw the Beatles, for instance, Brian Epstein "sensed something big —if it could be at once harnessed and at the same time left untamed."* For six years, Epstein nurtured and molded the Beatles in this image, and the group gradually fulfilled and then surpassed their manager's vision. They have been receptive to the contributions of their associates, in film, in publicity, as well as in ideas and in music. But this very receptiveness is one aspect of their genius.

The English Scene: Other Groups

Together with the Beatles, a great many English groups swarmed over the American record market in 1964. They included the Dave Clark Five, the Rolling Stones, Herman and His Hermits, the Zombies, the Yardbirds, the Animals, the Honeycombs, Gerry and the Pacemakers, the Moody Blues, the Unit Four Plus Two, and many others. Among the individual vocalists were Dusty Springfield, Cilla Black, Marianne Faithful, and Petula Clark. The influx was unprecedented in the history of rock. Of all these artists, however, none displayed the sustained inventive power of the Beatles, and none affected the overall music scene so dramatically, although several inspired large and devoted audiences.

The only group to offer a consistent challenge to the Beatles' dominance of the English and American rock scenes has been the Rolling Stones. Like the Beatles, the Rolling Stones benefited from the advice of a musical producer who was in basic sympathy with their music and

* *Time*, September 8, 1967, p. 54.

was able to develop with it: Andrew Loog Oldham. In addition, two members of the group, Mick Jagger and Keith
Richard, have written most of the Rolling Stones' songs.
The number does not match the production of John Lennon and Paul McCartney, but it has provided an important element of consistency in the Rolling Stones' development. But the Stones' public image has been radically different from that of the Beatles. Since their emergence, the
Rolling Stones have presented the image of an aggressive,
hostile group, ragged in comparison to the Beatles' elegance, and noncommunicative in comparison to the Beatles' glibness and quotability. The respective images of the
two groups have been so different, but at the same time so
compelling, that their audiences have viewed them as opposing, mutually exclusive forces.

The difference between the Rolling Stones and the
Beatles involves more than public images. The music of
the Rolling Stones has been clearly different from that of
the Beatles and from most other English groups, and this
has been largely a matter of their strong allegiance to the
Negro Rhythm and Blues tradition. I have already mentioned that this tradition played a crucial role in the formation of the English scene generally. With the Rolling
Stones, however, it was more than a routine, formative
element in their first songs; rather, it provided the primary direction for nearly all of their songs between 1964
and 1966. Moreover, their music was oriented not only
toward the songs of the older representatives of this tradition, Chuck Berry, Bo Diddley, and Sam Cooke, but to the
Rhythm and Blues artists who emerged in the 1960's—
Otis Redding, Wilson Pickett, and Marvin Gaye. To illus-
trate this, in addition to "Carol," "Mona," and "Good
Times," the Stones' songs have included "That's How
Strong My Love Is," "If You Need Me," and "Hitch
Hike."

it. But forcefulness of content is only one factor in the final judgment of a work's quality.

The individual who has defined the Rolling Stones' public and artistic image most clearly and forcefully is Mick Jagger. As their lead vocalist, Jagger has emphasized a rough and sensual style of blues singing, and he has epitomized the disdain and aloofness of the entire group. His performances in concerts combined these elements and he brilliantly projected them in "Satisfaction," commercially one of the most successful records of 1965 and in the entire history of rock music as well. The phenomenal success of this record, making it a classic in the music's history, was largely due to the fact that it "explained" Mick Jagger and the Rolling Stones. As Jagger described his frustration and alienation, he spoke to youth's similar feelings about the world, and he helped young people understand why the Stones looked and acted the way they did. The song functioned like traditional folk music, expressing a life situation more immediately than it expressed a 1960's version of the Rhythm and Blues musical tradition.

The Rolling Stones' records have been consistently high in quality during the late 1960's, but they have not shown the stylistic development that is evident in the Beatles' music. More than the Beatles, they have remained closely aligned to traditional folk expression, working within a restricted format that they have explored but not essentially altered. This is not to say that the Stones' music has not changed. Between their first albums and their 1968 *Beggars Banquet*, the group has reflected the style and subject matter fluctuations of the late sixties rock scene: "Lady Jane" shows a classical music orientation; "We Love You" responds to the general love generation sensibility; "Goin' Home" utilizes well the extended format of the 33 rpm medium; and the entire *Beggars Banquet* album reveals a sympathy for the Nashville country style

which was revived during 1967 and 1968. Moreover, the
Rolling Stones' 1968 album exhibits the internal unity of
a recorded rock symphony, and in this sense it is reminiscent, as was their earlier *Their Satanic Majesties Request*,
of the Beatles' *Sgt. Pepper*. For their changes, however,
the Stones have usually drawn upon the innovations of
other groups, particularly the Beatles. In spite of the
changes, at the same time, the basic public image of the
Rolling Stones has remained constant: They share the
growing sophistication of late-sixties rock, but they remain
"beggars" nevertheless. Their musical shifts have neither
demonstrated nor elicited an art-consciousness. Whatever
art awareness they possess at any rate does not inform the
content of their songs.

Apart from the Beatles and the Rolling Stones there are
many other British contributors to the current rock style.
There is, for instance, the embellished ballad style of
Petula Clark, one of the few refreshing contributions to
the Pop vocalist tradition. Herman and His Hermits have
transformed the smoothness of the English sound into the
cuteness of novelty performances. Other groups, the Dave
Clark Five, Gerry and the Pacemakers, and Manfred
Mann, enjoyed occasional hit records during the middle
sixties but featured styles that were more ordinary than
innovative. At the same time, Eric Burdon and the Animals emerged with a blues-based sound similar to the
Rolling Stones but less consistent in its power. Experi-
ments in electronic rock have been tried by the Who, a
group which, like the Doors in the United States, has also
developed a highly theatrical live performance style. During the late sixties, Cream was a leading group in the
trend toward a jazz-like, improvisatory style. And there
are the groups and individuals who produce the one-shots,
the two-shots, and the occasional hits that constitute the
folk music of England today. A history of them all lies out-

side the scope of the present study. The point in the present context is that the Beatles and the Rolling Stones have defined the major outlines of England's contribution to the rock development.

Bob Dylan

As the Beatles represent the most important English contribution to rock in the 1960's, Bob Dylan is the most important American contributor. This is true in spite of the fact that, commercially, he has never staggered the record industry in the way the Beatles have. Dylan's music possesses an artistic significance which is comparable to that of the Beatles. And he has stimulated an audience commitment which is spiritually as deep, if not deeper, than that of Beatle fans.

Bob Dylan emerged from the popular folk movement during 1962 and 1963. His first two albums for Columbia, *Bob Dylan* and *The Freewheelin' Bob Dylan*, appeared in those years and established his national reputation. This reputation grew slowly, and was helped by personal appearances around New York City and at college concerts, and by countrywide and international record sales. The growth of Dylan's reputation was accompanied by the steady development of a personal style which became increasingly independent from the folk styles, although not the folk functions, of the past. As early as 1962, Dylan became known for the quality and abundance of his songwriting. In this sense, he is like the Beatles. But Dylan's material has reflected a consistent social awareness and has always involved protest against racial, intellectual, and human injustice. It has stimulated a broad trend of similar songs in the present-day market. Furthermore, his writing has provoked extensive discussion about the notion of "poetry" within the context of the current rock scene, and he has been called the "first poet of the mass media."[*] These elements, in combination with Dylan's particular *sound*, have made him one of the most exceptional figures in the history of rock.

By postponing the issue of Dylan's subject matter, the significance of his musical development can be clearly grasped. Generally, his songs fall into two stylistic groups: those which were sung with electronic accompaniment and those which were not. Among Dylan's audience, the distinction is sometimes made between his folk style and his rock style, although this is misleading because it fallaciously implies that folk and rock are essentially separate artistic enterprises. On the contrary, Dylan's music unequivocably demonstrates that rock *is* folk.

The change in Dylan's stylistic development came in 1965, at the Newport Folk Festival of that year, which was Dylan's first public demonstration of his rock style. But there has been a real consistency in his development nevertheless. Where the Beatles' music has always been cool and aloof and has resisted direct links between the artists and their creations, Bob Dylan's records have always been decidedly close to his personal life and thought. Where the Beatles' art is classical and cerebral, Dylan's is expressionistic and emotive. His interviews and quotations are directly related to his songs, and he has actually commented on specific numbers. This practice is best exemplified by the album, *The Freewheelin' Bob Dylan*, which contains extensive personal statements about the songs Dylan recorded in it. The song's feelings about war, preju-

[*] Ralph Gleason, "The Children's Crusade," *Ramparts*, IV, no. 11 (March 1966), p. 28.

idea that an ordinary wall may be regarded as a work of fine art is not new—Leonardo suggested it in the fifteenth century. The occurrence of this idea in the writings of Bob Dylan, however, is significant because it suggests an awareness of comparable developments in contemporary artistic thought, an awareness which was foreign to rock artists in the 1950's. Similarly the fact that Dylan's album notes are consistently printed in lower case type implies an awareness of the e. e. cummings poetry tradition which cannot be found among earlier folk expressions. This type of sophistication surrounds but does not determine the character of Dylan's music. That is, his sophistication is not forced self-consciously upon his songs; it never blocks or diverts their aesthetic impact in the way that social or political awareness frequently obscured the expressions of the popular folk movement, making their records more like manifestos than music.

Like the Beatles, Dylan was at first strongly influenced by his teachers, and then he subsequently moved toward a more personal type of expression. For Dylan, Woodie Guthrie was a primary inspiration, and the "talking blues" became a common format in his songs, as exemplified by "Talkin' New York" and "Talkin' World War III Blues," from his first two albums respectively. Dylan's raw sensibility, which gave his more overt rock style of 1965 its special character, was apparent in these early songs. It is especially clear in the rusty, sandpaper quality of his voice and in the rocking harmonica sections that punctuate such songs as "Talkin' World War III Blues" and "Honey Just Allow Me One More Chance." The latter, recorded in 1963, possesses the typical hard beat of rock, although Dylan's audience, which was generally unsympathetic to rock, did not experience it as such when the song was released. At that time, the response to Dylan's style usually emphasized the idea that his voice was "bad" but his "message" was important. Such a distinction emphasizes the restricted, academic concept of folk style which pervaded the popular folk movement: Vocals were not considered "good" unless they conformed to a pattern of refinement and elegance. Nevertheless, Dylan's sandpaper voice and untamed harmonica, as well as his general stylistic awareness of the blues and of country music, was already announcing the direction of his later development. As these features became more openly expressed in his music, they showed that authentic folk music is never academic or restricted.

When Dylan changed to an overt rock style in 1965, his audience was at first bitterly disappointed. At the Newport Folk Festival in that year, Dylan completed the first half of his performance with the acoustic guitar, the harmonica, and the song style to which his listeners had become accustomed. But when he returned for the second half of his concert, accompanied a set of electric guitars, he was jeered and driven from the stage. He returned, in tears, sang one of his greatest songs 'Mr. Tambourine Man," and temporarily regained the support of his audience. This event was crucial in the development of rock in the 1960's. The popular folk movement had the stylistic support of its most talented and promising artist the folk movement lost, however, the whole rock movement gained.

The gain became apparent within months after the Newport incident, when Dylan began releasing fine records in the electronic manner, "Subterranean Homesick Blues," for instance, "Like A Rolling Stone," and others. By the end of 1965, the term "folk-rock" had become popular and, for both rock and popular folk enthusiasts, its use symbolically established the importance of Dylan's change. At an intuitive level, Dylan questioned the identity of folk music, as it was interpreted by the popular folk movement and as he felt it pulsating within rock. The shift to electronic accompaniment reflected his decision that rock was as authentically folk-like as the music he had previously created. Dylan returned again to the acoustic guitar and the harmonica, in the remarkable 1968 album, *John Wesley Harding*. So by 1968, after constant experimentation with different types of accompaniment, Dylan's music showed clearly that folk music is not dependent upon superficial trappings or sounds, but upon a commitment to reality. In consciously pursuing the nature of folk art, Dylan has, paradoxically, pushed his music increasingly close to the domain of fine art.

Rising through the rawness of Dylan's music runs an element of softer lyricism that should not be overlooked. It is clearly exemplified by his early "Girl From The North Country," by his 1967 "Just Like A Woman," and by one of his most penetrating songs, "Mr. Tambourine Man." There is a tenderhearted hardness in these songs, and a reluctant escapism which is exceptional in the context of Dylan's generally more realistic aesthetic. They present an honest and poignant uncertainty, particularly in their overt but futile struggle to avoid the expression of romantic feeling. In spite of Dylan's overall toughness, this sensitive aspect of his music periodically emerges, even in some of his more pointed social protests.

Dylan's protest writing has stimulated more discussion than has the development of his musical style.* It is in this area that the commitment of his followers has been centered, because Dylan has in many ways been the spokesman for youth's complaints about the world they inherited in the 1960's. Dylan's attacks have been directed at the Federal Government ("Masters Of War"), the nu-

---

* See *The American Folk Scene: Dimensions of the Folksong Revival*, ed. David A. DeTurk and A. Poulin, Jr. (New York: Dell, 1967), particularly the editors' essay, "Dylan as Poet," pp. 274-79.

clear threat ("A Hard Rain's A-Gonna Fall," "Talkin'
World War III Blues"), the law ("The Lonesome Death
Of Hattie Carroll"), racial prejudice ("Blowin' In The
Wind," "Oxford Town," and others), the shallowness of
ordinary boy-girl relationships ("It Ain't Me Babe,"
"Don't Think Twice, It's All Right," and others), and the
standardization of Christian values ("With God On Our
Side"). These issues are topical and of a kind that young
people have become deeply concerned about, and Dylan
has expressed them with a forcefulness that is without
precedent in the folk music of the past decade and a half.

Critics who do not share Dylan's vision of the current
world, or who remain unconvinced by his statements, legitimately point out that his protests have numerous parallels in the art, the literature, the politics and the sociology
of the past.* Those who side with Dylan legitimately defend his music by saying that he is the first socially-
conscious singer of his generation to utilize such a range
of media in contemporary culture, and particularly the
mass media.** Some critics view his work as fine art,
others as folk art. Regarding it as fine art necessitates relating it to poetry, painting, and essays from the current
period or from the larger history of art which have similarly dealt with protest material. Regarding it as folk art,
on the other hand, means treating it as an extension and
enrichment of a totally different tradition, one that is not
subject to the same kinds of critical demands that prevail
in fine art. Fine art or folk art? It is the question that the
Beatles have raised also. But Dylan's songs have provoked
more confusion and controversy regarding the question
than the Beatles have. The resulting debate about Dylan is

* Ewan MacColl states this position in "Topical Songs and Folk-
singing, 1965: A Symposium," in DeTurk and Poulin, pp. 156-8.
** Ralph Gleason represents this position in *Ramparts*, IV, 11, p.
28.

a phenomenon in itself, but a brief examination of it can, I believe, help to illuminate the nature of its cause—that is, Dylan's art.

The extraordinary interest in Dylan's songs is centered on the idea that he is a poet. Ralph Gleason, for instance, has written the following:

> Dylan has already made the kind of searing impression upon this generation that any poet in history would have been proud to make . . . Dylan has done the impossible . . . He is the first poet of that all-American artifact, the jukebox, the first American poet to touch everyone, to hit all walks of life in this great sprawling society. The first poet of mass media.*

In a similar spirit, Robert Shelton wrote:

> One day, it can be predicted, the John Ciardis, the Louis Untermeyers, the Maxwell Geismars will address themselves to the topical-protest-poetic movement of the last five years when they attempt to estimate "the poetic situation." If and when they do, it is also predictable that they will find Dylan as the most important poetic voice of the time.**

From a very different point of view, Ewan MacColl concluded:

> What poetry? The cultivated illiteracy of his topical songs or the embarrassing fourth-grade schoolboy attempts at free verse?†

It is interesting that neither Gleason nor Shelton say what *kind* of poet Dylan is. They mention his subject matter and the media through which he speaks, and they are obviously convinced that his writing possesses high quality.

* *Ibid.*
** Quoted in DeTurk and Poulin, p. 275.
† *Ibid.*, p. 157.

By comparison, Ewan MacColl is not convinced about the
quality of Dylan's writing, and so he wants to deny it the
title of 'poetry" in the first place.

In this controversy, the word "poet" plays a central role.
It seems to carry certain inherent critical implications, the
most important of which is an aura of dignity, respect-
ability, and fine art. That is, the word itself is synonymous
with artistic quality. Hence, critics who like Dylan's
music express their response to it by calling it "poetry,"
while opposing critics simply refuse to accord it this distinction. But in either case, the word is used unconsciously,
without distinguishing between folk poetry and fine art
poetry. In these terms, the Dylan controversy is symptom-
atic of the sophistication of the rock sensibility of the
1960's. In the 1950's, rock artists such as Chuck Berry and
Fats Domino were never called "poets." Today, however,
they are, and this fact signals a new awareness of fine art
traditions and values which were irrelevant to rock artists,
audiences, and critics a decade ago. But as long as the term
"poet" is employed without consciousness of its associations and meanings—that is, without an awareness of folk
art-fine art distinctions—its use is itself a variety of folk
response.*

* In *The Poetry Of Rock* (New York: Bantam Books, 1969), p. 6,
Richard Goldstein discusses Dylan as the most influential writer in
modern rock, arguing that his "intention is to reconcile poetry with
song." These terms seem peculiar, since they imply that poetry and
song had not been reconciled before Dylan, which is not the case.
Chuck Berry, for instance, also reconciled poetry with song. The difference lies in the fact that Berry wrote folk poetry, while Dylan's
poetry has gradually become conscious, like fine art poetry. Goldstein touches upon this difference, calling Chuck Berry's songs "acci-
dental art." However, he does not pursue it. Instead, he deals with
the stylistic changes in rock lyrics, the ways in which songs have
become more complex, sophisticated, and personalized. While his
book treats this question intelligently and admirably, it does not
shed light on what is to me a more basic problem: the *kind* of
poetry rock lyrics consist of.

These distinctions are necessary for understanding Dylan's significance within the rock of the sixties. That significance resides first of all in the overall quality of his music, which I consider to be of the highest order. Still, the specific terms of Dylan's significance are not clarified merely by calling his work "poetry." From the point of view of this study, the consciousness of his poetry, like the consciousness of his music, must receive primary emphasis. In Dylan's writing, this consciousness is most apparent in the way his images, his wild associations, and his confusing syntax draw attention to themselves as language manipulations and artistic ends in themselves. Together, these elements indicate a clear inclination toward fine art.

As I said before, Dylan's 1968 album, *John Wesley Harding*, achieves the consciousness of fine art to a greater extent than any of his earlier productions. It is, so to speak, a conscious return to an idiom that he initially practiced unconsciously. While returning to his own past, however, Dylan does not seem to make anything out of the return. That is, he does not use it to make any statement about earlier music, as the Beatles do, for instance, in their 1968 album. Rather, Dylan's return to the past, to what seems to be his original folk style, serves the purpose of liberating him as an artist. In *John Wesley Harding*, he declares his freedom to practice whatever style he wishes, whatever instrumentation and subject matter. This declaration of freedom takes precedence over any declaration about past music, and it becomes the point of the album. In these terms, the album bears comparison to *Sgt. Pepper*, which similarly announced a freedom to manipulate whatever musical elements the Beatles chose. But both records, it seems to me, *suggest* an awareness of their own enterprises rather than *compelling* it. I must emphasize that this conclusion does not undermine Dylan's contribution to rock. Like *Sgt. Pepper*, *John Wesley Harding* is one of the most significant and high-quality records in the history of rock music. Moreover, Dylan is one of that history's most significant and high-quality artists. Along with the Beatles, he has changed the shape of folk music and has pushed it to the present limits of its identity.

General Trends between 1964 and 1968

Bob Dylan's incisive style inspired a general trend of socially-conscious music in the years between 1965 and 1967. The trend was based essentially on songs of protest against war, for instance, and racial prejudice, but it also included several amusing anti-protest records such as Senator Everett Dirksen's "The Gallant Men" and Sgt. Barry Saddler's "Ballad Of The Green Berets." Both records defended traditional American values with reactionary political messages, and both lacked musical impact. They were more like sermons than songs in avoiding singing almost entirely. But they unconsciously recognized the power of the rebellious rock beat, and they sought to counter its meaning to youth with their own messages.

The protest songs also exhibited some of this unconsciousness, especially in the way they combined political messages with the beat of rock. Two fascinating examples of this were Barry McGuire's "Eve Of Destruction" and Glen Campbell's "Universal Soldier," both of which were popular during the second half of 1965 when the protest trend was at its height. "Eve Of Destruction" was written by P. F. Sloan; it openly damned the death, violence, and hatred that are spread around the globe and suggested that the world was about to destroy itself. This provoked widespread controversy, and the song was banned from many radio stations and from ABC television as well. "Universal Soldier" was written by Buffy St. Marie, and similarly lashed out against war and killing. In the case of "Eve Of Destruction," articles in teen newspapers expressed youth's indignation about the banning of the song and stressed the validity of its lyrics. The musical sound of the record was invariably taken for granted, indicating how the folk orientation to tangible realities had persisted in the 1960's. But the "Eve Of Destruction" sound was interesting. It featured an accelerating beat which slowly developed into the impact of a forceful marching song. This effect was enhanced by McGuire's strongly felt vocal, but it resulted in the paradoxical and disturbing aesthetic impression that the predicted destruction might be a glorious and appealing event, something like the sensuous violence of James Bond films, professional football, or *Life* magazine war photos. The same ambivalent aesthetic mixture characterized Glen Campbell's recording of "Universal Soldier." Its rousing and inspired style inadvertently provided an apotheosis for the song's object of criticism. These examples provoke speculation about the locus of protest music's appeal: Does it lie primarily in the lyrics, as the folk audience seems to think, or in the musical beat, as the actual experience of the records suggests? Of course, both aspects are important, but on different levels. While songwriting became a conscious enterprise in the 1960's, the beat of a rock accompaniment continued to be relished in a spontaneous, folk manner.

The majority of socially-conscious songs from the mid-sixties did not take the form of overt protest characteristic of "Eve Of Destruction" and "Universal Soldier." They concentrated on the immediate concerns of young people, which were of course generally social in origin, as they had been in the 1950's. I have already mentioned several of the Beatles' songs, especially "Nowhere Man," "Eleanor Rigby," and "She's Leaving Home," and I should also include the Rolling Stones' "Satisfaction," "Mother's Little

Helper," and "Have You Seen Your Mother, Baby, Standing In The Shadows," all of which question the social values of the adult generation. Similarly, Janis Ian's hit record, "Society's Child," raised the issue of interracial dating and its shocking effect on parents, teachers, and other adults.

As an extension of these socially-oriented songs, others were devoted to specific activities and preoccupations of young people, particularly to LSD, marijuana, and other drugs. During 1966 and 1967, numerous records dealt with these subjects indirectly, by describing experiences which could be regarded as drug-induced but which did not have to be explained in this way: for instance, "Mr. Tambourine Man" by Bob Dylan; Donovan's "Mellow Yellow" and "Sunshine Superman"; the Jefferson Airplane's "White Rabbit"; the Rolling Stones' "Something Happened To Me Yesterday"; and the Beatles' "Yellow Submarine," "Lucy In The Sky With Diamonds," and "A Day In The Life."

Like the socially-minded songs, those implying drug experiences reveal the traditional folk orientation of rock music in the 1960's. After all, these are the subjects with which the lives of the rock audience are intimately involved. At the same time, the method of treating these subjects has the distinctive character of recent sophisticated rock style. For instance, many of the drug references are coded in a special jargon: the Beatles' "Lucy In The Sky With Diamonds" must be shortened to LSD; likewise, the Association's "Along Comes Mary" uses "Mary" for marijuana. These disguised references will no doubt force future music critics to do research in order to discover the actual meaning of different lyrics, just as literary and art critics presently search to uncover the hidden significance in Shakespeare's sonnets and in the painted forms of van Eyck, van der Weyden, and Poussin. During the late sixties, however, rock music iconography represented more of a life activity than a scholarly enterprise. Those who knew the jargon used it to distinguish themselves from those who did not. It became a method whereby young people defined their personal world and excluded adults from it. This practice extended rock's folk function in the sense that the music's "real" meanings were employed primarily in the service of life rather than art.

As I have tried to suggest, an awareness of meaningful statements and serious subjects is inherent in the rock music of the late sixties. In the 1950's, rock artists and audiences did not generally think about meaning as such. The songs worked on an unconscious level; their meaning was taken for granted. Moreover, that meaning was usually negated or forgotten when young people entered college; it was replaced by the more sophisticated concept of meaning which they learned from a structured study of fine art. Of course, my contention is that rock has been profoundly meaningful since its inception, even when it did not overtly express concerns of the intellect and consciousness that it expresses today. Clearly, the sophistication of late-sixties rock is linked to the growing sophistication of youth in general, and this fact carries crucial implications. For instance, the pervasive sophistication of rock suggests that the college "dropout" trend is not so much a reaction against the concerns of the intellect, as many young people claim, but possibly against the standardizing of them through outdated educational methods. In addition, the music's growing consciousness suggests that the new youth may not so easily deny the meaning they find in current rock. In response to protest songs and other socially-oriented records in recent years, many adults have claimed, "Wait until they grow up . . . they'll forget their idealism." But if they have been really consciously gripped by the music's meaning, they will have developed a deeper, more total commitment. This partially explains the phenomenal, constant and faithful commitment exhibited by the audiences of Bob Dylan and the Beatles, the artists who have created the most conscious music in rock history. But these questions are the concern of sociology; the problem for rock music, as opposed to the rock audience, is this: While consciousness may lead to stronger commitment in one's beliefs, it is not necessarily translated into stronger or better art. The qualitative uniqueness of Bob Dylan and the Beatles demonstrates this. point.

A consciousness of meaning pervaded the so-called "folk-rock" movement of the late sixties. Folk-rock was an undefined style which included artists as different as Sonny and Cher, the Byrds, Simon and Garfunkle, the Turtles, the Animals, the Mamas and the Papas, Donovan, and the Lovin' Spoonful. For a variety of reasons, each of these has appealed to the increasingly sophisticated audience of the 1960's and has touched on the sense of commitment that pervades the thinking of the young generation.

Because Bob Dylan provided its spiritual impetus and many of its songs, the folk-rock trend might be said to have begun with his 1965 performance at the Newport Folk Festival. Certain records anticipated this incident, however, and the beginning of the movement is hard to pinpoint. In the summer of 1964, for instance, the English group, the Animals, released a rock version of the traditional folk ballad, "House Of The Rising Sun," and the record became a commercial success in the American market. In June, 1965, the Byrds' electronic version of "Mr. Tambourine Man" became their first nationwide hit. If all sources of folk-rock are to be mentioned, finally, even the Pop Singer Trini Lopez should be cited, particularly his recordings of "If I Had A Hammer" and "Lemon Tree" in 1963 and 1964.

In 1965 folk-rock meant a combination of songs from the popular folk movement with the beat and instrumentation of rock. Dylan was the first artist to use this combination consistently and well, so he should be credited as the primary force in the trend. He definitely exerted the greatest influence on other groups. In 1965, numerous versions of his songs appeared. With "Mr. Tambourine Man," the Byrds released a recording of "All I Really Want To Do," a song that was also covered by Cher; and the Turtles recorded "It Ain't Me Babe." But as the movement continued to expand, with records by the Mamas and the Papas, the Lovin' Spoonful, Simon and Garfunkle, and others, folk-rock became more than a phenomenon of Dylan covers. Part of it was influenced by the "poetic" aspect of Dylan's writing, and part explored the inspired rock sound of his music. Still, the records of both sub-trends primarily represented a way of life for their followers, and this provided a common bond for stylistic orientations that differed superficially. Here again, both the folk character of early rock music and the sophistication of the 1960's have asserted themselves, in that folk-rock was largely a conscious style, but a style more closely related to life than art.

The importance of life style in the mid-sixties was clearly exemplified by the career of Sonny and Cher. The Southern California couple were recognized nationally in the summer of 1965 and, by the end of September, had five songs on the charts simultaneously. They were: "I Got You Babe," "All I Really Want To Do," "Just For You," "Laugh At Me," "Baby Don't Go." While these records were influenced by Bob Dylan, the main characteristic of their content was Sonny and Cher's love for one another. They were a married couple, Sonny arranged their records, and their publicity constantly stressed the idea that they were actually singing to one another as well as to young couples throughout the country. In particular, this is the point of "I Got You Babe," although it is reemphasized in Sonny's "Laugh At Me," which he begins with a spoken dedication to his wife. The life aspect of the Sonny and Cher image was also enhanced by their clothes, a sort of folk-mod combination which made them pacesetters in the world of youth fashions. As this total image developed, then, it created an increasingly tight relation between the lives of the artists and the songs they performed. The couple seemed a perfect symbol for the music-minded love generation.

During 1966 and 1967, however, the Sonny and Cher hits became less frequent. The decline in their commercial success was partly due to the decreasing artistic quality of their records. Sonny and Cher began to reflect the recurrent pattern in which rock artists become self-conscious about their style and create only embellished versions of their first songs. This is especially true of Sonny and Cher's "Bang Bang" and "Alfie." Both records were arranged by Sonny and both contain a confused mélange of compositional and musical effects indicative of a folk artist who vainly tries to make complex and intricate fine art. But the decline of Sonny and Cher's popularity was also related to their personal life image. As the style of love evolved in the 1960's, it steadily took the form of cool and detached involvement, the kind I mentioned in the context of the Beatles. In contrast to this style, Sonny and Cher appeared increasingly conservative and "middle class," because they stressed their marriage, their careers, and their suburban home in Southern California luxury. These values were inherent in their songs, and they did not coincide with the changing values of the new youth. It gradually became apparent that the life style of Sonny and Cher was based on the fifties rather than the sixties, a distinction the rock audience sensed in spite of the currency of the couple's wardrobe.

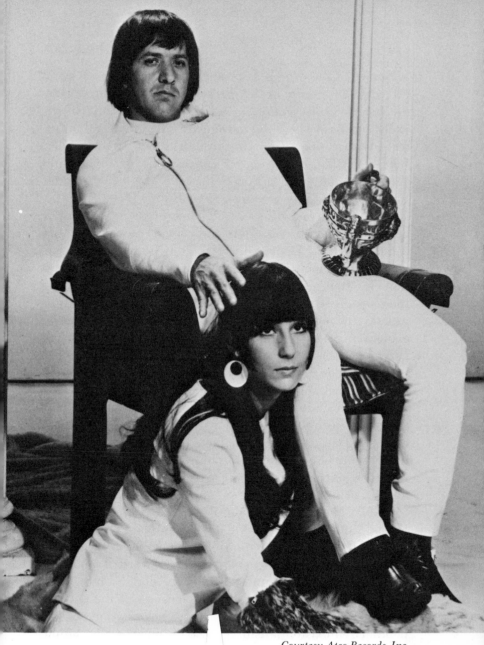

Sonny and Cher

Not all of the groups associated with the folk-rock trend projected as specific an image as Sonny and Cher. Nevertheless, the projection of a general kind of folk image pervaded most aspects of the movement. The Lovin' Spoonful, for instance, particularly through their writer-leader, John Sebastian, has produced a steady flow of albums and singles, including "Do You Believe In Magic," "Summer In The City," "Day Dream," "You Didn't Have To Be So Nice," and "Nashville Cats." These records present a broad stylistic range, from traditional rock to a pure country sound. Their subject matter is generally easygoing and nonpolitical, and the combination demonstrates that, by 1966 and 1967, folk-rock had expanded beyond the scope of its 1965 definition. Yet, the Lovin' Spoonful's link to the original meaning of the trend was clearly evident in their public image, especially in the look of naturalness that they popularized. Similarly, the Mamas and the Papas subscribed to the 1965 image of folk-rock in their physical appearance more than in their music, which is neither socially nor politically oriented. Folk-rock became increasingly associated with life styles rather than musical styles. By 1967, in fact, the term possessed virtually no meaning in relation to music; songs qualified as folk-rock on the basis of their artists' personal images, not on the basis of their sound or subject matter.

Unlike the Lovin' Spoonful or the Mamas and the Papas, Simon and Garfunkle have been more consistent in pursuing the musical notion of folk-rock as it existed in 1965. Their best-selling singles, "Homeward Bound," "I Am A Rock," and "Sounds Of Silence," for instance, have the "message" and the social consciousness of the popular folk movement. The message in these records consists of a popularized existentialism, a sense of loneliness, isolation, and inability to communicate caused by the fast-paced world of twentieth-century urban America. In addition,

Paul Simon's writing has been cited as an important contribution to the "poetic" aspirations of the current scene. In the album notes for *Simon and Garfunkle: Parsley, Sage, Rosemary and Thyme*, journalist Ralph Gleason defended the pair on this basis and in terms of their "intellectuality" and realism. Simon and Garfunkle's "I Am A Rock," claims that love brings tears and disappointment; the message in this song is stated in elegant and educated terms, and the writing is sophisticated when it is viewed against the background of the 1950's. But when it is viewed against the background of Dylan or the Beatles, it can at best be called accomplished. And by those criteria, Simon and Garfunkle, like the other folk-rock artists I have mentioned, have created many good records, but very few great ones.

The Rhythm and Blues Revival: Art and Integration

To understand an artistic movement or an individual work of art, it is necessary to separate the art from its audience and from the artists who created it. This becomes more important as a culture becomes more sophisticated, when artists and audiences assume greater responsibility for explaining the material they create or appreciate. This is especially true for the historian of rock since 1964. It is essential for an understanding of the development of Negro music during the late 1960's, particularly the Rhythm and Blues revival and its relation to the larger history of rock. Negro music has always been more inextricably bound up with social developments than has white music. Thus, distinguishing between art and society in this case is at once more difficult and more necessary—if one wishes to understand the music *as* music.

During the 1960's a whole field of Negro music became nationally popular and commercially successful. This music is "soul," and the term actually refers to an entire cultural trend. It is Negro music, played by Negro artists, on Negro radio stations, and publicized by Negro magazines and newspapers. The trend parallels the larger Black Power movement of the 1960's.

In broad social terms, the history of rock during the 1950's reflects the integration efforts which took place in those years. On the basis of the music itself, I have said that rock began in 1954, the year that the United States Supreme Court made its first major decision to prohibit segregation in the public schools. I have pointed out that this year marked the beginning of a steady convergence of the Pop and Rhythm and Blues fields, with the latter making a constant impact on the national market for the first time in its history, which is remarkable in view of the fact that the blues tradition had been an integral part of American music for more than half a century. Finally, I have indicated how Rhythm and Blues provided the fundamental beat that persisted throughout the development of the rock style. These musical developments parallel the integration struggles of the 1950's, although the connection was never consciously experienced at the time. Songs from the middle fifties do not refer to integration or segregation in their subject matter; and the hostility which rock aroused was directed toward juvenile delinquency and similar youth phenomena, not toward Negro-white relations. Admittedly, the rock controversy had overtones of racial prejudice, especially in the efforts to censor certain Rhythm and Blues songs. By the middle of the decade, however, such attacks diminished as the public became more familiar with the new idiom.

While a type of musical integration took place in the 1950's, it did so in decidedly white terms. For a Negro group or individual to succeed meant that their popularity had to spread from the Rhythm and Blues field to the Pop field and its national market, according to the pattern I described for the 1954 to 1956 period. These terms of success are understandable in view of the relative sizes of the Pop and the Rhythm and Blues audiences. Nevertheless, they had devastating effects on the Rhythm and Blues field itself. As early as 1958, Paul Ackerman noted these effects in the following way:

> The integrated musical scene is not without its touch of sadness and irony. As Negro and country cultures contribute to the main current of pop music, they are themselves in danger of losing their essential folk quality.*

With the exception of the rockabilly trend, the country field resisted this development and, as I have said, retreated into a generally self-defined area after the late 1950's. On the other hand, the Rhythm and Blues field suffered, not so much from the loss of its folk quality, as Ackerman says, but from the loss of a sense of cultural identity. Between 1954 and the early sixties, the charts of the Rhythm and Blues field changed as dramatically as the Pop charts. In fact, the two fields revealed an identical pattern of stylistic "integration." With increasing regularity, the Rhythm and Blues lists included white artists such as Bill Haley, Elvis Presley, and the Everly Brothers. Some of these inclusions can be explained by the high quality of the artists' recordings and by their basic folk style. Besides Bill Haley and Elvis Presley, however, Pat Boone, Ricky Nelson, and, incredible as it may seem, David Seville and the Chipmunks were also included, artists who represented the *kitsch* or popular art tradition instead of the folk tradition of rock. These developments in the Rhythm and Blues charts provoke disbelief among

* *High Fidelity Magazine*, June 1958, p. 108.

today's listeners; needless to say, they were impossible to predict in 1954. Nevertheless, they reveal the remarkable extent to which the Pop and Rhythm and Blues fields converged before 1963.

Because of the increasing similarity between the charts of the two fields, *Billboard* magazine discontinued its separate listing of Rhythm and Blues music in November, 1963. To the national audience, it probably seemed that the Rhythm and Blues tradition had died, that it had been absorbed by rock, and that its contribution to rock was in turn eclipsed by the popular folk movement. But this was not the case. In July, 1964, *Billboard* reinstated a weekly Rhythm and Blues page containing a market analysis for different cities, although the magazine did not include a chart of the national best sellers as it formerly had. The Rhythm and Blues pages also featured stories about various radio stations that had shifted to all-Negro programming with only Negro disk jockeys. In addition, the term "soul" gradually became a symbol for the revived, but still largely underground, Rhythm and Blues trend. For instance, the May 23, 1964 issue of *Billboard* contained the following statement by disk jockey Magnificent Montague, in answer to the question, "What is it the Negro DJ has that cannot be captured by the white DJ?"

> It's SOUL, man, SOUL. Now what is soul? It's the last to be hired, the first to be fired, brown all year-round, sit-in-the-back-of-the-bus feeling. You've got to live with us or you don't have it. The Black Brothers are the mainstay of our pop music today. Artists like John Lee Hooker, Otis Redding and others are heavy on soul—one thing our English friends can't imitate.*

In January 1965, *Billboard* expanded its Rhythm and Blues page and, for the first time in more than a year,

---

* *Billboard*, May 23, 1964, p. 25.

published the Top 40 national best-selling Rhythm and Blues hits. All of the records were by Negro artists, indicating that they had reclaimed the field with which they were traditionally associated. By 1965, the year of the Watts riots, the "soul" movement was no longer underground.

Although 1965 marks an important turning point in the Rhythm and Blues revival, the phenomenon itself is not defined merely by the chart changes during the years between 1954 and 1965. Other aspects of the whole development of rock are important. One of these concerns the popular folk trend which evolved between 1958 and 1963, and it provides an object lesson in the importance of separating a musical style from its audience and artists. As the folk movement developed, it became steadily conscious of Civil Rights issues, and it openly linked itself with the Negro social cause. The trend expressed this alignment in the subject matter of its songs and in protest demonstrations, many of which were accompanied by singing "We Shall Overcome." The hearts of folk artists and audiences were deeply committed to the cause of freedom and equality, regardless of race. Yet, the music of the folk movement manifested a different meaning, one which the Negro audience possibly sensed.

In spite of its commitment to the Negro, the popular folk movement was stylistically white, more thoroughly white, in fact, than the rock style which it hoped to replace. For instance, it consisted almost exclusively of white artists. When it included Negro folk singers, they were Josh White, Leadbelly, and others who had worked in the folk idiom for many years and could be resurrected as safe, historical prototypes. The Negro songs that became popular with the folk movement belonged to an older tradition, and were appreciated like nostalgic glimpses of the past. Finally, the style of the popular folk

singers was radically different from the style of Negro
folk blues. It was clean, elegant, and arty, and it possessed
none of the raw immediacy of the Negro tradition. With a
harsh, rock basis, Bob Dylan's music was an exception to
the arty folk style, but this was not generally realized
until later, when Dylan personally shifted to electronic
accompaniment. At the peak of the popular folk trend,
then, it was apparently inconceivable to include a current
Negro style, rock, in a television hootenanny. Chuck
Berry, James Brown, Fats Domino, and other Negro artists
were inadvertently excluded from the folk tradition to
which they rightfully belonged.

Negro artists were also absent from the trend which followed the popular folk movement, namely the English
craze. Like the folk trend, English music drew heavily on
the contributions of Negro artists. The Beatles and the
Rolling Stones clearly acknowledged their Rhythm and
Blues sources and, as I have said, this led to a revival of
interest in Negro artists among white audiences in England and the United States. Like most socially-based
changes, however, the revival came about slowly, and it
was never as widespread as the Negro contribution to rock
actually deserved. Chuck Berry, Bo Diddley, and B. B.
King have each experienced it, but other Negro artists
from the fifties have not, because by the late sixties, sadly,
they were no longer making music.

The cumulative effect of these developments, the ab-
sorption of the Rhythm and Blues tradition by the Pop
field, the predominantly white style of the popular folk
movement, and the extraordinary enthusiasm for the
white English groups, partly explains why Negroes have
claimed their musical heritage as forcefully as they have
claimed their political, economic, and social rights. Of
course, these developments cannot account completely for
the Rhythm and Blues revival of the 1960's or the grow-

ing importance of the "soul" designation. The question of Negro identity is intimately linked with a myriad of other questions in contemporary American society. But the Rhythm and Blues revival provides an important insight into the unsettled Negro-white relations of the past decade and a half.

The Music of the Rhythm and Blues Revival

Rock in the sixties contains numerous signs of a growing sophistication, particularly in the music of the Beatles and Bob Dylan, but also among its audience generally. The Negro Rhythm and Blues scene has exhibited less of this sophistication, remaining closer to the folk norms that prevailed in the past. With a few exceptions such as Jimi Hendrix and Charles Lloyd, there has been relatively little concern about "soul poetry" or fine art among current Rhythm and Blues artists. Moreover, while white audiences have fragmented into a variety of musical subcultures such as surf, psychedelic, folk-rock, and acid-rock, Negroes have faced the task of defining their culture in its broadest terms. The 1966 music of the hippies, for instance, was largely irrelevant to the Negro, because it presupposed cultural values with which he was neither familiar nor sympathetic.

A symbol of the Negro's effort to achieve cultural definition concerns the term "soul." During the middle sixties, soul became a vital expression in the Negro cultural scene. Artists were referred to as "soul brothers" and "soul sisters," radio stations proclaimed the "soul sound," bumper stickers designated members of the "soul community," and a *Soul* newspaper, comparable in many ways to the *Beat*, provided weekly coverage of the Negro music world. The pages of *Soul* constantly contained articles about the meaning of the term soul, who "owns" it, who is "king" of it, and whether it is possible for white artists to have it. According to reporter Bobbi Jean Lewis,

> Soul is the music that tells it like it is . . . This isn't really a long way around of explaining rhythm and blues, because that's what R&B is. It communicates the soulfulness of the Negro people. The Beatles don't own it, and neither do the Stones or the Animals or any of the other British groups which have invaded American shores. But these English long-hairs cut their musical teeth on American rhythm and blues.*

In another *Soul* article, Little Richard openly praised the English groups, particularly the Beatles and the Rolling Stones, and he defined soul in the following terms:

> To me, soul is not tricks; to me, soul is *more* than that. Soul is when a man sings from his heart and it reaches another heart. When you sing with feeling and you really *feel* what you're singing, that's soul.**

Similarly, Otis Redding, who was tragically killed in 1968, and was one of the most powerful Negro Rhythm and Blues artists, found soul quality in the English music, as shown by his recording of the Mick Jagger-Keith Richard song, "Satisfaction." Like Little Richard, Otis Redding emphasized the idea that soul represents a feeling or attitude:

> Soul is something that you really have to bring up from your heart; it's not something that you can just think of. It's really something that you think of and you get in your mind and you *see* it, and you *feel* it, and you *say* it just right—and really *mean* it . . . that's soul.†

These statements, like many others which were inspired by the soul phenomenon, indicated that soul is more

* *Soul*, June 9, 1966, p. 5.
** *Ibid.*, May 19, 1966, p. 7.
† *Ibid.*, May 5, 1966, p. 3.

Courtesy Leacock-Pennebaker, Inc. From the film Monterey Pop

Otis Redding

of a general feeling than a particular musical style. The same conclusion is urged by the records which were contained in the charts of the Negro market between 1965 and 1967. The best-selling songs ranged stylistically from the traditional blues approach of Joe Tex to the polished manner of the Supremes, and from the authentic, funky sound of James Brown to the *kitsch* jazz of the Ramsey Lewis Trio. In spite of their stylistic variety, each of these artists was regarded as expressing soul. A precise, objective meaning of the word was impossible to isolate, since its use depended upon personal and individual responses. Still, many of these responses were linked to a concept of authenticity. In this sense, soul was not unlike the term "folk" which evolved between 1958 and 1963. With folk, authenticity was also a primary concern among artists and audiences. There were different clues for establishing authenticity—the topicality of subject matter, the artist's background, the fact that a singer wrote his own material, the kinds of instruments that were used—but most of them were arbitrary, based on audience tastes rather than the music itself. As a result, ideas about authenticity changed rapidly as the folk movement developed. Similarly, soul had, and continues to have, shifting meanings. For the Magnificent Montague and for many Negroes, it clearly means black. In discussions of music, however, the meaning of soul is more evasive, more closely related to an aesthetic experience than to the color of an individual artist.

The use of the term soul reflected the Negro's growing self-consciousness about his relation to contemporary American society. It is interesting that this self-consciousness has not generally been expressed in the Rhythm and Blues music of the 1960's. The sophistication of the white music has frequently resulted in artificial, self-conscious songs with poetic lyrics. But Negro music has remained a

Courtesy Atlantic Records, Inc.

Wilson Pickett

more thoroughly traditional folk expression. Negro Rhythm and Blues has possessed a consistency which is not present in the white music of the 1960's. And a listener hears a higher percentage of *good* records on the soul stations than on white or integrated programs, although he does not hear anything as artistically advanced as the Beatles.

An area in which Rhythm and Blues music has clearly demonstrated its lack of self-consciousness is that of protest lyrics. In spite of the racial awareness that pervades our society and that inspires many white songs, Negro music has devoted surprisingly little attention to these problems. Some of the best Rhythm and Blues songs of the late sixties concentrate on the subjects which were the concern of blues singers before the 1960's, especially on the problems and feelings of people in love: The Four Tops' "Baby I Need Your Lovin' "; Wilson Pickett's "The Midnight Hour"; Otis Redding's "I Can't Turn You Loose"; Percy Sledge's "When A Man Loves A Woman"; James Brown's "It's A Man's, Man's, Man's World"; Smokey Robinson and the Miracles' "Come 'Round Here—I'm The One You Need"; the Supremes' "Back In My Arms Again"; Aretha Franklin's "Respect"; Martha and the Vandellas' "Love (Makes Me Do Foolish Things)"; Bobby Moore and the Rhythm Aces' "Searching For My Love," are all examples. The concept of love in these songs is not cool and cerebral as it is in white music. On the contrary, it is earthy and direct, not necessarily more realistic, but certainly reflective of a different sensibility from that of the "love generation."

There have been exceptions to the lack of self-consciousness which usually characterizes the new Rhythm and Blues music. For instance, Lee Dorsey's "Workin' In The Coal Mines" tried too hard to make listeners appreciate the hardship of being a Negro. Lou Rawls's song about growing up in Chicago was more inclined to propaganda than musical spontaneity, and Ramsey Lewis's "In Crowd" gave the impression of existing in order to show whites what it's "really" like when Negro musicians get together in a jam session. But these are exceptions; subject matter and attitude in the majority of Rhythm and Blues songs have avoided protest and social consciousness, just as they have avoided calling attention to their artists' race. Negroes have permitted their music to function in the traditional folk manner. A protest is implicit in the very existence of Rhythm and Blues music. It does not have to be stated literally in order to be communicated. If social and political justice do not exist, music does. It may not change the world—a lesson the popular folk movement learned—but it enables artists and audiences to relate to the world in a way that does not recognize prejudice and injustice.

Consciousness about soul has been as common with white artists as it has with Negroes. During 1966 and 1967, this led to a phenomenon called "blue-eyed soul." The category included the Rolling Stones and the Animals, primarily because of their deep respect for the Negro Rhythm and Blues tradition and because of their ability to create authentic, personal expressions in this idiom. But the category also included a handful of records which were not by blues-oriented artists, but which superficially *sounded* as if they were. Examples of this trend were the Righteous Brothers, in particular their early hit, "You've Lost That Lovin' Feeling"; the Young Rascals' recording of "Groovin' "; and the song "A Whiter Shade Of Pale" by the English group, Procol Harum. When they were first released, these records sounded as if their artists were Negroes. They were reminiscent of a white group known as the Diamonds, who, in the later 1950's, also produced an imitation Negro sound in records such as "Little Darlin'." These songs broke into the Rhythm and Blues charts when other white Rhythm and Blues songs did not, including those which clearly showed their indebtedness to the Negro tradition in musical terms. Their distinguishing ingredient, in other words, was that they had the *sound* of a Negro vocal, and on this level they fooled Negro audiences as well as whites.

With the few exceptions of "blue-eyed soul," the Rhythm and Blues charts have essentially listed Negro music since they returned to the *Billboard* pages in 1965. At the same time, numerous Rhythm and Blues hits have continued to appear in the Pop charts of national best sellers. The crossovers have been generally one way and it can be concluded that here Negroes have defined their cultural sphere. A symbol of this cultural self-definiton is the Motown Record Company. Under the guidance of Berry Gordy, Jr., Motown has grown phenomenally during the past ten years and has become a major power within the record industry, one that is completely controlled by Negroes. Along with its subsidiary firms, Tamla and Gordy, Motown has also been responsible for producing the "Detroit Sound," a big-band, gospel- and blues-derived style which has provided much of the impetus for soul music as it is generally known today. But the situation is not without complications of both a musical and a commercial nature. Commercially, the highest level of success still entails popularity among the white audience. This is evidenced by Diana Ross and the Supremes, the Four Tops, Smokey Robinson and the Miracles, the Temptations, and other Motown groups who have been accepted by Negro and white audiences alike. These artists have enjoyed the economic fruits of both markets, but in varying and delicate degrees they have been confronted by the challenge of retaining their Negro identity and of not selling out to white values. The musical implications of the Rhythm and Blues situation are not entirely divorced

Courtesy Motown Records Corporation

Smokey Robinson and the Miracles

from the commercial ones. There is evidence that Negro
artists, like white artists, risk the loss of their stylistic
identity as the commercial rewards become increasingly
enticing. The Supremes have gained an enormous audience among both Negroes and whites during the late
sixties. They have appeared in concerts and nightclubs
throughout the world, they have been publicized by magazines, and they have sold millions of single records and
albums. But during this period the quality of their music
has deteriorated. "Baby Love," "Come See About Me,"
"Stop In The Name Of Love," and "Back In My Arms
Again" are among the best records of the 1960's, but gradually the Supremes' songs have become stylized and superficially complicated, as shown by "The Happening" from
1967, and "Love Child" from 1968.

It should be emphasized that the decline of the Supremes' style is not necessarily characteristic of Negro
artists who achieved success in both the Rhythm and
Blues and Pop fields. Most have maintained their own
style and quality. Moreover, the Supremes' development
cannot be considered peculiar to the Negro field of music.
The history of rock contains many examples of groups and
individuals whose records similarly gravitated from folk
art to popular art. As I pointed out earlier, Elvis Presley is
a prime example. But in the shifting and troubled social
atmosphere of the 1960's, both Negroes and whites view
this transformation of folk art to popular art as more than
a musical phenomenon. They view it as a betrayal of
identity, as a sellout. Peculiarly, and irrationally, the
transformation of a Negro artist's style in this way is
thought to be especially tragic, as if Negroes have a
greater responsibility to their racial identity than whites.
At this moment in history, perhaps they do; certainly,
many Negroes and whites subscribe to this feeling. Without attempting to analyze the motivations of current so-

Courtesy Motown Records Corporation

Diana Ross and the Supremes

ciety, however, I want to make one point: The link which
is established between musical change and racial integrity
is unquestionably based upon a folk response—a response
which unknowingly equates art with life instead of regarding them separately.

An exception to the pattern whereby Negro artists have
achieved popularity with both Negro and white audiences
is James Brown. Over the past ten years, in fact, James
Brown has gradually and unequivocally earned the title
of "The King of Soul." Most significantly, however, he has
done so without the support of the white audience. Certainly, he has enjoyed occasional hit records in the Pop
field—"Papa's Got A Brand New Bag," for instance, and
"I Feel Good"—and he has also appeared on various "integrated" television variety shows and in Hollywood films
featuring rock performers. But James Brown's real and
most consistent popularity is among Negroes. Generally,
white audiences do not understand or feel the impact of
his music: It has a funky, unrefined quality that separates
it from the elegant, sophisticated smoothness of the Supremes, the Miracles, and most Negro groups who are
well-known among whites.

To me, the James Brown phenomenon contains an important lesson: It means that the Negro claim of possessing
a distinct, separate, and unique black culture, one that is
foreign to whites and generally unknown to them, is certainly justified. Much of the long and varied musical
career of Ray Charles is also explained by this distinction.
Via rock, gospel, and jazz expressions, Ray Charles's records have periodically become popular with whites as well
as Negroes. But his tremendous stature in the music world
cannot be explained from a white point of view. To fully
understand Ray Charles or James Brown, not to mention
the countless Negro groups and individuals whose music
is still unfamiliar to whites, requires a separate study.

Courtesy Rogers, Cowan, and Brenner, Inc.

James Brown

During the present decade, Negro writers have frequently looked back at the fifties and minimized the significance of rock. In *Blues People*, LeRoi Jones dismissed
rock in a couple of paragraphs, suggesting that it is generally a commercialization of Rhythm and Blues, and
comparing it to the commercialization of swing in the
1940's, although he concluded that rock is not as meaningless as swing.* In the newspaper *Soul*, Bobbi Jean Lewis
expressed the same general attitude, but showed even less
sympathy for rock:

> Not so long ago, no one wanted the real thing. Rock and
> roll of the 50s was just a commercialized form of the
> most bland R&B. It was like soup with too much water—
> just not very satisfying. So rhythm and blues remained
> for a long time neglected and isolated—appreciated and
> participated in by Negroes only.**

This attitude toward rock is understandable, especially
from the sociological view that interprets rock as a cultural rape of the Negro by white society. But of course this
view does not do musical justice to a great many very fine
songs.

More important, socially based criticisms fail to ac-
knowledge the indebtedness of the Rhythm and Blues of
the 1960's to the tradition of rock. The new Rhythm and
Blues music consists of more than the traditional blues
style of B. B. King or Muddy Waters. The big beat and
heavy sound in the songs of Wilson Pickett and Otis Redding for instance, have undeniable parallels in the 1950's.
The compelling rebellious beat of rock in the 1950's, especially in the music of Ray Charles, Fats Domino, and Bo
Diddley provided a clear precedent for the music of Wilson Pickett and Otis Redding.

* *Blues People: Negro Music in White America* (William Mor-
row and Company: New York, 1963), p. 223.
** *Soul*, June 9, 1966, p. 5.

This does not mean that the new Rhythm and Blues is the same as the rock of the 1950's. The current Rhythm and Blues music possesses a distinct character of its own. It is earthy, smooth and natural, qualities that are generally foreign to present-day rock music. An appropriate term for the music is "groovy," a folk term which is commonly used to denote any kind of pleasurable experience, but which in Negro music refers specifically to an easiness of expression and a flowing, sensuous feeling. It is implicit in music which issues forth effortlessly, with a folk quality that is emotionally overpowering and free from the self-conscious desire to make "meaningful" statements or fine art. The unique combination is brilliantly summarized by the Gordy record label, which proclaims, "It's what's in the grooves that count."

The San Francisco Scene

In 1965, a scene featuring live band performances and dances began to develop in San Francisco. The scene was highly complex, providing material for students of art, music, politics, sociology, and economics. There were many cultural phenomena, but their most important common bond was the rock music which emerged in the city. Since 1965, similar developments have taken place in Los Angeles, New York, Detroit, Boston, and other American cities, but San Francisco has remained a leading center for live rock. In fact, it has been called the Liverpool of the West.*

San Francisco was perfectly suited for the rock culture which exploded there during the middle 1960's. For many decades, the city had slumbered peacefully in the

* Ralph Gleason, popular music critic for the *San Francisco Chronicle*, has periodically expressed this concept.

atmosphere of nineteenth-century culture. With the Golden Gate Bridge and other scenic attractions, it had been a traditional mecca for tourists. Moreover, its atmosphere of nostalgia had been preserved—in the 1936 Clark Gable film which bears the city's name, in Tony Bennet's famous song, "I Left My Heart In San Francisco," and elsewhere. Annually, the city's most important cultural event was the opening of the opera season, another event which looked to the past more than the present or the future. These qualities dominated the foreground of the San Francisco scene and they symbolized the traditional, conventional values which young people persistently questioned during the 1960's. The city was an excellent target for a rock rebellion.

Another aspect of San Francisco culture contributed to the development of its rock artists. For more than a decade, the city had lacked the structure of a real vanguard art scene. Admittedly it had launched the Beat poets; and many fine painters, sculptors, and theater people lived in the area, but apart from City Lights bookshop it contained very few well-established outlets through which these artists could display or market their work. Patronage for contemporary art was relatively limited, because San Franciscans characteristically devoted their cultural energies to traditional artistic expressions. For some artists, this situation was ideal because it enabled them to work outside the high pressure atmosphere of New York, Los Angeles, and other cities. But many artists left because San Francisco offered limited opportunities for public recognition. For rock artists, however, the situation was perfect. They had an audience among the youth of Haight-Ashbury and Berkeley; they had numerous unofficial places where their music could be heard; and they had no competition.

Between 1965 and 1968, the San Francisco rock scene became highly sophisticated in its overall character, although it retained strong elements of folk culture. Generally, the development liberated rock music from the strict domain of records and gave it the three-dimensionality of a total way of life. In doing so, it embellished the way of life with a variety of artistic accoutrements.

The most popular sites for the appearance of rock bands in San Francisco were the Fillmore Auditorium and the Avalon Ballroom, directed by Bill Graham and Chet Helms respectively. Because of the presence of these two entrepreneurs, there has probably been a greater sponsorship of rock music in San Francisco than in any city in the world. In their programs, the Fillmore and the Avalon had similar formats: Three bands generally appeared on a given night and through a given weekend; the halls provided ample dancing space; and the music was accompanied by a glittering light show. The latter consisted of colored projections, stroboscopic lights, experimental films, and slides of paintings and drawings, all of which were cast on the walls of the auditoriums and surrounded the spectator with a constantly-changing visual environment. In many cases, the music and visual imagery were directly linked by projectionists who attempted to keep their forms evolving with the same rhythm as the rock sound. In fact, each dance became a total environment, similar to the happenings and environments directed by New York artists Alan Kaprow and Claes Oldenburg in the late fifties and early sixties.

The San Francisco dance environments represented a sophisticated development over the balloon-and-crepe-paper style characteristic of record hops in the 1950's. As I said, they inspired comparisons with fine art happenings in their combination of music, art, drama, and life in a multi-media aesthetic statement. Still, they possessed folk elements. The light shows, for instance, were originally created to simulate psychedelic experiences. That is, they dealt primarily with life instead of with art. After 1965 the light shows gradually shifted toward an awareness of art. The term "psychedelic" became consciously used in reference to the broad artistic style of the light shows, a dense and optical style which dazzled the viewer, and was clearly related to the Op Art trend which became briefly important in fine art during 1965 and 1966. In itself, the evolution of this style reflected a remarkable sophistication, and it was an important symptom of the movement from folk art to fine art thinking that I discussed earlier. Despite their increased art-consciousness, however, the light shows have not materialized as a genuine fine art phenomenon. In the first place, the light shows are usually sporadic in effect, their visual events rarely fusing into a powerful aesthetic whole. And although elements have been added to the shows, more colored lights, and more movies, for instance, singular effects have not been investigated or carried through as artistic ends.

The same is true of the posters that announced the San Francisco rock dances. These are also called psychedelic in style, and their creators, among them Wes Wilson, Mouse Studios, and Victor Moscosso, have received widespread attention in *Time*, *Life*, *Ramparts*, *Art International*, and other magazines. The posters began as innocent folk expressions: Bill Graham commissioned them for the Fillmore dances, and Chet Helms quickly followed at the Avalon. By the end of 1966, however, they had become popular. They were used for almost every dance in the entire San Francisco area, and they were distributed throughout the country. Rock now had its own pictorial art, in the form of inexpensive, easily distributed items which could be owned by anyone. This development marked another facet of youth's independence; with their own art, they no longer had to rely on prints of Renoir or Picasso masterpieces in order to enrich their environmental surroundings.

Courtesy Jay F. Good

The Fillmore East, New York. The group performing is Chicago, the light show by Joshua Light Show.

Excitement about these posters quickly removed them from the strict domain of the rock scene, and they were exhibited in art galleries and museums around the country. These displays represented more than an adult attempt to appreciate youth culture. The rock posters obviously belong in the long tradition of poster expression, more so for instance than the oversized photographs of movie stars that also became popular in the late sixties, because their initial function and inspiration was to provide information about an event outside of themselves. Like the Toulouse-Lautrec posters, or those of the German Expressionists, their task was to draw the attention of the man-on-the-street and to direct that attention to a particular event. They were not conceived as self-contained artistic entities, although artistic quality certainly played an important role in their success or failure. In fact, artistic aspects of the rock posters are especially fascinating. For many viewers, the information content of the posters is difficult or impossible to decipher. Letters, dates, human figures, and design elements generally flow together so thoroughly that a special effort is required to separate the different parts. But for young people there is no such problem. Accustomed to the overallness of rock music itself, they immediately sense the information within the posters. In fact, it can be argued that the best posters are the ones that are the most difficult to "read" in the conventional manner.

In artistic terms, the rock posters are highly sophisticated examples of folk expression. They are thoroughly eclectic, containing a dense mixture of Pop, Op, and Art Nouveau elements which are used liberally and are taken from varied sources in both fine art and the mass media. Such eclecticism is generally foreign to the best fine art in the twentieth century, although this does not deny the visual excitement which the posters occasionally exhibit.

Like traditional folk artists, Wes Wilson and his colleagues have arrived unconsciously at a stylistic solution to which they adhere doggedly in spite of its eclecticism. A major difference between the poster artists and their folk predecessors, at the same time, is that the former are aware of a broader range of visual conventions. They share the sophistication of recent rock in comparison to rock from the 1950's. However, like the light shows, the posters have not changed substantially since 1965 or 1966. In fact, they have gradually lost their sense of visual challenge and specialness. For the most part, they have been better than the light shows, but they have not been able to sustain quality in the way that rock music has.

Despite the interest provoked by light shows and posters, the music of the San Francisco scene has been its most important contribution to the history of rock. This music, it should be noted, has nothing to do with records such as Eric Burdon's "San Francisco Nights" or Scott McKenzie's "San Francisco (Be Sure To Wear Some Flowers In Your Hair)," both of which exploited the city's hippy culture, but belonged stylistically in the popular art tradition of Tony Bennett's "I Left My Heart In San Francisco."

While there are numerous rock bands in the San Francisco area, only a handful have thus far achieved distinction. These include the Jefferson Airplane, the Grateful Dead, the Moby Grape, Big Brother and the Holding Company, and Country Joe and the Fish. Each of these groups has issued singles and albums which have brought them national recognition. Before they were recorded, however, most of the groups spent several years developing their music at local dance performances. In fact, this live-scene emphasis has been the most distinctive feature of the entire San Francisco development. The San Francisco groups have earned recording contracts, but the record companies have been faced with the difficult task of adapting their medium to an environmental sound. As I pointed out earlier, this represents a reversal of the former pattern by which most rock music has come into being.

The difference between records and live performances imparts shifting meanings to the San Francisco music. When the first albums by the Grateful Dead and Country Joe and the Fish appeared in the San Francisco area, they sold with unprecedented speed. For many listeners, the records offered an opportunity to relive a night at the Fillmore Auditorium or the Avalon Ballroom. Frequently, however, these listeners had to adjust their phonograph systems in order to compensate for the altered impact of the music on records: They had to play the records at extremely high volume. For listeners outside the San Francisco area, the same adjustment was not necessary, because there was no in-person performance to use as a point of reference. Because there was not, at the same time, records by the San Francisco groups did not stun the country-wide market when they were first released. This situation has gradually changed. With television appearances and with concert performances in New York, Los Angeles, and other cities, the San Francisco groups have begun to sell records at an increasing rate. In other words, their music legitimately functions on two distinct levels: records and live performances. And to the extent that the records are played *as if* they were live performances, the latter can be said to distinguish the San Francisco contribution to rock.

After 1965, the style of live performances in San Francisco gradually changed. Concerts by certain groups, the Jefferson Airplane for instance, were attended by an audience who sat and consciously *listened* to the music instead of dancing. This phenomenon has crucial bearing on the question of the fine art aspirations of rock in the 1960's. To the artists, the audience response was at first disturbing and on several occasions they actually invited

Courtesy Rogers, Cowan, and Brenner, Inc.

The Jefferson Airplane

a prototype for developments in other cities across the country. But one qualitative issue remains: Is San Francisco in fact the "Liverpool of the West?" Certainly, the city has spawned a large number of new rock groups; moreover, its light shows, posters, and live concerts have provided evidence of a significant shift in the rock of the late sixties in the direction of heightened sophistication and a consciousness of fine art. However, the Jefferson Airplane, the Grateful Dead, and other groups have not yet made as much good music as the Beatles.

5

A Troubled Period: 1969 through 1971

At the end of 1968 rock music appeared to be enjoying its fullest moment. The Beatles had just released their most ambitious album; Bob Dylan had returned after an absence of over a year; the Rolling Stones' production showed no signs of slackening; and an array of exciting new groups offered added promise for the music's future development. In many ways, rock had matured: It possessed, and shaped, a vast and still-growing audience; writers had begun to chronicle its separate history; it had begun a re-discovery of its own country roots; and, with an awareness of both jazz and modern classical music, it had effectively broadened its stylistic range. The sophistication which informed these trends had largely obscured the music's humble- folk beginnings.

The promise which characterized rock at the end of 1968 dissipated considerably during the next three years. This is not to say that the music simply declined. Compared with the feverish pace of its development between 1964 - 1968, however, it began to seem disillusioned, dir~ ? lacking new artists of the Beatles' or Dylan' ....ure, and

d by uncertainty about its own identity—particu-
in relation to pop commercialism. The years between
9 and 1971 had their own share of good, bad, and even
agic events.

The problematic nature of the period became evident in
the summer of 1969 at the Woodstock Music and Art Fair.
The weekend celebration assembled a majority of the year's
most popular groups and offered rock to crowds estimated
as high as half a million people. The event became known
as "Woodstock" and the young people who were there in
fact or in spirit became "Woodstock Nation." It was a spectacular statement of what young people had claimed
throughout the sixties: that they possessed their own culture, a world filled with music, drugs and love, most of
which were free. During a three-day period, the dream materialized. Against a background of music—by the Jimi
Hendrix Experience, Blood, Sweat and Tears, the Jefferson
Airplane, Janis Joplin, Joan Baez, Arlo Guthrie, and Ravi
Shankar, among others—rock fans roamed the pastures of
the Catskills, sharing food and water, bathing in the nude,
and, most important for the event's public image, shunning
violence of any kind. Woodstock was a model of rock's com-
munal message—folk-like perhaps in its naïve belief that it
could affect the larger system of American society, but
moving nevertheless.

But the Woodstock story had other facets which, as they
became known, generated skepticism about the meaning of
the event. In the aftermath of the weekend, stories circulated about Woodstock's promoters—Michael Lang, John
Roberts, Joel Roseman, and Artie Kornfeld—who claimed
they had lost more than $1 million by the end of the fes-
tival. "Then," as Jon Weiner has written, "they started trying to buy each other out, and it was reported that Albert
Grossman, manager of Dylan, Janis Joplin, and The Band,
among others, was offering $1 million for one-fourth of the

business. Albert Grossman is the most successful money-maker in rock music; he doesn't make mistakes. Why, *Variety* asked, would Grossman offer $1 million to acquire a debt of $1.3 million? The answer was that there was no debt, that the promoters' report of their expenses was filled with lies."* For Andrew Kopkind, the event was also tainted by commercialism: "Woodstock was, first of all, an environment created by a couple of hip entrepreneurs to consolidate the cultural revolution and . . . extract the money of its troops."**

For many of its participants, Woodstock thus prophesied a glowing future for the rock culture; for others it meant disillusionment—the music had opted for commercial rewards. Of course, Woodstock was not the first example of rock's susceptibility to commercialism. But as an event with far-reaching, yet paradoxical implications, it was probably more awesome than any comparable phenomenon in the music's history.

Like the Monterey Pop Festival before it, Woodstock was translated into a film which spread a one-sided picture of the festival, at the same time tapping still further its commercial potential. Other films quickly followed the example, employing rock as background music (*Easy Rider*) or concentrating on the appeal of its personalities as they perform (for instance *Gimme Shelter*, *Mad Dogs and Englishmen*, *Let It Be*, and *Soul To Soul*). A more unique cinematic use of the music was *Alice's Restaurant*, possibly the first film in the history of the medium for which a record provided the scenario! Like *Woodstock*, however, these films have little bearing on the history of the music itself; they serve primarily to mark its enormous popularity and, secondly,

---

* Jon Wiener, "Woodstock Revisited," in *The Age of Rock* 2, ed. Jonathan Eisen (New York: Random House, 1970), pp. 170-71.
** Andrew Kopkind, "Woodstock Nation," *ibid.*, p. 313.

they stand as testaments to the ingenuity of its financially oriented producers. Certainly, the recent films are more sophisticated than *Rock Around the Clock*, *Don't Knock the Rock*, and other cinematic oddities of the 1950's, but, like their predecessors, their relation to the music is essentially parasitic.

The period between 1969 and 1971 witnessed other examples of rock profiteering. The promotion of James Taylor as an authentic and original folk singer and of Johnny Winter as a master of the Delta blues are cases in point. More disturbing, however, are those groups or individuals who might have contributed significantly to the rock tradition, but who instead gravitated toward popular music— for instance, Blood, Sweat and Tears.

The group was created by the ubiquitous and talented Al Kooper as a jazz-rock merger. To achieve the union, Kooper added a quartet of horns to the basic rock combo. The result was an authentic and powerful big-band sound that had remained unexplored through most of rock history. In 1968 it also promised a new direction for the music's future. But after the release of the group's first album, *The Child Is Father To The Man*, Kooper left Blood, Sweat and Tears and was replaced by vocalist David Clayton-Thomas. During 1969 and 1970 the group became enormously successful with singles, including "Spinning Wheel," albums, and public performances. In the process, however, Blood, Sweat and Tears failed to develop the potential of Kooper's original idea, choosing instead to work within a safe, popular formula. Other groups, Chicago, for instance, have subsequently adopted the formula, and have also shunned its innovational possibilities.

The popularization of rock trends was more blatant in other areas. During 1970 and 1971 a group called Sha-Na-Na successfully exploited the "rock 'n' roll revival" which had been stimulated by the Beatles' White Album,

Photograph Chuck Pulin

Al Kooper, at the Village Gaslight

the publication of several rock histories, Elvis Presley's return as a live performer, Frank Zappa's parodies of fifties'
ballads, and the reappearance of several vocal groups who
had been away from the rock scene for almost a decade.
Sha-Na-Na sought to re-create the style and feeling of early
rock. With slicked-back hair, white socks, and cigarettes
rolled in the sleeves of their T-shirts, they presented a physical image of mid-fifties "hoods" and "greasers"; an array
of dip-dips, do-be-do-bes, and frantic dance steps provided
the act with its musical counterpart. Whatever their mo-
tivation, however, the group's interpretation of the fifties
invariably seemed satirical; they seemed to view early rock
and its life styles as inherently ridiculous. But that is a popular view, shared by those who did not experience the music's beginnings or whose self-consciousness irretrievably
distances them from an understanding of folk innocence.

There were other self-conscious efforts to expand rock
into larger cultural and artistic formats. In 1969 The Who
produced the first rock opera, *Tommy*. Written by Peter
Townshend, its principal character is a deaf, dumb, and
blind boy who undergoes a series of surrealistic experiences
including a seduction by his uncle and a miracle cure, and
whose major talent is his pinball wizardry. Typical of The
Who, the story is brutal and menacing, but not without
some morbid fascination. Unfortunately, the music of
Tommy fails to match the story in either weirdness or fascination. It is largely repetitious, suggesting that Townshend had forced rock into an over-ambitious and unnatural structure. Of course, if the opera had been fully
performed instead of merely "played," The Who's wild
and absorbing personal theatrics may have altered this
impression.

The rock opera *Jesus Christ-Superstar* was an even
greater commercial success than *Tommy*, reportedly selling over 4,000,000 albums in 1971. With music by Andrew

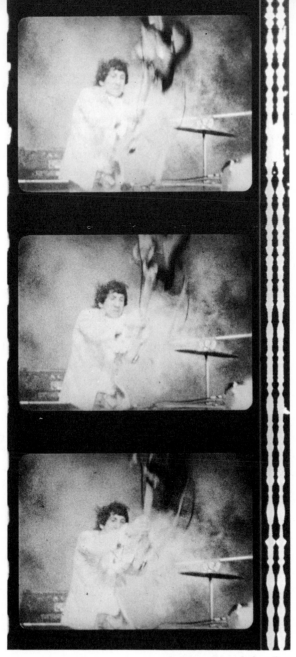

Courtesy Pennebaker, Inc.

Peter Townshend of The Who

Lloyd Webber and lyrics by Tim Rice, the story is based on the last seven days of the life of Jesus; the music, called rock, is inspired more by Broadway shows like *Hair* than by any authentic rock sounds. In other words, *Jesus Christ-Superstar* is a pure popular culture phenomenon. Still, it is a landmark in the history of the period, an archetype of the way rock can be manipulated to sell not only "high culture," but even religion.

In view of the precarious relationship between rock and pop, the commercialization of the music is not surprising. But although the vastness of this commercialism may have been disillusioning to many rock followers, other events cast a more ominous pall over the period. Jimi Hendrix and Janis Joplin died, needlessly it seemed, through neither quirk of fate nor natural catastrophe, but from overdoses of drugs. Their deaths seemed to symbolize the tragic aspect of the glamorous work life style.

Hendrix and Joplin were first of all live performers, a fact which became dramatically apparent to vast audiences at the Monterey Pop Festival in 1967 and in the film which documented the event and subsequently circulated throughout the world. Actually, Hendrix first attracted attention in London early in 1967. When he returned to this country, where he had worked as a backup musician for several years, his act generated an immediate enthusiasm. It consisted of pure theater: Hendrix writhed and moaned, attacking his guitar with savagely erotic gestures, even burning the instrument in a love-death ritual which concluded his performance. Although his three-man group, the Jimi Hendrix Experience, issued a number of albums, their records rarely captured the lusty spontaneity of the in-person events. The tragedy of Hendrix' death was that it deprived the rock world of one of its ablest concert figures. Along with The Who, Hendrix offered the most promise for a convincing rock theatricality. At the same time, he was a vir-

notice, the Rolling Stones had announ\ that they would give a free afternoon concert. An estima 300,000 people attended, probably thinking the event \ ould match the spiritual meaning of Woodstock while a iding its commercial excesses. But Altamont took a di: 'e nt course. The concert created huge traffic jams and w \ larred by numerous fights, most of them involving \ nbers of the Hell's Angels, who were hired by the Rol \ Stones to police the event. At the end of the day, four p le were dead, scores were injured, and many were recove. ng from bad drug trips. Amidst the violence, the rock world lost much of the respect it had gained at Woodstock.

Less tragic for the music, though no less disillusioning, was the breakup of the Beatles in 1970. For five years they had been the premier rock group, constantly advancing their music and exerting an unprecedented influence over other artists. Their development reached a highpoint in 1968 with the controversial White Album, an intensely conscious survey of their own past and of rock history in general. But subsequent albums were unable to match the White Album's concentration, intensity, or range. *Abbey Road*, for instance, contains good individual selections such as "Carry That Weight" and "The End," but does not exhibit the internal cohesiveness of their best previous material. Even on the medley side of the record, cohesiveness is achieved more by stringing songs together and by lyrical repetition than by establishing a consistent musical position in relation to a fixed subject or genre.

Accounting for the Beatles' breakup must necessarily be speculative. Despite lengthy interviews with members of the group—most notably, John Lennon's in *Rolling Stone* and Paul McCartney's in *Life*—the story appears cloudy and elusive, perhaps too personal, finally, to yield to mass media explanations. Obviously, the Beatles' world changed radically between 1964 and 1970. From a quartet of musicians they evolved into a gargantuan business complex, producing films, other artists, and their own songs, and managing their own record company, among other ventures. In addition, each member of the group had a personal life, which meant that wives, attorneys, and special interests began increasingly to clash with the carefree public image the Beatles were content to maintain in their first years. Such changes are natural enough in the world of rock music, but the Beatles seem to have needed a special cohesive force or buffer to insulate them from the inevitable conflicts between public and private lives. In retrospect, Brian Epstein seems to have fulfilled that role. His death marked the beginning of a steady withdrawal of the group from public appearances and, apparently, the start of internal difficulties that could not be resolved.

Apart from the complexities of the Beatles' business and personal lives, I estimate that the group's breakup also hinged on the respective feelings of Lennon and McCartney about music. During the late sixties, Lennon became particularly involved with social and political issues and seemed to want his music to express those concerns. McCartney, by comparison, was not a politically-minded artist; on the contrary, he seemed, in the course of the Beatles' development, to become increasingly interested in *music as music*. Works of art which successfully combine these two attitudes are exceedingly rare—with *Guernica*, even Picasso failed at the task. Rather than struggle with it, however, Lennon and McCartney seemed to feel they could make better music by occupying separate positions.

Separately, neither demonstrated a unique individual talent. Teamed with his second wife, Yoko Ono, and the Plastic Ono Band, Lennon produced several "message" songs, including "Give Peace A Chance" and "Power To The People." Like most political songs, they fail on formal grounds. In Lennon's case, it appears that his personal and artistic lives have not meshed productively. Through Yoko Ono's influence, he has become both an intensely personal, almost an autobiographical artist, and at the same time a didactic artist, working in an idiom which is foreign to his creative sensibility and to rock music generally. He has also become interested in the plastic arts, but in the sort that are susceptible to popular fashion, like Duchampian ready-mades, environments, and other superficially seductive enterprises. As Phil Spector, one of the production geniuses of rock, said of Lennon in 1969, "I have a feeling that Yoko may not be the greatest influence on him. I mean, I don't know, but I have a feeling that he's a far greater talent than she is."* McCartney, at the same time, produced two albums, *McCartney* and *Ram*, neither of which is as good as those on which he collaborated with John Lennon. The songs on both albums are pleasant and accomplished, though they occasionally give the impression of leaning toward the "easy listening" ballads of popular artists. Apparently, McCartney is uncomfortable working as a solo artist. In his *Life* interview he remarked that he was teaching his wife, Linda, to become a song writer. More recently, he announced that he was forming a new group. Whether or not these new conditions will allow him to recover the natural spark of his creative genius, however, remains to be seen.

Together, Lennon and McCartney constituted an extraordinary team, combining power and poetry, authority and lyricism. Separately, each sounds like another "one-shot" rock artist of the late sixties or early seventies. Lennon seems to need McCartney's control, and McCartney seems to need Lennon's drive.

Not all of the rock events of the period were as implicitly lugubrious as the ones I have just mentioned. New artists emerged and several established groups and individuals

* *Ibid.*, p.

continued to create the high-quality material their earlier
work promised. Carole King represents a fascinating combination of both categories.

Before 1971 Carole King was a background figure in rock
music, relatively unknown to the public that either purchased records or attended concerts. She enjoyed a minor
hit record in 1962, called "It Might As Well Rain Until
September," but she did not pursue a career as a vocalist at
that time. Within the music business, however, she was
well known as a song writer. In collaboration with Gerry
Goffin, she wrote numerous hits during the 1960's, includ-
ing "Will You Love Me Tomorrow" (The Shirelles),
"Every Breath I Take" (Gene Pitney), "Point Of No Re-
turn" (Gene McDaniels), "Take Good Care Of My Baby"
(Bobby Vee), "Chains" (The Cookies), "Go Away, Little
Girl" (Steve Lawrence), "The Loco-Motion" (Little Eva),
"Up On The Roof" (The Drifters), "Don't Say Nothin' Bad
About My Baby" (The Cookies), "Hey Girl" (Freddie
Scott), "I Can't Stay Mad At You" (Skeeter Davis), "One
Fine Day" (The Chiffons), and "I'm Into Something Good"
(Herman's Hermits). The list is formidable in length and
in stylistic and emotional range.

During 1971 Carole King emerged as a vocalist. She first
appeared on a touring show that featured James Taylor,
but she soon generated enough enthusiasm to earn independent top billing. Her single, "It's Too Late," and the album, *Tapestry*, were among the best-selling records of the
year. The style of her songs is simple and direct; it is dominated by a voice that is deeply expressive, suggesting that
the artist feels her lyrics on an intensely personal level.
Moreover, the fact that she performs her own material
aligns her with the best artists of the more traditional folk
idiom.

Crosby, Stills, Nash and Young were also stylistically
closer to traditional folk music than to conventional rock of

Carole King

the fifties or sixties. The group appeared in 1969 when it consisted of David Crosby, formerly of the Byrds, Steven Stills of the Buffalo Springfield, and Graham Nash of the Hollies. Neil Young, also from the Buffalo Springfield, joined the group after a first album, called simply *Crosby, Stills and Nash*, had appeared.

During the late sixties, the Crosby, Stills and Nash style offered a refreshing alternative to the art-conscious or acid-rock styles which were popular at the time. With genuine elegance and reserve, they produced "Suite: Judy Blue Eyes" and "Marrakesh Express," two of the best songs from the first album. Their emphasis on acoustic guitars and vocal harmonies was also reminiscent of the folk revival of the early sixties, albeit without the latter's implied criticism of rock's gritty expressionism.

The Band also tended to look back, for the most part to country rock, rather than push the music toward new heights of lyrical or artistic complexity. Originally The Hawks, and later the backup musicians for Dylan's "electric" style, they emerged on their own late in 1968 with an album titled *Music From Big Pink*—"Big Pink" referring to the house in West Saugerties, New York, where the group lived and worked at that time. The album contains the best-known single recording of the group, "The Weight," which is a quasi-religious, but fully convincing and modern folk ballad executed in a strong and controlled rock style.

While The Band's subsequent albums sold well, the group's primary significance lay in their live performances. Robbie Robertson, Rick Danko, Richard Manuel, Garth Hudson, and Levon Helm, all first-rate musicians, gave the impression of enjoying their work. Without theatrics, they demonstated that rock can fully accept its folk identity and can express itself richly within those limits.

Along with Dylan, The Band was instrumental in ignit-

Crosby, Stills, Nash and Young

ing a renewed interest in Country and Western and "mountain music" during the late sixties, especially in the richly textured variety associated with Nashville. On records and television shows, Johnny Cash re-emerged as part of the phenomenon, and various groups, including San Francisco's Grateful Dead, have been influenced by it.

Among newer groups, Creedence Clearwater Revival was probably the most consistent and successful in terms of record production. Though they originated in San Francisco, they eschewed the convoluted style characteristic of the best-known Bay Area groups like the Jefferson Airplane and the Grateful Dead, opting instead for a direct, almost "old fashioned" kind of rock. Their first single, "Suzie Q," which was issued in 1968, set the pattern for their subsequent development. Based closely on the original Dale Hawkins hit, the song features a strong vocal and pounding, unaffected guitar work. Their second single, "Proud Mary," was even more exciting and it demonstrated that Creedence was not simply a "rock revival" group. The song was written by lead-vocalist John Fogerty, and its success catapulted the group into the spotlight of national recognition in 1969. It inspired numerous adaptations by other artists, the most spectacular being the Ike and Tina Turner version which appeared in 1971.

The quality and effectiveness of the Creedence style reveals that recent rock had not completely jettisoned its folk roots. Most of their songs are cut from the same mold— "Suzie Q" and "Proud Mary" were followed by "Lodi," "Bad Mood Rising," "Who'll Stop The Rain," "Lookin' Out My Back Door," and others which expressed a deep commitment to vintage rock. Not that vintage rock represents the music's only legitimate or authentic style. Rather, the group's authority simply showed that that style need not be considered exhausted. Like some of the great rock masters, Chuck Berry or Fats Domino, for instance, Creedence Clear-

The Band

water Revival refused to change their style or force it into
unnatural directions.

The Rolling Stones deserve mention here for several reasons: first, they provide one of the few threads of continuity
between the sixties and the seventies; second—and here
they are like Creedence Clearwater Revival—they demonstrate that high-quality music can be continuously produced within a restricted, unchanging idiom. The Stones'
albums, *Let it Bleed*, *Get Yer Ya-Ya's Out*, and *Sticky Fingers*, revealed no significant change from their best earlier
work. If anything, they appeared to settle on the earthy
blues style which defined their original contribution to
rock, at the same time resisting the electronic or psychedelic innovations which occasionally plagued their previous music, particularly at those times when they seemed
to be competing with the Beatles. The group's name now
appears to have been prophetic: They kept rolling along,
creating great music in a folk idiom they at once understood and enjoyed.

Bob Dylan also provided continuity between the sixties
and the seventies. His later musical position was largely defined by the 1968 album, *John Wesley Harding*, which expressed commitment to an essentially country style informed by both rock and traditional folk music. *Nashville
Skyline*, *Self Portrait*, and *New Morning* broadened and
stabilized this position. They also contained several of Dylan's finest performances: "Lay Lady Lay," "Nashville
Skyline Rag," "Peggy Day," "Blue Moon," "The Mighty
Quinn," "New Morning," "If Dogs Run Free," and "If Not
For You."

Like the Rolling Stones, Dylan apparently settled into an
idiom within which he could maneuver and express himself freely. His fans may have looked for more innovations
or dramatic shifts of style in his work, but he seemed determined to make the kind of music he personally enjoyed

Photograph Gianfanco Montena, Globe Photos, Inc.

Tina Turner

Bibliographical Essay

After 1968 a number of rock books appeared on the American market. In itself the phenomenon is revealing. In the first place, it was largely unprecedented: The history of rock had evolved naturally; attempts to chart it were initiated unconsciously, by record companies which re-issued forgotten singles or albums of "oldies," and by radio stations which played increasing numbers of past hits, thus inspiring a random sense of rock history among their listeners. Not surprisingly, radio produced one of the first systematic histories of the music, RKO's "The History of Rock and Roll," an ambitious, well-informed, twenty-four-hour program which was first presented in 1969. Unlike jazz or traditional folk music, however, rock enjoyed no written history until the last years of the sixties.

During this period the number of rock periodicals also proliferated. These magazines tended to lead a precarious existence, appearing and disappearing as fast as rock groups or records. Amidst the vast turnover, *Rolling Stone* deserves mention for its longevity and reliability. Published bi-weekly in San Francisco, the magazine contains

news of the rock world, record reviews, and extensive interviews with rock personalities. The latter constitute the
magazine's most important feature. *Rolling Stone* gets the
"exclusive" when other periodicals usually cannot, a fact
which underscores the respect which the magazine has
generated among both fans and musicians. The interviews
are also seriously conducted; together they contain a
wealth of information and insight into the music itself.
Aware of this, editors of the magazine published a collection of the interviews in 1971: *The Rolling Stone Interviews*, New York (Paperback Library), 1971. The volume
includes discussions with John Lennon, Eric Clapton, Bob
Dylan, Frank Zappa, Chuck Berry, Jim Morrison, Peter
Townshend, John Fogerty, Little Richard, and Phil Spector, among others. It's one of the most important collec-
tions in the entire rock bibliography.

Crawdaddy! was a precursor *Rolling Stone*. It ceased
publication at the end of sixties, but was revived again.
The format is similar to *Rolling Stone*, with interviews the
most distinctive and significant feature. Between them,
Rolling Stone and *Crawdaddy!* provide thorough coverage
of current rock.

1. Cohn, Nik. *Rock from the Beginning*. New York (Stein
   and Day), 1969.
An "impressionistic" history than a documented
one, by a British journalist. Does not actually cover
rock from the beginning. While it includes brief chapters
on Bill Haley, Elvis Presley, "Classic Rock" (Little
Richard, Fats Domino, Chuck Berry), the bulk of his
text deals with rock during the sixties. Whatever the osten-
sible subject, however, the content *from the Beginning* consists of Cohn's responses: to personalities, performances, and the "rock scene" in general. In these areas the
author offers some engaging material. His writing style is

lively, humorous, and rich with feeling, although his penchant for hyperbole occasionally leads to descriptions that appear formulized.

As far as the music itself is concerned, Cohn has no thought-out notions about its meaning or development. Clearly, he loves the music—particularly its "sexy," "evil," "frightening" qualities—but he employs analytical tools, usually socio-economic in origin, randomly. On youth: "When kids had had nothing at all, they had somehow accepted it. Now that life was easier, they began to riot. Juvenile delinquency became all the rage" (p. 15). On Elvis Presley: "His big contribution was that the brought home just how economically powerful teenagers really could be" (p. 22). Obviously, these remarks are not meant to be taken too seriously. But Cohn's coyness, lack of documentation, and imprecision finally affect his whole subject: *Rock from the Beginning* does not take rock seriously. It is more like a commercialized, autobiographical novel than a history or description.

2. Eisen, Jonathan (ed.). *The Age of Rock.* New York (Random House), 1969.
A collection of essays written during 1967 and 1968 for such publications as *Esquire, Jazz and Pop, The New York Review of Books, Partisan Review, Crawdaddy!, The Village Voice, Ramparts, High Fidelity,* and others. Writers include Nat Hentoff, Ralph Gleason, Murray Kempton, Ned Rorem, Robert Christgau, Richard Meltzer, Tom Wolfe, and Paul Williams. Most of the essays consist of popular sociology, using rock music as evidence for explaining late-sixties culture in general. Bob Dylan, the Beatles, and Frank Zappa's Mothers of Invention receive the most attention. More important than the content of any indi-

vidual essay, however, is the phenomenon of the book as a whole. Like a volume of old magazines, it unconsciously offers the profile of an era now past.

3. Eisen, Jonathan (ed.). *The Age of Rock* 2. New York (Random House), 1970.

In what appears to be a desperate effort to keep pace with taste, Eisen's second volume wanders even more randomly through contemporary culture than did the first. That the book is merely a commercial venture is revealed in the editor's introduction: "Rockwrite itself is the most boring trash imaginable unless it is linked with other equally boring concepts about the way we live or think we're supposed to and then it makes for a more interesting time."

4. Gabree, John. *The World of Rock*. Greenwich, Connecticut (Fawcett Publications), 1968.

A rapid-fire account of rock groups and individuals active during the second half of the 1960's. A survey of earlier rock and blues figures is included, and the book is illustrated with numerous photographs.

Of particular interest is Gabree's initial chapter, "Underachieving with the Beatles," in which he argues that the group's enormous popularity is the result of their musical and lyrical safeness. In comparison, he finds the Rolling Stones more significant, "mostly because they provide a musical parallel to the civil rights movement, the anti-Vietnam protesters, and the sexual and drug revolutions" (p. 27). This vaguely political vision of art recurs sporadically in *The World of Rock*, although the position is not developed in any systematic way. As a result, the aesthetic opinions which fill the book remain more platitudinous than challenging.

5. Gillett, Charlie. *The Sound of the City*. New York (Outerbridge and Dienstfrey), 1970.

A serious study which, unlike any other book on this list, contains a wealth of facts and documentation. The author may reach the same conclusions as other writers, but his bear the authority that comes only through substantive research.

Gillett covers the history of rock from its inception around 1954 to the beginning of 1970. In doing so, he places strong emphasis on the record companies, both majors and independents, who made rock available to the American public. He also devotes considerable attention to the Rhythm and Blues tradition, and it is this portion of the study that is especially valuable and welcome in that he traces the idiom back to its high point in the 1940's. Few books on rock have provided such comprehensive coverage of this aspect of the rock heritage.

Gillett is a professional sociologist, as opposed to most writers who, like Gleason or Cohn, use the methods of that discipline unconsciously and arbitrarily. His book thus contains a special vision of art, one that I occasionally find troublesome. For the sociologist, art is a function of social conditions; its meaning and development are explained in terms of those conditions. Such explanations are often persuasive. For instance, Gillett writes that, "During 1954 and 1955, black vocal groups and their companies sought to satisfy the taste of the white record-buying audience by adapting as closely as they could the singing style that appealed to it" (p. 46). We have no reason to doubt this statement; it may, in fact, describe precisely what the individual singers and record-company executives had in mind when they produced records like "Sh-Boom," "Gee," and others. In other words, I am not arguing that Gillett's approach to the material is in any sense "wrong." Rather, I want to point out that, for someone who values works of art as objects worthy of study *in and of themselves*, the sociological approach may seem to limit the aesthetic significance of the works, treating them like pawns in a frustratingly amorphous cultural fabric rather than as ends in themselves. While reading *The Sound of the City*, I occasionally found myself making such a complaint, feeling that the artistic meaning of individual records had been neglected, or treated summarily, because the author's primary concerns lay elsewhere. But such complaints are not finally criticisms, because it is only by examining different methodological positions in relation to the same material that we can gain new insights into the kind of objects that works of art—including rock records—are.

6. Gleason, Ralph. *The Jefferson Airplane and the San Francisco Sound*. New York (Ballantine), 1969.
Ralph Gleason has been a jazz critic for the *San Francisco Chronicle* for a number of years. During the mid-sixties he became a rock convert and has since written regularly on the subject. One of his best-known articles, "Like a Rolling Stone," is included in the Jonathan Eisen anthology, *The Age of Rock*, mentioned above. The piece represents a distillation of Gleason's position: He believes the most immediate expression of the "youth revolution" can be found in rock music. His heroes are Bob Dylan, John Lennon, and various San Francisco groups, and his vision of art is sociopolitical. Rock "tells it the way it is," whether *it* refers to the "generation gap," the war in Vietnam, "adult hypocrisy," "dropping out" of society, drugs, or whatever. Such a position puts a tremendous burden on the music; in addition, it is often linked with fashionable issues rather than real ones, and the writing which supports it risks becoming dated. This is one of the problems with Gleason's book. It is largely a defense of the "San Francisco Sound," and thus refers to a debate which seemed more pressing in the late

sixties than it does today. The other problem concerns editing, or the lack thereof. Most of the book consists of interviews with members of the Jefferson Airplane. But the interviews run on endlessly; while they contain some revealing insights, their impact is usually lost in the text's excessive verbiage.

7. Goldstein, Richard. *The Poetry of Rock*. New York (Bantam), 1968.

A collection of rock lyrics dating from the mid-fifties to the late sixties. The selection of over seventy-five examples is extremely comprehensive and includes many of the best-known songs of the entire rock history. At the same time, the title of the book is misleading. In his introduction, Goldstein deals not with question of rock lyrics as poetry, but with the way lyrics have broadened their scope and become increasingly conscious and sophisticated in relation to the world at large. As far as poetry is concerned, the author states his position: "I do not claim that these selections constitute a body of 'undiscovered' poetry. . . . But I do assert that there is an immense reservoir of power here, an impressive awareness of language, and a profound sense of rhythm; I call those qualities 'poetic' " (p. xii).

At the time Goldstein's book was published, the "poetry" of rock was a topical issue. Today it is not. By finally divorcing himself from the question, Goldstein revealed sound judgment—the same judgment which informed and governed his selections.

8. Hopkins, Jerry. *The Rock Story*. New York (Signet), 1970.

At first glance, this appears to be another commercially oriented, superficial "history" like Cohn's or Gabree's. But Hopkins does not try to cover everything. Instead, he provides a picture of the rock world by focusing on selected details within it. The approach is unique and refreshing. For instance, the late fifties unfold through a chapter on Dick Clark ("The *Other* Philadelphia Story"); record production is illuminated in an account of the genesis of Aretha Franklin's "I Never Loved A Man" ("The Story of a Hit"); the enormity of rock's commercial ramifications is treated in "We're Only in It for the Money"; aspects of rock's social scene are revealed in a description of "groupies" ("The Story of the Electric Fan"); and the complex experiences of being in a rock group are documented in a history of the Buffalo Springfield ("The Rise and Fall of a Group").

By concentrating on such details, Hopkins' book quietly evolves into a fully three-dimensional and convincing account. His writing style allows it to do so. With neither defensiveness nor hostility, he accepts the variety of rock phenomena—whether they are confused teenagers or manipulative business moguls—and presents them through objective and meaningful descriptions. The book's serious and unpretentious manner respects both its subject matter and its reader.

9. Marcus, Greil (ed.). *Rock and Roll Will Stand*. Boston (Beacon), 1969.

A collection of essays by individuals who were located in Berkeley during the second half of the sixties. Most of the discussions are therefore inspired by, or linked to, events in the Bay Area and are correspondingly restricted by that context. As a whole, the book is thoroughly folk, an expression of how deeply the music can be felt and the lengths to which its meaning can be stretched. For instance, in a taped conversation called "Chuck Berry Brings You the Free Speech Movement," someone says, "—*Fanny Hill* I thought was a good book . . . 'Victorian pornography' . . . The Who are doing that in a way. It's like unexpurgated Gilbert and Sullivan." Such spontaneous and enthu-

siastic cultural leaps could only issue from an unconscious
folk sensibility.

10. Meltzer, Richard. *The Aesthetics of Rock*. New York
    (Something Else Press), 1970.
Of all the books mentioned here, this is the most bizarre.
The book's cover calls it "A kaleidoscope of the rock experience." Meltzer himself says, "I have deemed it a necessity
to describe rock 'n' roll by allowing my description to be
itself a parallel artistic effort. In choosing rock 'n' roll as
my original totality I have selected something just as eligi-
ble for decay as my work, and I will probably embody this
work with as much incoherency, incongruity, and downright self-contradiction as rock 'n' roll itself, and this is
good" (p. 7). The book is intended as a work of art whose
content parallels the content, history, and experience of
rock music.

As Meltzer predicts, *The Aesthetics of Rock* is filled with
"incoherency, incongruity and downright self-contradiction." Without direction, he rambles among records, lyrics,
groups, and individuals, offering interpretations of their
meanings and using as support or foil such sources as Aris-
totle's *Poetics*, Bergson's *Time and Free Will*, Wittgen-
stein's *Philosophical Investigations*, and Unamuno's *Tragic
Sense of Life*, as well as thoughts from Kant, Kierkegaard,
Schopenhauer, Warhol, Duchamp, and others. In spanning
the history of western culture, Meltzer thus implies that
the meaning of rock has neither limits nor integrity.

In certain ways, *The Aesthetics of Rock* realizes Meltzer's ambition to create a work that is an artistic parallel to
rock music. The book is thoroughly folk-like in its naïve
vision of what constitutes philosophy, aesthetics, literature,
traditional and modern art, music, etc. More specifically,
however, one wonders which rock style, or record, the book
parallels. My personal suggestion is: Richard Harris' 1968

single, "MacArthur Park," an unnecessarily long, preten-
tious song which attempts to combine symphonic organiza-
tion, rock, poetry, surrealism, art, and deep "meaning" into
a single 45 rpm record. Both works end as self-conscious attempts to dignify rock by relating it to established, but finally irrelevant, cultural traditions. The attempts may be
sincere but, lacking quality and conviction, they are not
serious.

11. Robinson, Richard, and Zwerling, Andy. *The Rock
    Scene*. New York (Pyramid), 1971.
A superficial survey of the most popular groups and individuals around 1970-71. Among others, these include
Grand Funk Railroad, the Jefferson Airplane, the Flamin
Groovies, Led Zeppelin, Joe Cocker, the Stooges, Sly and the
Family Stome, The Who, Elton John. More like a fan magazine than a serious survey, the book develops no particular
critical position. Some music is good because it is commercially successful, some because it is honest, some because it
is undiscovered, some because its performers are out-
rageous, some just because. In trying to cover everything,
moreover, the writers seem to be groping for a group or individual who might crystallize the direction of current rock
or enable predictions about its future. The book demonstrates that folk spontaneity can become popularized and
self-conscious in rock writing just as easily as it occasionally
has in the music.

12. Roxon, Lillian. *Rock Encyclopedia*. New York (Grosset
    and Dunlap), 1969.
An alphabetical listing of rock groups, individual performers, and related phenomena. The entries are individually described, or defined, in short essays that range
from a couple of sentences to three or four pages, depending
on the subject's importance. Performer entries also include

extensive discographies. A series of appendices list the top-selling singles for the period 1950 to 1968 and albums from 1960 to 1968. With more than 1200 entries, the book thus represents a gargantuan research effort. Moreover, it is written in an engaging and witty style which facilitates easy, occasional reading. One example will suffice: "ARLO GUTHRIE/ Arlo Guthrie, star, was born on New York's underground station WBAI in the spring of 1967 when that station first played a tape of *Alice's Restaurant*."

In spite of its extensiveness, the *Rock Encyclopedia* has been criticized because it is incomplete. While it covers the sixties thoroughly, it overlooks many artists from the first decade of rock history. The Clovers, the Platters, and the Coasters are not included, nor is Ruth Brown or Laverne Baker; song writers, including Jerry Lieber and Mike Stoller, are overlooked, as are rock personalities such as Phil Spector and Dick Clark. Such omissions reveal that the book is limited by late-sixties taste.

13. Shaw, Arnold. *The Rock Revolution*. London (Collier-Macmillan), 1969.

Like Cohn's *Rock from the Beginning*, this is only nominally a history of rock from the mid-fifties to the late sixties. While short sections are devoted to the fifties, the bulk of the text concentrates on Dylan, the Beatles, and other stars of the past decade. Shaw's interpretative position is more or less socio-psychological: He stresses the sexual content of rock, the way it reflects child-parent relations, feelings of alienation, and so forth, though invariably on a superficial level. Still, the book is not without value. In the past, Shaw has been professionally involved in the music business—he mentions that in 1954 he was Vice President and General Professional Manager of Hill and Range Songs and in 1955 he was General Professional Manager of the Edward B. Marks Music Corporation. In those years and in those positions he enjoyed first-hand experiences of the beginnings of rock. Some of those experiences creep into his text, though usually in the form of anecdotes or asides. When they do, the reader often wishes they had been expanded, perhaps forming the basis for a history of rock written from a business point of view. Such a book would be a welcome addition to the field. Unfortunately, however, *The Rock Revolution* does not pursue the area of its greatest potential.

14. Williams, Paul. *Outlaw Blues*. New York (Dutton), 1969.

A collection of essays written between 1966 and 1968 and originally published in *Crawdaddy!* magazine. Williams founded the magazine and his essays consist largely of record reviews written in a sophisticated but rambling folk style. The most valuable section of the book is a long interview between Williams and David Anderle, a business advisor for the Beach Boys during 1966 and 1967. The subject is almost exclusively Brian Wilson, and the article presents him in a sensitive, occasionally moving portrait—a rarity for interviews connected with the world of rock music.

Selected Discography: 1953-1971

The following contains a list of rock singles for the decade, 1953 to 1963. Since 1963, rock has become increasingly dominated by albums, so a selected list of LPs only is included for the 1964 to 1968 period. For a more complete listing of singles records, the reader is referred to the comprehensive studies edited by Nat Shapiro, *Popular Music: An Annotated Index of American Popular Songs*, Vol 1: 1950-1959, and Vol 3: 1960-1964 (New York: The Adrian Press, 1967). Shapiro's studies place folk music (rock) and popular music within the same category, namely popular art. The following list consists of folk music (by my definition) alone.

1953

"Crazy Man, Crazy," Bill Haley and His Comets; words and music by Bill Haley; Eastwick Music Co.; Essex Records.

"Crying In The Chapel," The Orioles; words and music by Artie Glenn; Valley Publishers, Inc.; Jubilee Records.

"Good Lovin'," The Clovers; words and music by Leroy Kirkland, Danny Taylor, Ahmet Ertegun, and Jesse Stone; Raleigh Music, Inc.; Atlantic Records.

"Mama (He Treats Your Daughter Mean)," Ruth Brown; words and music by Johnny Wallace and Herbert J. Lance; Marvin Music Co.; Atlantic Records.

"Money Honey," Clyde McPhatter; words and music by Jesse
     Stone; Walden Music Co.; Atlantic Records.
"Shake A Hand," Faye Adams; words and music by Joe Mor-
     ris; Merrimac Music Corp.; Herald Records.

1954

"Annie Had A Baby," The Midnighters; words and music by
     Henry Glover and Lois Mann; Jay and Cee Music
     Corp.; Federal Records.
"Dim, Dim The Lights," Bill Haley and His Comets; words
     and music by Beverly Ross and Julius Dixon; Republic
     Music Corp.; Decca Records.
"Gee!," The Crows; words and music by Viola Watkins, Dan-
     iel Norton, and William Davis; Patricia Music Publish-
     ing Corp.; Rama Records.
"Goodnight, Sweetheart, Goodnight," The Spaniels; words and
     music by Calvin Carter and James Hudson; Arc Music
     Corp./Conrad Publishing Co., Inc.; Vee Jay Records.
"Honey Love," The Drifters; words and music by Clyde Mc-
     Phatter and J. Gerald; Progressive Music Publishing Co.,
     Inc.; Atlantic Records.
"I Love You Madly," The Four Coins; words and music by
     Charles Jones; Angel Music, Inc.; Epic Records.
"Lovey Dovey," The Clovers; words and music by Ahmet Erte-
     gun and Memphis Curtis; Progressive Music Publish-
     ing Co., Inc.; Atlantic Records.
"Work With Me Annie," The Midnighters; words and music
     by Henry Ballard; Lois Publishing Co.; Federal Rec-
     ords.
"Your Cash Ain't Nothin' But Trash," The Clovers; words and
     music by Charles Calhoun; Progressive Music Publish-
     ing Co., Inc.; Atlantic Records.
"Pledging My Love," Johnny Ace; words and music by Ferdi-
     nand Washington and Don D. Robey; Wemar Music
     Corp./Lion Publishing Co., Inc.; Duke Records.
"Sexy Ways," The Midnighters; words and music by Henry
     Ballard; Armo Music Corp.; Federal Records.

"Shake, Rattle and Roll," Joe Turner; words and music by Charles Calhoun; Progressive Music Publishing Co., Inc.; Atlantic Records.

"Sh-Boom," The Chords; words and music by James Keyes, Claude Feaster, Carl Feaster, Floyd F. McRea, James Edwards; St. Louis Music Corp./Progressive Music Publishing Co., Inc.; Cat Records.

"Things That I Used To Do," Guitar Slim; words and music by Eddie "Guitar Slim" Jones; Venice Music, Inc.; Specialty Records.

1955

"Ain't That A Shame," Fats Domino; words and music by Antoine "Fats" Domino and Dave Bartholomew; Travis Music Co.; Imperial Records.

"Black Denim Trousers And Motorcycle Boots," The Cheers; words and music by Mike Stoller and Jerry Leiber; Quintet Music, Inc.; Capitol Records.

"Bo Diddley," Bo Diddley; words and music by E. McDaniels; Arc Music Corp.; Checker Records.

"Devil Or Angel," The Clovers; words and music by Blanche Carter; Progressive Music Publishing Co., Inc.; Atlantic Records.

"Earth Angel," The Penguins; words and music by Jesse Belvin; Dootsie Williams, Inc.; Dooto Records.

"The Great Pretender," The Platters; words and music by Buck Ram; Panther Music Corp.; Mercury Records.

"It's Almost Tomorrow," The Dream Weavers; words by Wade Buff, music by Eugene H. Adkinson; Northern Music Corp.; Decca Records.

"Maybellene," Chuck Berry; words and music by Chuck Berry, Russ Fratto and Alan Freed; Arc Music Corp.; Chess Records.

"Most Of All," The Moonglows; words and music by Alan Freed and Harvey Fuqua; Arc Music Corp.; Chess Records.

"Only You," The Platters; words and music by Buck Ram and Ande Rand; Wildwood Music, Inc.; Mercury Records.

"Rock Around The Clock," Bill Haley and His Comets; words and music by Max C. Freedman and Jimmy DeKnight; Meyers Music; Decca Records.

"Speedo," The Cadillacs; words and music by Esther Navarro; Benell Music Publishing Co.; Josie Records.

"Story Untold," The Nutmegs; words and music by LeRoy Griffin and Marty Wilson; Tideland Music Publishing Corp.; Herald Records.

"This Little Girl Of Mine," Ray Charles; words and music by Ray Charles; Progressive Music Publishing Co., Inc.; Atlantic Records.

"Tutti Frutti," Little Richard; words and music by Richard Penniman, D. LaBostrie, and Joe Lubin; Venice Music, Inc.; Specialty Records.

1956

"Ain't Got No Home," Clarence "Frogman" Henry; words and music by Clarence Henry; Arc Music Corp.; Argo Records.

"Be-Bop-A-Lula," Gene Vincent; words and music by Gene Vincent and Sheriff Tex Davis; Lowery Music Co.; Capitol Records.

"Blue Suede Shoes," Carl Perkins; words and music by Carl Lee Perkins; Hi-Lo Music, Inc./Hill and Range Songs, Inc.; Hi-Lo Records. Also recorded by Elvis Presley on RCA Victor Records.

"A Casual Look," The Six Teens; words and music by Ed Wells; Limax Music, Inc.; Flip Records.

"Church Bells May Ring," The Willows; words and music by Morty Craft and The Willows; Ray Maxwell Music Publishing Co.; Melba Records.

"Don't Be Cruel," Elvis Presley; words and music by Otis Blackwell and Elvis Presley; Travis Music Co./Elvis Presley Music, Inc.; RCA Victor Records.

"Eddie, My Love," The Teen-Queens; words and music by Aaron Collins, Maxwell Davis, Sam Ling; Modern Music Publishing Co.; RPM Records.

"Fever," Little Willie John; words and music by Eddie Cooley and John Davenport; Jay and Cee Music Corp.; King Records.

"Hallelujah I Love Her So," Ray Charles; words and music by Ray Charles; Progressive Music Publishing Co., Inc.; Atlantic Records.

"Heartbreak Hotel," Elvis Presley; words and music by Mae Boren Axton, Tommy Durden and Elvis Presley; Tree Publishing Co., Inc.; RCA Victor Records.

"Honky Tonk," Bill Doggett; words by Henry Glover; music by Bill Doggett, Billy Butler, Shape Sheppard, and Clifford Scott; Islip Music Publishing Co./W&K Publishing Corp.; King Records.

"Hound Dog," Elvis Presley; words and music by Jerry Leiber and Mike Stoller; Elvis Presley Music, Inc./Lion Publishing Co., Inc.; RCA Victor Records.

"I Want You, I Need You, I Love You," Elvis Presley; words by Maurice Mysels, music by Ira Kosloff; Elvis Presley Music, Inc.; RCA Victor Records.

"I Want You To Be My Girl," Frankie Lymon and the Teenagers; words and music by George Goldner and Richard Barrett; Nom Music, Inc.; Gee Records.

"I'm In Love Again," Fats Domino; words and music by Antoine "Fats" Domino and Dave Bartholomew; Travis Music Co.; Imperial Records.

"In The Still Of The Night," The Five Satins; words and music by Fredericke Parris; Angel Music, Inc.; Ember Records.

"Let The Good Times Roll," Shirley and Lee; words and music by Leonard Lee; Travis Music Co./Atlantic Music Corp.; Aladdin Records.

"Long Tall Sally," Little Richard; words and music by Enotris Johnson, Richard Penniman and Robert A. Blackwell; Venice Music, Inc.; Specialty Records.

"Love Love Love," The Clovers; words and music by Teddy

McRae, Sid Wyche, and Sunny David; Progressive Music Publishing Co., Inc.; Atlantic Records.

"Love Me Tender," Elvis Presley; words and music by Elvis Presley and Vera Matson; Elvis Presley Music, Inc.; RCA Victor Records.

"No Money Down," Chuck Berry; words and music by Chuck Berry; Arc Music Corp.; Chess Records.

"Rip It Up," Litle Richard; words and music by Robert A. Blackwell and John Marascalco; Venice Music, Inc.; Specialty Records.

"Rock Island Line," Lonnie Donegan; new words and music by Lonnie Donegan; Hollis Music, Inc.; London Records.

"Roll Over Beethoven," Chuck Berry; words and music by Chuck Berry; Arc Music Corp.; Chess Records.

"Since I Met You Baby," Ivory Joe Hunter; words and music by Ivory Joe Hunter; Progressive Music Publishing Co., Inc.; Atlantic Records.

"Slippin' and Slidin'," Little Richard; words and music by Richard Penniman, Edwin Bocage, James Smith, and Albert Collins; Venice Music, Inc./Bess Music Co.; Specialty Records.

"Stranded In The Jungle," The Cadets; words and music by Ernestine Smith and James Johnson; Shag Publications/Peer International Corp.; Modern Records.

"A Thousand Miles Away," The Heartbeats; words and music by James Sheppard and William H. Miller; Nom Music, Inc.; Rama Records.

"Too Much Monkey Business," Chuck Berry; words and music by Chuck Berry; Arc Music Corp.; Chess Records.

"Transfusion," Nervous Norvus; words and music by Jimmy Drake; Paul Barrett Music, Inc.; Dot Records.

"Treasure Of Love," Clyde McPhatter; words and music by J. Shapiro and Lou Stallman; Progressive Music Publishing Co., Inc.; Atlantic Records.

"When You Dance," The Turbans; words and music by Andrew Jones and L. Kirkland; Angel Music, Inc.; Herald Records.

"Why Do Fools Fall In Love," Frankie Lymon and the Teenagers; words and music by Frank Lymon and George Goldner; Patricia Music Publishing Corp.; Gee Records.

1957

"All Shook Up," Elvis Presley; words and music by Otis Blackwell and Elvis Presley; Travis Music Co./Elvis Presley Music, Inc.; RCA Victor Records.

"At the Hop," Danny and The Juniors; words and music by A. Singer, J. Medora, and D. White; Sea-Lark Enterprises, Inc./Singular Music Publishing Co., Inc.; ABC Paramount Records.

"Banana Boat Song" ("Day-O"), Harry Belafonte; words and music by Erik Darling, Bob Carey, and Alan Arkin; Edward B. Marks Music Corp./Bryden Music, Inc.; RCA Victor Records. Also recorded by The Tarriers on Glory Records.

"Blueberry Hill," Fats Domino; words and music by Al Lewis, Larry Stock, and Vincent Rose; Chappell & Co., Inc.; Imperial Records.

"Blue Monday," Fats Domino; words and music by Dave Bartholomew and Antoine "Fats" Domino; Travis Music Co.; Imperial Records.

"Bony Moronie," Larry Williams; words and music by Larry Williams; Venice Music, Inc.; Specialty Records.

"Book Of Love," The Monotones; words and music by Warren Davis, George Malone, and Charles Patrick; Arc Music Corp./Keel Music Co.; Argo Records.

"Bye Bye Love," The Everly Brothers; words and music by Felice Bryant and Boudleaux Bryant; Acuff-Rose Publications; Cadence Records.

"Come Go With Me," The Del Vikings; words and music by C. E. Quick; Gil Music Corp./Fee Bee Music; Dot Records.

"Freight Train," The Clyde McDevitt Skiffle Group, vocal by Nancy Wiskey; words and music by Paul James and Fred Williams; The Peter Maurice Music Co., Ltd., New York; Chic Records.

"Get A Job," The Silhouettes; words and music by The Silhouettes; Wildcat Music, Inc./Kae Williams Music Inc.; Ember Records.

"Great Balls Of Fire," Jerry Lee Lewis; words and music by Jack Hammer and Otis Blackwell; Hill and Range Songs, Inc.; Sun Records.

"Happy, Happy Birthday Baby," The Tune Weavers; words and music by Margo Sylvia and Gilbert Lopez; Arc Music Corp./Donna Music Publishing Co.; Checker Records.

"I'm Gonna Be A Wheel Someday," Fats Donimo; words and music by Dave Bartholomew and Antoine "Fats" Domino; Travis Music Co.; Imperial Records.

"I'm Walkin'," Fats Domino; words and music by Antoine "Fats" Domino and Dave Bartholomew; Travis Music Co.; Imperial Records.

"Jailhouse Rock," Elvis Presley; words and music by Jerry Leiber and Mike Stoller; Elvis Presley Music, Inc.; RCA Victor Records.

"Jenny, Jenny," Little Richard; words and music by Enotris Johnson and Richard Penniman; Venice Music, Inc.; Specialty Records.

"Jim Dandy," LaVern Baker; words and music by Lincoln Chase; Raleigh Music, Inc./Progressive Music Publishing Co., Inc.; Atlantic Records.

"Jingle-Bell Rock," Bobby Helms; words and music by Joe Beal and Jim Boothe; Rosarita Music, Inc.; Decca Records.

"Just Because," Lloyd Price; words and music by Lloyd Price; Pamco Music, Inc.; ABC Paramount Records.

"Keep A-Knockin'," Little Richard; words and music by Richard Penniman; Venice Music, Inc./Duchess Music Corp.; Specialty Records.

"Little Bitty Pretty One," Thurston Harris; words and music by Robert Byrd; Recordo Music Publishers; Aladdin Records.

"Little Darlin'," The Diamonds; words and music by Maurice Williams; Excellorec Music Co.; Mercury Records.

"Long Lonely Nights," Lee Andrews and the Hearts; words and music by Lee Andrews, Bernice Davis, Douglas Henderson, and Mimi Uniman; Arc Music Corp./G&H Music Publishing House, Inc.; Chess Records.

"Love Is Strange," Mickey and Sylvia; words and music by Ethel Smith and Mickey Baker; Jonware Music Corp.; Groove Records.

"Lucille," Little Richard; words and music by Albert Collins and Richard Penniman; Venice Music, Inc.; Specialty Records.

"Mr. Lee," The Bobbettes; words and music by Heather Dixon, Helen Gathers, Emma Ruth Pough, Laura Webb and Jannie Pought; Progressive Music Publishing Co., Inc.; Atlantic Records.

"My Special Angel," Bobby Helms; words and music by Jimmy Duncan; Blue Grass Music; Decca Records.

"Over The Mountain, Across The Sea," Johnnie and Joe; words and music by Rex Garvin; Arc Music Corp.; Chess Records.

"Party Doll," Buddy Knox; words and music by Jimmy Bowen and Buddy Knox; Patricia Publishing Corp.; Roulette Records.

"Peanuts," Little Joe and the Thrillers; words and music by Joe Cook; Cranford Music Corp.; Okeh Records.

"Peggy Sue," Buddy Holly; words and music by Jerry Allison, Buddy Holly and Norman Petty; Nor Va Jak Music, Inc.; Decca Records.

"Raunchy," Bill Justice; music by Bill Justice, Jr. and Sidney Manker; Hi-Lo Music, Inc.; Phillips-International Records.

"Rock and Roll Music," Chuck Berry; words and music by Chuck Berry; Arc Music Corp.; Chess Records.

"School Day," Chuck Berry; words and music by Chuck Berry; Arc Music Corp.; Chess Records.

"Searchin'," The Coasters; words and music by Jerry Leiber and Mike Stoller; Tiger Music, Inc.; Atco Records.

"Short Fat Fannie," Larry Williams; words and music by Larry Williams; Venice Music, Inc.; Specialty Records.

"Short Shorts," The Royal Teens; words by Bob Gaudio and Bill Dalton, music by Bill Crandall and Tom Austin; Figure Music, Inc./Admiration Music, Inc.; ABC Paramount Records.

"Silhouettes," The Rays; words and music by Frank C. Slay, Jr. and Bob Crewe; Regent Music Corp.; Cameo Records.

"Susie Q," Dale Hawkins; words and music by Dale Hawkins, Stanley Lewis, and Eleanor Broadwater; Arc Music Corp.; Checker Records.

"Swanee River Rock," Ray Charles; words and music by Ray Charles; Progressive Music Publishing Co., Inc.; Atlantic Records.

"Teddy Bear," Elvis Presley; words and music by Bernie Lowe and Kal Mann; Gladys Music, Inc.; RCA Victor Records.

"That'll Be The Day," Buddy Holly and the Crickets; words and music by Jerry Allison, Buddy Holly, and Norman Petty; Nor Va Jak Music, Inc.; Brunswick Records.

"To The Aisle," The Five Satins; words and music by Billy Dawn Smith and Stuart Wiener; Wemar Music Corp.; Ember Records.

"Wake Up, Little Susie," The Everly Brothers; words and music by Boudleaux Bryant and Felice Bryant; Acuff-Rose Publications; Cadence Records.

"Whispering Bells," The Del Vikings; words and music by C. E. Quick; Gil Music Corp./Fee Bee Music; Dot Records.

"White Sport Coat And A Pink Carnation," Marty Robbins; words and music by Marty Robbins; Fred Rose Music, Inc.; Columbia Records.

"Whole Lot-ta Shakin' Goin' On," Jerry Lee Lewis; words and music by Dave Williams and Sunny David; Valley Publishers, Inc./Cherio Music Publishers, Inc.; Sun Records.

"You Send Me," Sam Cooke; words and music by L. C. Cooke; Higuera Publishing Co.; Keen Records.

"Young Blood," The Coasters; words and music by Jerry Leiber, Mike Stoller, and Doc Pomus; Tiger Music, Inc.; Atco Records.

1958

"All I Have To Do Is Dream," The Everly Brothers; words and music by Boudleaux Bryant; Acuff-Rose Publications; Cadence Records.

"All-American Boy," Bill Parsons; words and music by Bill Parsons and Orville Lunsford; Buckeye Music, Inc.; Fraternity Records.

"Baby Talk," Jan and Dean; words and music by Melvin H. Schwartz; Admiration Music, Inc./Ultra Music/Hillary Music, Inc.; Dore Records.

"Beep, Beep," The Playmates; words and music by Donald Claps and Carl Cicchetti; Patricia Music Publishing Corp./H&L Music Corp.; Roulette Records.

"Bird Dog," The Everly Brothers; words and music by Boudleaux Bryant; Acuff-Rose Publications; Cadence Records.

"Carol," Chuck Berry; words and music by Chuck Berry; Arc Music Corp.; Chess Records.

"Chantilly Lace," The Big Bopper; words and music by J. P. Richardson; Glad Music Co.; Mercury Records.

"Do You Want To Dance?," Bobby Freeman; words and music by Bobby Freeman; Clockus Music, Inc.; Josie Records.

"Donna," Ritchie Valens; words and music by Ritchie Valens; Kemo Music Co.; Del-Fi Records.

"Endless Sleep," Jody Reynolds; words and music by Jody Reynolds and Dolores Nance; Johnstone-Montei, Inc./ Elizabeth Music; Demon Records.

"Johnny B. Goode," Chuck Berry; words and music by Chuck Berry; Arc Music Corp.; Chess Records.

"La Bamba," Ritchie Valens; words and music by William Clauson; Beechwood Music Corp.; Del-Fi Records.

"La Dee Dah," Billy and Lillie; words and music by Frank C. Slay, Jr. and Bob Crewe; Conley Music, Inc.; Swan Records.

"Little Star," The Elegants; words and music by Vito Picone and Arthur Venosa; Keel Music Co.; Apt Records.

"Lonely Teardrops," Jackie Wilson; words and music by Berry Gordy, Jr., Gwen Gordy, and Tyran Carlo; Pearl Music Co., Inc.; Brunswick Records.

"Lover's Question, A," Clyde McPhatter; words and music by Brook Benton and Jimmy Williams; Eden Music, Inc./ Progressive Music Publishing Co., Inc.; Atlantic Records.

"Maybe," The Chantels; words and music by George Goldner; Figure Music, Inc.; End Records.

"My True Love," Jack Scott; words and music by Jack Scott; Starfire Music Corp.; Carlton Records.

"Poor Little Fool," Ricky Nelson; words and music by Shari Sheeley; Eric Music, Inc.; Imperial Records.

"Problems," The Everly Brothers; words and music by Boudleaux Bryant and Felice Bryant; Acuff-Rose Publications; Cadence Records.

"Rockin' Robin," Bobby Day; words and music by Jimmie Thomas; Recordo Music Publishers; Class Records.

"Skinny Minnie," Bill Haley and His Comets; words and music by Bill Haley, Arrett "Rusty" Keefer, Catherine Cafra, and Milt Gabler; Valley Brook Publications, Inc.; Decca Records.

"So Fine," The Fiestas; words and music by Johnny Otis; Eldorado Music Co.; Old Town Records.

"Splish Splash," Bobby Darin; words and music by Bobby Darin and Jean Murray; Travis Music Co.; Atco Records.

"Stagger Lee," Lloyd Price; words and music by Harold Logan and Lloyd Price; Travis Music Co.; ABC-Paramount Records.

"Summertime Blues," Eddie Cochran; words and music by Eddie Cochran and Jerry Capehart; American Music, Inc.; Liberty Records.

"Summertime, Summertime," The Jamies; words and music by Tom Jameson and Sherm Feller; Roxbury Music Co.; Epic Records.

"Talk To Me, Talk To Me," Little Willie John; words and music by Joe Seneca; Jay and Cee Music Corp.; King Records.

"Tears On My Pillow," Little Anthony and the Imperials; words and music by Sylvester Bradford and Al Lewis; Gladys Music, Inc./Tricky Music, Inc.; End Records.

"Tequila," The Champs; music by Chuck Rio; Jat Music, Inc./ Modern Music Publishing Co.; Challenge Records.

"To Know Him Is To Love Him," The Teddy Bears; words and music by Phil Spector; Hillary Music, Inc./Bamboo Music, Inc.; Dore Records.

"Tom Dooley," The Kingston Trio; arranged by Dave Guard; Beechwood Music Corp.; Capitol Records.

"Western Movies," The Olympics; words and music by Cliff Goldsmith and Fred Smith; Elizabeth Music/Aries Music Co.; Liberty Records.

"Yakety Yak," The Coasters; words and music by Jerry Leiber and Mike Stoller; Tiger Music, Inc.; Atco Records.

"You Cheated," The Shields; words and music by Don Burch; Balcones Publishing Co.; Dot Records.

1959

"Almost Grown," Chuck Berry; words and music by Chuck Berry; Arc Music Corp.; Chess Records.

"Along Came Jones," The Coasters; words and music by Jerry Leiber and Mike Stoller; Tiger Music, Inc.; Atco Records.

"Bongo Rock," Preston Epps; music by Preston Epps and Arthur Egnoian; Drive-In Music Co., Inc.; Original Sound Records.

"Charlie Brown," The Coasters; words and music by Jerry Leiber and Mike Stoller; Tiger Music, Inc.; Atco Records.

"Dream Lover," Bobby Darin; words and music by Bobby Darin; Fern Music, Inc./Progressive Music Publishing Co., Inc./T.M. Music, Inc.; Atco Records.

"Everybody Loves To Cha Cha Cha," Sam Cooke; words and music by Barbara Campbell; Kags Music Corp.; Keen Records.

"Here Comes Summer," Jerry Keller; words and music by

Jerry Keller; Jaymar Music Publishing Co., Inc.; Kapp Records.

"I'm Gonna Get Married," Lloyd Price; words and music by Harold Logan and Lloyd Price; Lloyd and Logan, Inc.; ABC-Paramount Records.

"It Was I," Skip and Flip; words and music by Gary Paxton; T.M. Music, Inc./Desert Palms Publishing Co./Brent Music Corp.; Brent Records.

"Kansas City," Wilbert Harrison; words and music by Jerry Leiber and Mike Stoller; Armo Music Corp.; Fury Records.

"Love Potion Number Nine," The Clovers; words and music by Jerry Leiber and Mike Stoller; Quintet Music, Inc.; United Artists Records.

"Poison Ivy," The Coasters; words and music by Jerry Leiber and Mike Stoller; Tiger Music, Inc.; Atco Records.

"Poor Jenny," The Everly Brothers; words and music by Boudleaux Bryant and Felice Bryant; Acuff-Rose Publications; Cadence Records.

"Red River Rock," Johnny and the Hurricanes; music by Tom King, Ira Mack and Fred Mendelsohn; Vicki Music, Inc.; Warwick Records.

"Sea Of Love," Phil Phillips; words and music by George Khoury and Phil Battiste; Kamar Publishing Co.; Mercury Records.

"Since I Don't Have You," The Skyliners; words and music by James Beaumont, Janet Vogel, Joseph Verscharen, Walter Lester and John Taylor, music by Joseph Rock and Lennie Martin; Calico Records, Inc.; Calico Records.

"16 Candles," The Crests; words and music by Luther Dixon and Allyson R. Khent; Coronation Music, Inc./January Music Corp.; Co-ed Records.

"Sleep Walk," Santo and Johnny; music by Ann Farina, John Farina and Santo Farina; T.M. Music, Inc.; Canadian-American Records.

"Sorry, I Ran All The Way Home," The Impalas; words and music by Harry Giosasi and Artie Zwirn; Figure Music, Inc.; Cub Records.

"Sweet Nothin's," Brenda Lee; words and music by Ronnie Self; Champion Music Corp.; Decca Records.

"Tallahassee Lassie," Freddy Cannon; words and music by Frank C. Slay, Jr., Bob Crewe and Frederick A. Picariello; Conley Music, Inc.; Swan Records.

"Teen Angel," Mark Dinning; words and music by Jean Surrey and Red Surrey; Acuff-Rose Publications; M-G-M Records.

"Teenager In Love," Dion and the Belmonts; words and music by Jerome "Doc" Pomus and Mort Shuman;; Rumbalero Music, Inc.; Laurie Records.

"There Goes My Baby," The Drifters; words and music by Benjamin Nelson, Lover Patterson, and George Treadwell; Jot Music Co./Progressive Music Publishing Co., Inc.; Atlantic Records.

"Tragedy," Thomas Wayne; words and music by Gerald H. Nelson and Fred B. Burch; Bluff City Music Publishing Co./Dorothy Music; Fernwood Records.

"What'd I Say," Ray Charles; words and music by Ray Charles; Progressive Music Publishing Co., Inc.; Atlantic Records.

"You've Got Personality," Lloyd Price; words and music by Harold Logan and Lloyd Price; Lloyd and Logan, Inc.; ABC-Paramount Records.

1960

"Angel Baby," Rosie and the Originals; words and music by Rose Hamlin; Figure Music, Inc.; Highland Records.

"Cathy's Clown," The Everly Brothers; words and music by Don Everly and Phil Everly; Acuff-Rose Publications, Inc.; Warner Brothers Records.

"Chain Gang," Sam Cooke; words and music by Sol Quasha and Herb Yakus; George Pincus Music Corp.; RCA Victor Records.

"Fannie Mae," Buster Brown; words and music by Waymon Glasco; Frost Music Corp./Olivia Publishing Co.; Fire Records.

"Finger Poppin' Time," Hank Ballard and the Midnighters; words and music by Hank Ballard; Lois Publishing Co.; King Records.

"Gee Whiz!" Carla Thomas; words and music by Carla Thomas; East Publications/Bais Music; Atlantic Records.

"Image Of A Girl," The Safaris; words by Marvin Rosenberg, music by Richard Clasky; Eldorado Music Co.; Eldo Records.

"(I Wanna) Love My Life Away," Gene Pitney; words and music by Gene Pitney; Sea-Lark Enterprises, Inc.; Musicor Records.

"Money, That's What I Want," Barrett Strong; words and music by Berry Gordy, Jr. and Janie Bradford; Jobete Music Co., Inc.; Anna Records.

"New Orleans," U. S. Bonds; words and music by Frank J. Guida and Joseph F. Royster; Rock Masters, Inc.; Le-Grand Records.

"Only The Lonely," Roy Orbison; words and music by Roy Orbison and Joe Melson; Acuff-Rose Publications, Inc.; Monument Records.

"Spanish Harlem," Ben E. King; words and music by Jerry Leiber and Phil Spector; Progressive Music Publishing Co., Inc./Trio Music Co., Inc.; Atco Records.

"Stay," Maurice Williams and the Zodiacs; words and music by Maurice Williams; Windsong Music; Herald Records.

"Step By Step," The Crests; words and music by Ollie Jones and Billy Dawn Smith; Paxwin Music Corp.; Co-ed Records.

"Swingin' School," Bobby Rydell; words by Kal Mann, music by Bernie Lowe and Dave Appell; Columbia Pictures Music Corp.; Cameo Records.

"This Magic Moment," The Drifters; words and music by Doc Pomus and Mort Shuman; Rumbalero Music, Inc./Tiger Music, Inc./Tredlew Music, Inc.; Atlantic Records.

"The Twist," Chubby Checker; words and music by Hand Ballard; Lois Publishing Co.; Parkway Records.

"Walk, Don't Run," The Ventures; words and music by John H. Smith, Jr.; Forshay Music; Dolton Records.

"Wild One," Bobby Rydell; words and music by Bernie Lowe, Kal Mann, and Dave Appell; Lowe Music Corp.; Cameo Records.

"You Got What It Takes," Marv Johnson; words and music by Berry Gordy, Jr., Gwen Gordy and Tyran Carlo; Fidelity Music Co.; United Artists Records.

"You Talk Too Much," Joe Jones; words and music by Joe Jones and Reginald Hall; Nom Music, Inc./Ben-Ghazi Enterprises, Inc.; Roulette Records.

1961

"Bristol Stomp," The Dovells; words by Kal Mann, music by Dave Appell; Kalmann Music Corp.; Parkway Records.

"Calendar Girl," Neil Sedaka; words and music by Howard Greenfield and Neil Sedaka; Screen Gems-Columbia Music, Inc.; RCA Victor Records.

"Candy Man," Roy Orbison; words and music by Fred Neil and Beverly Ross; January Music Corp.; Monument Records.

"Crying," Roy Orbison; words and music by Roy Orbison and Joe Melson; Acuff-Rose Publications, Inc.; Monument Records.

"Dum Dum," Brenda Lee; words and music by Jackie De Shannon and Sharon Sheeley; Metric Music Co.; Decca Records.

"Ebony Eyes," The Everly Brothers; words and music by John Loudermilk; Acuff-Rose Publications, Inc.; Warner Brothers Records.

"Gypsy Woman," The Impressions; words and music by Curtis Mayfield; Curtom Publishing Co., Inc.; ABC Paramount Records.

"Happy Birthday, Sweet Sixteen," Neil Sedaka; words and music by Neil Sedaka and Howard Greenfield; Screen Gems-Columbia Music, Inc.; RCA Victor Records.

"Hats Off To Larry," Del Shannon; words and music by Del

Shannon; Vicki Music Co./McLaughlin Publishing Co.; Big Top Records.

"Hello Mary Lou," Ricky Nelson; words and music by Gene Pitney; January Music Corp.; Imperial Records.

"His Latest Flame," Elvis Presley; words and music by Doc Pomus and Mort Shuman; Elvis Presley Music, Inc.; RCA Victor Records.

"Hit The Road, Jack," Ray Charles; words and music by Percy Mayfield; Tangerine Music Corp.; ABC-Paramount Records.

"Hundred Pounds of Clay," Gene McDaniels; words and music by Bob Elgin, Luther Dixon, and Kay Rogers; Gil Music Corp.; Liberty Records.

"Last Night," The Mar-Keys; words and music by T. Johnson and the Mar-Keys; East Publications/Bais Music; Satellite Records.

"Let's Twist Again," Chubby Checker; words by Kal Mann, music by Kal Mann and Dave Appell; Kalmann Music Co.; Parkway Records.

"Little Bit Of Soap," The Jarmels; words and music by Bert Russell; Robert Mellin, Inc.; Laurie Records.

"Look In My Eyes," The Chantels; words and music by Richard Barrett; Atlantic Music Corp.; Carlton Records.

"Mama Said," The Shirelles; words and music by Luther Dixon and Willie Dennson; Ludix Publishing Co., Inc./Betalbin Music Publishing Corp.; Scepter Records.

"Mother-in-Law," Ernie K. Doe; words and music by Alan Toussaint; Minit Music Co.; Minit Records.

"The Mountain's High," Dick and Deedee; words and music by Dick Gosting; Odin Music Co.; Liberty Records.

"Peppermint Twist," Joey Dee and the Starliters; words and music by Joey Dee and Henry Glover; Frost Music Corp.; Roulette Records.

"Point Of No Return," Gene McDaniels; words and music by Gerry Goffin and Carole King; Screen Gems-Columbia Music, Inc.; Liberty Records.

"Quarter To Three," U. S. Bonds; words and music by Frank Guida, Joe Royster, Gene Barge, and Gary Anderson; Rock Masters, Inc.; LeGrand Records.

"Runaway," Del Shannon; words by Del Shannon, music by Max Crook and Del Shannon; Vicki Music, Inc.; Big Top Records.

"Sad Movies (Make Me Cry)," Sue Thompson; words and music by John D. Loudermilk; Acuff-Rose Publications, Inc.; Hickory Records.

"School Is Out," U. S. Bonds; words and music by Gary Anderson and Gene Barge; Rock Masters, Inc.; LeGrand Records.

"Shop Around," The Miracles; words and music by Berry Gordy, Jr. and Smokie Robinson; Jobete Music Co., Inc.; Tamla Records.

"There's A Moon Out Tonight," The Capris; words and music by Al Striano, Joe Luccisano, and Al Gentile; Rob-Ann Music, Inc./Maureen Music, Inc.; Old Town Records.

"Those Oldies But Goodies Remind Me Of You," Little Caesar and the Romans; words and music by Paul Politti and Nick Curinga; Maravilla Music, Inc.; Del-Fi Records.

"Tossin' and Turnin'," Bobby Lewis; words and music by Malou Rene and Ritchie Adams; Harvard Music, Inc./Viva Music, Inc.; Beltone Records.

"Tower of Strength," Gene McDaniels; words by Bob Hilliard, music by Burt F. Bacharach; Famous Music Corp.; Liberty Records.

insistor Sister," Freddie Cannon; words and music by Frank C. Slay, Jr. and Chuck Dougherty; Claridge Music, Inc.; Swan Records.

hat's Your Name," Don and Juan; words and music by Claude Johnson; Hill and Range Songs, Inc.; Big Top Records.

"Who Put The Bomp (In The Bomp Ba Bomp Ba Bomp)," Barry Mann; words and music by Barry Mann and Gerry Goffin; Screen Gems-Columbia Music, Inc.; ABC Paramount Records.

"Ya Ya," Lee Dorsey; words and music by Lee Dorsey, Clarence Lewis, and Morgan Robinson; Frost Music Corp.; Fury Records.

1962

"Baby, It's You," The Shirelles; words and music by Mack David, Burt Bacharach, and Barney Williams; Dolfi Music, Inc./Mary Jane Music; Sceptor Records.

"Beachwood 4-5789," The Marvelettes; words and music by William Stevenson, George Gordy, and Marvin Gaye; Jobete Music Co., Inc.; Tamla Records.

"Bring It On Home To Me," Sam Cooke; words and music by Sam Cooke; Kags Music; RCA Victor Records.

"Chains," The Cookies; words and music by Gerry Goffin and Carole King; Screen Gems-Columbia Music, Inc.; Dimension Records.

"Do You Love Me?" The Contours; words and music by Berry Gordy, Jr.; Jobete Music Co., Inc.; Gordy Records.

"Don't Play That Song," Ben E. King; words and music by Ahmet M. Artegun and Betty Nelson; Progressive Music Publishing Co., Inc.; Atco Records.

"Duke Of Earl," Gene Chandler; words and music by Earl Edwards, Bernie Williams, and Eugene Dixon; Conrad Publishing Co., Inc./Aba, Inc.; Vee Jay Records.

"He's A Rebel," The Crystals; words and music by Gene Pitney; January Music Corp.; Philles Records.

"He's Sure The Boy I Love," The Crystals; words and music by Barry Mann and Cynthia Weil; Screen Gems-Columbia Music, Inc.; Philles Records.

"If I Had A Hammer," Peter, Paul and Mary; words and music by Pete Seeger and Lee Hays; Ludlow Music, Inc.; Warner Brothers Records.

"Let Me In," The Sensations; words and music by Yvonne Baker; Arc Music Corp./Kae Williams Music, Inc.; Argo Records.

"Loco-Motion," Little Eva; words and music by Gerry Goffin and Carole King; Screen Gems-Columbia Music, Inc.; Dimension Records.

"Mashed Potato Time," Dee Dee Sharp; words and music by Jon Sheldon and Harry Land; Rice Mill Publishing Co., Inc./Jobete Music Co., Inc.; Cameo Records.

"On Broadway," The Drifters; words and music by Barry Mann, Cynthia Weil, Jerry Leiber, and Mike Stoller; Screen Gems-Columbia Music, Inc.; Atlantic Records.

"The One Who Really Loves You," Mary Wells; words and music by William Robinson; Jobete Music Co., Inc.; Motown Records.

"Papa-Oom-Mow-Mow," The Rivingtons; words and music by Al Frazier, Carl White, Turner Wilson, Jr. and John Harris; Beechwood Music Corp.; Liberty Records.

"Party Lights," Claudine Clark; words and music by Claudine Clark; Rambed Publishing Co., Inc.; Chancellor Records.

"Please Mr. Postman," The Marvelettes; words and music by Brian Holland and Freddy C. Gorman; Jobete Music Co., Inc.; Tamla Records.

"Slow Twistin'," Chubby Checker; words and music by Jon Sheldon; Woodcrest Music, Inc.; Parkway Records.

"Smoky Places," The Corsairs; words and music by Abner Spector; Arc Music Corp./Winlyn Music, Inc.; Tuff Records.

"Surfin' Safari," The Beach Boys; words and music by Mike Love and Brian Wilson; Guild Music Co.; Capitol Records.

"Suspicion," Terry Stafford; words and music by Doc Pomus and Mort Shuman; Elvis Presley Music, Inc.; Crusader Records.

"Telstar," The Tornadoes; music by Joe Meek; Ivy Music, Ltd., London, England/Campbell-Connelly, Inc.; London Records.

"Twist And Shout," The Isley Brothers; words and music by Bert Russell and Phil Medley; Robert Mellin, Inc./Progressive Music Publishing Co., Inc.; Wand Records.

"Twistin' The Night Away," Sam Cooke; words and music by Sam Cooke; Kags Music; RCA Victor Records.

"Up On The Roof," The Drifters; words and music by Gerry Goffin and Carole King; Screen Gems-Columbia Music, Inc.; Atlantic Records.

"Uptown," The Crystals; words and music by Barry Mann and

Cynthia Weil; Screen Gems-Columbia Music, Inc.; Philles Records.

"Wah-Watusi," The Orlons; words by Kal Mann, music by Dave Appell; Kalmann Music, Inc./Lowe Music Corp.; Cameo Records.

"You Beat Me To The Punch," Mary Wells; words and music by William Robinson and Ronald White; Jobete Music Co., Inc.; Motown Records.

"You'll Lose A Good Thing," Barbara Lynn; words and music by Barbara Lynn Ozen; Jamie Music Publishing Co./ Crazy Cajun Music Co.; Jamie Records.

1963

"Be My Baby," The Ronettes; words and music by Jeff Barry, Ellie Greenwich and Phil Spector; Trio Music Co., Inc./ Mother Bertha Music, Inc.; Philles Records.

"The Bird Is The Word," The Rivingtons; words and music by Al Frazier, Carl White, Turner Wilson, Jr., and John E. Harris; Beechwood Music Corp.; Liberty Records.

"Blowin' In The Wind," Peter, Paul and Mary; words and music by Bob Dylan; M. Witmark & Sons; Warner Brothers Records.

"Da Doo Ron Ron," The Crystals; words and music by Jeff Barry, Ellie Greenwich, and Phil Spector; Trio Music Co., Inc./Mother Bertha Music, Inc.; Philles Records.

"Come Get These Memories," Martha and the Vandellas; words and music by Brian Holland, Lamont Dozier, and Eddie Holland; Jobete Music Co., Inc.; Gordy Records.

"Don't Say Nothin' Bad About My Baby," The Cookies; words and music by Gerry Goffin and Carole King; Screen Gems-Columbia Music, Inc.; Dimension Records.

"Easier Said Than Done," The Essex; words and music by William Linton and Larry Huff; Nom Music, Inc.; Roulette Records.

"Fingertips (Part I)," Little Stevie Wonder; music by Henry Cosby and Clarence Paul; Jobete Music Co., Inc.; Tamla Records.

"Fingertips (Part II)," Little Stevie Wonder; words and music by Henry Cosby and Clarence Paul; Jobete Music Co., Inc.; Tamla Records.

"For Your Precious Love," Garnett Mimms and the Enchanters; words and music by Arthur Brooks, Richard Brooks, and Jerry Butler; Gladstone Music, Inc.; United Artists Records.

"Heat Wave," Martha and the Vandellas; words and music by Eddie Holland, Brian Holland, and Lamont Dozier; Jobete Music Co., Inc.; Gordy Records.

"Hello Stranger," Barbara Lewis; words and music by Barbara Lewis; McLaughlin Publishing Co./Cotillion Music, Inc.; Atlantic Records.

"I Can't Stay Mad At You," Skeeter Davis; words and music by Gerry Goffin and Carole King; Screen Gems-Columbia Music, Inc.; RCA Victor Records.

"If You Wanna Be Happy," Jimmy Soul; words by Carmela Guida, Frank J. Guida and Joseph Royster, music by Frank J. Guida and Joseph Royster; Rock Masters, Inc.; S. P. Q. R. Records.

"It's My Party," Lesley Gore; words and music by Herb Wiener, Wally Gold and John Gluck, Jr.; Arch Music Co., Inc.; Mercury Records.

"Land Of A Thousand Dances," Kris Kenner; words and music by Chris Kenner; Tune-Kel Publishing Co., Inc.; Instant Records.

"Louie Louie," The Kingsmen; words and music by Richard Berry; Limax Music, Inc.; Wand Records.

"Mama Didn't Lie," Jan Bradley; words and music by Curtis Mayfield; Curtom Publishing Co., Inc.; Chess Records.

"Mean Woman Blues," Roy Orbison; words and music by Jerry West and Whispering Smith; Excellorec Music Co.; Monument Records.

"Monkey Time," Major Lance; words and music by Curtis Mayfield; Curtom Publishing Co., Inc./Nicolet Music; Okeh Records.

"My Boyfriend's Back," The Angels; words and music by Robert Feldman, Gerald Goldstein, and Richard Gottehrer; Blackwood Music, Inc.; Smash Records.

"Nitty Gritty," Shirley Ellis; words and music by Lincoln Chase; Al Gallico Music Corp.; Congress Records.

"One Fine Day," The Chiffons; words and music by Gerry Goffin and Carole King; Screen Gems-Columbia Music, Inc.; Laurie Records.

"Pipeline," The Chantays; music by Bob Spickard and Brian Carman; Downey Music Publishing Co.; Dot Records.

"Sally Go 'Round The Roses," The Jaynettes; words and music by Zell Sanders and Lona Stevens; Winlyn Music, Inc.; Tuff Records.

"South Street," The Orlons; words by Kal Mann, music by Dave Appell; Kalmann Music, Inc.; Cameo Records.

"Surf City," Jan and Dean; words and music by Jan Berry and Brian Wilson; Screen Gems-Columbia Music, Inc.; Liberty Records.

"Surfer Girl," The Beach Boys; words and music by Brian Wilson; Guild Music Co.; Capitol Records.

"Surfer Joe," The Surfaris; words and music by Ron Wilson; Robin Hood Music Co./Miraleste Music; Dot Records.

"Surfin' U.S.A.," The Beach Boys; words by Brian Wilson, music by Chuck Berry; Arc Music Corp.; Capitol Records.

"Then He Kissed Me," The Crystals; words and music by Jeff Barry, Ellie Greenwich, and Phil Spector; Trio Music Co., Inc./Mother Bertha Music, Inc.; Philles Records.

"Two Faces Have I," Lou Christie; words and music by Twyla Herbert and Lou Sacco; Painted Desert Music Corp./ RTD Music; Roulette Records.

"Walking The Dog," Rufus Thomas; words and music by Rufus Thomas; East Publications; Stax Records.

"What's Easy For Two Is So Hard For One," Mary . Wells; words and music by William Robinson; Jobete Music Co., Inc.; Motown Records.

"Wild Weekend," The Rockin' Rebels; words and music by Tom Shannon and Phil Todaro; Tupper Publishing Co./ Embassy Music Corp.; Swan Records.

"Wipe Out," The Surfaris; music by Robert Berryhill, Patrick Connolly, James Fuller, and Ron Wilson; Miraleste Music/Robin Hood Music Co.; Dot Records.

"You've Really Got A Hold On Me," The Miracles; words and
    music by William Robinson; Jobete Music Co., Inc.;
    Tamla Records.

Selected Albums, 1964-1971

(All records are stereo unless otherwise noted.)

The Band

Music From Big Pink, Capitol Records (SKAO 2955).
Stage Fright, Capitol Records (SW-425).

The Beach Boys

Surfin' Safari, Capitol Records (DT 1808).
Surfer Girl, Capitol Records (ST 1981).
Little Deuce Coupe, Capitol Records (ST 1998).
All Summer Long, Capitol Records (ST 2110).
The Beach Boys Today, Capitol Records (ST 2269).

The Beatles

Meet The Beatles, Capitol Records (ST 2047).
The Beatles' Second Album, Capitol Records (ST 2080).
A Hard Day's Night, United Artists Records (UAS
    6366).
Something New, Capitol Records (ST 2108).
Beatles '65, Capitol Records (ST 2228).
Help!, Capitol Records (SMAS 2386).
Rubber Soul, Capitol Records (ST 2442).
Revolver, Capitol Records (ST 2576).
Sgt. Pepper's Lonely Hearts Club Band, Capitol Records
    (SMAS 2653).
The Beatles, Apple Records (SWOB 101).
Abbey Road, Apple Records (SO-383).

Big Brother and the Holding Company

Cheap Thrills, Columbia Records (KCS 9700).

Blood, Sweat and Tears

> *Child Is Father To The Man*, Columbia Records (CS 9619).

James Brown

> *James Brown "Live" At The Apollo*, King Records (826).
> *Please, Please, Please*, King Records (909).
> *Papa's Got A Brand New Bag*, King Records (938).
> *I Got You (I Feel Good)*, King Records (946).
> *It's A Man's, Man's, Man's World*, King Records (985).

Country Joe and the Fish

> *Electric Music For The Mind And Body*, Vanguard Records (VSD-79244).
> *Together*, Vanguard Records (VSD-79277).

Cream

> *Fresh Cream*, Atco Records (SD 33-206).
> *Disraeli Gears*, Atco Records (SD 33-232).
> *Wheels Of Fire*, Atco Records (SD 2-700).

Creedence Clearwater Revival

> *Bayou Country*, Fantasy Records (8387).
> *Green River*, Fantasy Records (8393).
> *Willy And The Poor Boys*, Fantasy Records (8397).
> *Cosmo's Factory*, Fantasy Records (8402).

Crosby, Stills and Nash

> *Crosby, Stills and Nash*, Atlantic Records (SD-8229).

Crosby, Stills, Nash and Young

> *Déjà Vu*, Atlantic Records (SD-7200).

The Doors

> *The Doors*, Elektra Records (EKS-74007).
> *Waiting For The Sun*, Elektra Records (EKS-74024).

Bob Dylan

> *Bob Dylan*, Columbia Records (CS 8597).
> *The Freewheelin' Bob Dylan*, Columbia Records (CS 8786).
> *The Times They Are A-Changin'*, Columbia Records (CS 8905).
> *Another Side Of Bob Dylan*, Columbia Records (CS 8993).
> *Bringing It All Back Home*, Columbia Records (CS 9128).
> *Highway 61 Revisited*, Columbia Records (CS 9189).
> *Blonde On Blonde*, Columbia Records (C2S 841).
> *John Wesley Harding*, Columbia Records (CS 9604).
> *Nashville Skyline*, Columbia Records (KCS 9825).
> *Self Portrait*, Columbia Records (C2X 30050).
> *New Morning*, Columbia Records (KC 30290).

The Four Tops

> *Reach Out*, Motown Records (660).
> *The Four Tops Greatest Hits*, Motown Records (662).

Aretha Franklin

> *Aretha Now*, Atlantic Records (SD 8186).

The Grateful Dead

> *The Grateful Dead*, Warner Brothers Records (W 1689-mono).
> *Aoxmoxoa*, Warner Brothers Records (WS-1790).
> *Live Dead*, Warner Brothers Records (WS-1830).
> *Workingman's Dead*, Warner Brothers Records (WS-1869).
> *American Beauty*, Warner Brothers Records (WS-1893).

The Jimi Hendrix Experience

> *Are You Experienced*, Reprise Records (6261).
> *Axis: Bold As Love*, Reprise Records (6281).
> *The Cry Of Love*, Reprise Records (MS 2034).
> *Smash Hits*, Reprise Records (MS 2025).

The Jefferson Airplane

> *The Jefferson Airplane Takes Off*, RCA Victor Records (LSP 3584).
> *Surrealistic Pillow*, RCA Victor Records (LSP 3766).
> *Crown Of Creation*, RCA Victor Records (LSP 4058).
> *After Bathing At Baxter's*, RCA Victor Records (LSO-1511).

Janis Joplin

> *I Got Dem 'Ole Kozmic Blues Again Mama!*, Columbia Records (KCS 9913).
> *Pearl*, Columbia Records (KC 30322).

Carole King

> *Tapestry*, Ode Records (SP 77009).

Martha and the Vandellas

> *Martha And The Vandellas' Greatest Hits*, Gordy Records (917).

Smokey Robinson and the Miracles

> *The Miracles Greatest Hits (From The Beginning)*, Tamla Records (254).
> *Going To A Go-Go*, Tamla Records (267).

The Mothers of Invention

> *Freak Out*, Verve Records (V6-5005-2X).
> *Absolutely Free*, Verve Records (V/V6-5013X).

Cruising With Ruben And The Jets, Verve Records (V6-5055X).

Wilson Pickett

The Exciting Wilson Pickett, Atlantic Records (SD 8129).

Otis Redding

Otis Blue: Otis Redding Sings Soul, Volt Records (S-412).
The History Of Otis Redding, Volt Records (S-418).
The Dock Of The Bay, Volt Records (S-419).
The Immortal Otis Redding, Atco Records (SD 33-252).
In Person At The Whisky A Go-Go, Atco Records (SD 33-265).

The Rolling Stones

The Rolling Stones, London Records (PS 375).
12 × 5, London Records (PS 402).
Out Of Our Heads, London Records (PS 429).
Aftermath, London Records (PS 476).
Got Live If You Want It, London Records (PS 493).
Between The Buttons, London Records (PS 499).
Flowers, London Records (PS 509).
Beggars Banquet, London Records (PS 539).
Let It Bleed, London Records (NPS-4).
Get Yer Ya-Ya's Out!, London Records (NPS-5).
Sticky Fingers, Rolling Stones Records (COC-59100).

Sam and Dave

Hold On, I'm Comin', Stax Records (708).
Soul Men, Stax Records (725).

The Supremes

Where Did Our Love Go, Motown Records (621).
Diana Ross And The Supremes' Greatest Hits, Motown Records (2-663).

The Temptations

>*Gettin' Ready*, Gordy Records (918).
>*The Temptations' Greatest Hits*, Gordy Records (919).

Vanilla Fudge

>*Vanilla Fudge*, Atco Records (SD 33-224).
>*The Beat Goes On*, Atco Records (SD 33-237).
>*Renaissance*, Atco Records (SD 33-244).

The Velvet Underground

>*The Velvet Underground And Nico*, Verve Records (V6-5008).

Index